Get a Hobby!

Get a Hobby!

101 All-Consuming Diversions for Any Lifestyle

Tina Barseghian

Collins

An Imprint of HarperCollinsPublishers

HarperCollins books may be purchased for educational, business, or sales promotional use. For information please write: Special Markets Department, HarperCollins Publishers, 10 East 53rd Street, New York, NY 10022.

FIRST EDITION

A QUIRK PACKAGING BOOK
Cover photography © Bill Milne 2006
Cover styling by Janet Prusa
Cover modeling by Myles Goldin and Barry Lehmann
Back cover illustration by Lynne Yeamans
Designed by Lynne Yeamans and Tanya Ross-Hughes
Illustrated by Nancy Leonard
Edited by Sarah Scheffel and Betsy Beier
Copyedited by Ana Deboo and Lianna Krissoff
Contributing researcher: Katherine Sharpe

Our thanks to the following people and organizations for their contributions:
Page 27: David Rudd, www.cycleback.com, for information about baseball card trading history; Page 39: Lucy Saunders, www.grillingwithbeer.com, for her amber cayenne-citrus marinade; Page 141: Enchanted Learning, www.enchantedlearning.com, for the mobile frame made from a wire coat hanger; Page 151: Herman Brown for his mushroom soup recipe; Page 157: Jeff Rutzky for his origami dollar-bill shirt project; Page 186–187: Rueul's Art & Frame, www.reuels.com, for basic silk-screening information.

Library of Congress Cataloging-in-Publication Data has been applied for.

ISBN-10: 0-06-121527-9
ISBN-13: 978-0-06-121527-8

10 9 8 7 6 5 4 3 2 1

I dedicate this book to my husband, Lloyd, who not only abandoned his own hobbies (woodworking and robot building), but kept the homestead intact and our daughter Lucine fed for the duration.

contents

foreword

In describing their lives, countless patients tell the familiar story of hurtling along from day to day, rushing from home to work and back, ticking off items on constantly regenerating to-do lists. They "relax" by going to the gym, celebrating holidays, or traveling, while occasionally fantasizing about that day in the future when they'll be a little less busy, finally able to enjoy the hobbies that they never quite have enough time for now.

My advice to these patients? Get a hobby now: it could save your life!

Here's why: reputable studies have shown that chronic stress contributes to poor health while regular relaxation promotes good health. A groundbreaking work published in 1975 by Herbert Benson, M.D., *The Relaxation Response*, definitively linked relaxation to improvements in health, from reduced blood pressure to better digestion. We now know that regular relaxation can improve and possibly even prevent an array of conditions and symptoms, including heart disease, high blood pressure, irritable bowel syndrome, ulcers, anxiety disorders, insomnia, and more. During the relaxation response, your heartbeat slows, your blood pressure goes down, your breathing is slower, your metabolism slows, your muscles become less tense and release less lactate, and the amount of oxygen in your bloodstream increases.

How can you experience this kind of relaxation?

The usual prescription is to learn a stress-management technique such as meditation, yoga, or biofeedback. These are all excellent methods. Nevertheless, they are not suitable for everyone—they require a significant time commitment to be learned as well as a quiet place to practice—luxuries that many people do not have. Other relaxation seekers are simply not comfortable with the spiritual or mind-body aspect of these practices.

However, almost everyone feels comfortable with the idea of a hobby. And regularly practicing a hobby can help induce a state of relaxation by focusing effortlessly, without the conscious sense of struggle often required in yoga or even in meditation.

A hobby is any thoroughly absorbing pastime that you engage in outside your regular activities that focuses your mind on something that is not your usual worries. A good hobby requires you to learn a skill that is not part of your working life (if you type on a computer all day, you will probably not find it relaxing to use one for your hobby); it also should put you into a state of focused, peaceful enjoyment, which is not to say it cannot have exciting moments (ahem, computer gamers—sorry, but most games put you into a prolonged state of physiological arousal that is the opposite of what we are looking for). A good, relaxing hobby is a personally pleasing occupation that brings you entirely into the moment. While you are practicing your hobby, you are not worrying about the difficult meeting you had today, criticizing yourself for not going to the gym, or planning your kids' soccer schedule. You are focused on accomplishing something right now, using your hands and mind in concert.

If you're going to practice your hobby often, you need to pick a pursuit you truly like. Helping you find a hobby that you will enjoy is the aim of this book. Tina Barseghian has done a terrific job of describing activities that appeal to all kinds of personality types, interests, aptitudes, schedules, and budgets—from birdwatching to knitting to geocaching to woodworking to origami to balloon twisting. Use this book to learn about a particular pursuit and give it a try. If it pleases you, keep going. If it turns out to be not so much fun, flip to a different page and try another.

When you find the right hobby, you'll know. You'll look forward to doing it. You may even find yourself making time (that you never thought you had) to enjoy it. And when you're thoroughly involved in your hobby, and have forgotten your cares, you'll finally be relaxed.

Miguel Figueroa, M.D.

MIGUEL FIGUEROA *is a neurologist who specializes in interventional pain management. Dr. Figueroa practices in Miami, Florida.*

introduction

to each a hobby

Have you ever built a car from a wooden crate and raced it down a hill? Knitted a scarf? Chased a brewing tornado? Learned how to connect the dots in the sky to find the Big Dipper? It's no surprise if these activities remind you of your less-encumbered youth, before you became distracted by work and other tediously adult responsibilities. As kids, we tried all sorts of activities, and we got to experience the pleasure of doing something for its own sake; whether the activity of choice was macramé or gerbil-raising, happiness was the main objective. *Get a Hobby!* invites you to revisit that unconstrained, pleasure-seeking state of mind. Just try a few of these hobbies until you find one that suits you. And if you are lucky enough to find more than one pleasureable pursuit, remember: you don't have to be monogamous with your hobby—feel free to indulge in more than one.

To help get you started down the road to hobby happiness, I've selected 101 hobbies that represent a broad sampling of the thousands of possibilities—from the traditional (birding, model railroading) to the unconventional (Dumpster diving, gravestone rubbing). This guide covers hobbies for crafters (crocheting, decoupage, scrapbooking); for aspiring artists (pottery, stained glass, watercolor painting); and for engineers (radio-controlled vehicles, robot building). There are hobbies for outdoorsy types (kite flying, mushroom hunting, beachcombing); for animal lovers (dog breeding, fish keeping); for woodworkers (framing, dollhouse building, whittling)—and anyone else who's willing to try something new. By casting such a wide net, I hope to encourage you to sample an assortment of these diversions.

These hobbies are meant to delight you—pure and simple. But as Dr. Miguel Figueroa discusses in his foreword, you'll reap additional benefits, too: practicing a hobby is a surefire way to decrease your anxieties and increase your mental and physical health overall. Who can object to that?

what to expect

Each entry presents everything you need to know in order to get started with a particular hobby—and determine whether it's right for you. You'll read an overview of what the hobby entails and the basics of the techniques associated with it; a brief history of where and how the hobby originated; a list of the tools and materials required; and finally, basic instructions for an easy project typical of this hobby. Some of the chapters also feature profiles of a hobbyist who is passionate about that particular pursuit, and I hope that enthusiasm is contagious. You'll also find a list of resources—books, magazines, and websites—that will guide you to more information. Our enterprising, do-it-yourself culture has yielded long lists of resources to choose from, and I've picked those I feel are most appropriate and helpful. But remember: Websites come and, as they're apt to do, websites go, so if a link has expired, I encourage you to conduct your own research. Most hobbies are associated with formal organizations and societies, but you'll also encounter many informal (but nonetheless useful) sites run by individual hobbyists who want to spread the word about their preferred proclivity.

Before you plunge right in, I encourage you to take our hobby personality quiz to guide you to hobbies that might interest you. Your answers will correspond to the hobbies that best suit your personality. You may discover that if you're interested in miniature wargaming, for example, you might also enjoy genealogy, or that a long-term interest in collecting might lead you to embrace beachcombing as a hobby.

Finally, I hope that reading this book will inspire you to make the most of the rarest of all luxuries—your free time.

Tina Barseghian

the quiz

what's your hobby personality?

With so many hobbies to choose from, how do you figure out which of these diversions is likely to be right for you? Start with this quiz. It will help you identify the personality traits that comprise your hobby personality. Then match your results to the hobby personality profiles that appear at the top of each hobby entry; these represent the most prominent characteristics of the many hobbyists who enjoy these pastimes. If two or more of your personality traits are represented, there's a good chance you'll enjoy that particular pastime, too. It's that simple.

Of course, even the most insightful test is no substitute for the real thing, so don't feel limited by the quiz results. Your hobby personality profile is only a starting point. If you allow yourself to experiment with a variety of different hobbies, you might discover a previously unsuspected aptitude or rekindle a long-buried obsession. Feel perfectly free to change your hobby preferences according to your schedule, mood, or even the weather.

1) A THRILLING VACATION WOULD BE:
   a) Trekking in the Alps.
   b) Driving around Napa Valley visiting vineyards.
   c) Watching the grass grow in my backyard.

2) WHICH BEST SUMS UP YOUR RELATIONSHIP WITH THE ANIMAL KINGDOM?
   a) Snakes are actually very sweet creatures.
   b) I can't resist an adorable puppy/kitten.
   c) Yeeeaaugh! There's a spider on me! Get it off! Is it gone!

3) THE LAST TIME YOU USED A PAINTBRUSH WAS:
   a) To create a replica of the Last Supper on my dining room wall.
   b) To apply "Breathless Nights" to my toenails.
   c) When I tripped over the one the contractor left in the hallway.

4) WHEN IT'S TIME TO WRAP A PRESENT, YOU PREFER TO:
   a) Stencil your own wrapping paper; a personal touch makes a gift truly special.
   b) Purchase a snazzy gift bag and matching card, then write a personal note.
   c) Ask the store clerk to gift wrap it.

5) HOW HANDY ARE YOU?
   a) I built a multi-level shed with individual compartments for my woodworking tools.
   b) I can assemble an Ikea chair.
   c) I can change a light bulb.

6) ARE YOU A GOOD COOK?
   a) Everyone says my duck à l'orange is out of sight.
   b) I can whip up a Betty Crocker box cake, with frosting.
   c) I burn frozen waffles.

7) DO YOU ENJOY PERFORMING?
   a) I have performed a one-man/woman show based on my life.
   b) I have sung karaoke in public.
   c) I sing to myself in the shower.

8) NAME ONE OF THE LEADERS OF THE PEASANT'S REVOLT OF 1381.
   a) Wat Tyler—that's why it's also called Tyler's Rebellion.
   b) I have no idea, but I know when WWII began and ended.
   c) Excuse me while I yawn.

9) WOULD YOUR FRIENDS AND FAMILY DESCRIBE YOU AS SELF-SUFFICIENT?
   a) Absolutely—they joke that I can entertain myself with some rubber bands and a ball of string.
   b) Yes, but I like a balance between "me time" and my social life.
   c) Are you kidding? If it were up to me, I wouldn't go to the mailbox without company.

10) HOW CONNECTED ARE YOU?

a) I spend three weeks each year at a Zen retreat in the mountains.

b) I occasionally enjoy a yoga class.

c) I sleep with my Blackberry.

11) WHAT BEST DESCRIBES YOUR ATTENTION TO DETAIL?

a) I have built a life-size model of my hometown with pistachio shells.

b) I can put together a jigsaw puzzle.

c) My shoelaces always come undone.

12) DESCRIBE THE ROLE OF MUSIC IN YOUR LIFE.

a) In my spare time, I compose operettas.

b) I can sing "Frère Jacques."

c) I can turn on the stereo.

13) YOUR IDEA OF A GOOD PLACE FOR A WALK IS:

a) The Appalachian Trail.

b) The beachfront at a Caribbean resort.

c) From the front door to my car.

14) DO YOU HAVE PETS?

a) A bunny would be a great companion for my three dogs and two cats.

b) I have a goldfish.

c) Our family cat ran away when I was seven.

15) AN EXCELLENT WAY TO SPEND A SUNNY SPRING DAY WOULD BE TO:

a) A morning jog through the woods, picnic lunch, afternoon at the ballpark, watch the sunset on the beach.

b) Be sure to get out in the garden for an hour or two.

c) Catch up on Star Trek reruns.

16) WHICH BEST DESCRIBES YOUR ATTENTION SPAN?

a) I enjoy the "hold" music my phone company plays.

b) I skip to the last page of a book to see how it ends.

c) I've already moved on to the next question.

17) MY IDEA OF A FUN FRIDAY NIGHT WOULD BE:

a) Hosting a party—the more the merrier.

b) Drinks with one or two of my closest friends.

c) Curling up with a good book and a cup of tea.

18) DESCRIBE YOUR MOST RECENT FORM OF EXERCISE.

a) I'm jogging on a treadmill as I read this.

b) A game of Frisbee in the park this weekend.

c) Does bending over to pick up some loose change count?

19) ARE YOU A TECHIE?

a) I rebuilt the engine of my 1969 VW Beetle.

b) I download all my own songs on my iPod.

c) I can successfully check my voicemail.

Every time you answered "a" above, circle the corresponding trait in the list below. String the traits together and you have your hobby personality: Some examples follow. Happy dabbling!

1) adventurous	**8)** history-loving	**15)** outdoorsy
2) animal-loving	**9)** independent	**16)** patient
3) artistic	**10)** meditative	**17)** social
4) crafty	**11)** meticulous	**18)** sporty
5) dexterous	**12)** musical	**19)** technical
6) epicurean	**13)** nature-loving	
7) extroverted	**14)** nurturing	

Are you artistic, dexterous, and meticulous?
You might like beading, model ships, or silk-screening.

Are you adventurous, sporty, and technical?
You might like caving, scuba diving, or soapbox derby.

Are you extroverted, history-loving, and social?
You might like docenting, historical reenactment, miniature wargaming.

Are you independent, nature-loving, and outdoorsy?
You might like birding, fly-tying, or mushroom hunting.

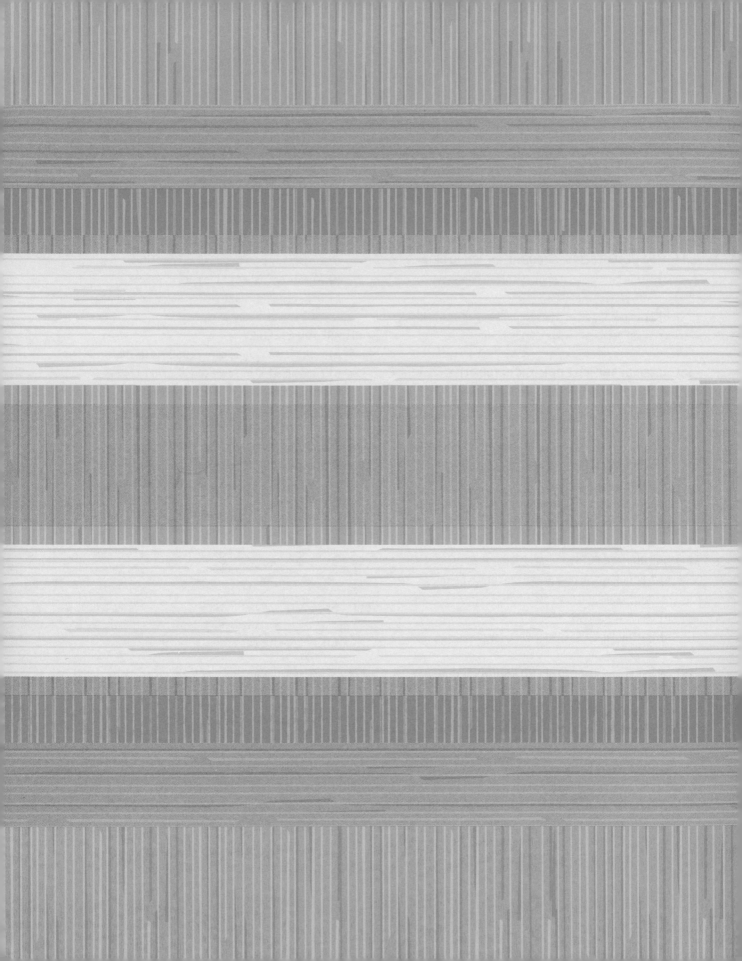

the hobbies

african violet cultivation

HOBBY PERSONALITY: adventurous ∘ animal-loving ∘ artistic ∘ crafty ∘ dexterous ∘ epicurean ∘ extroverted ∘ history-loving ∘ independent ∘ meditative ∘ meticulous ∘ musical ∘ **nature-loving** ∘ **nurturing** ∘ outdoorsy ∘ **patient** ∘ social ∘ sporty ∘ technical

GROWING A HOUSEPLANT CAN BE AS GRATIFYING—AND COMPLICATED—AS RAISING A CHILD. In the case of African violets, a temperamental but fetching plant, the parallels with child-rearing are particularly apt: They require tremendous patience, copious amounts of attention, and of course, buckets of love. But you'll dismiss the trouble as a small price to pay compared to the unquantifiable pleasures of seeing your little ones bloom.

what you'll need

- *An African violet plant (buy from a reputable nursery or start from a leaf cutting)*
- *Shallow flowerpot and large saucer*
- *Watering can with a small spout*
- *Soil (try special African violet potting soil)*
- *Pebbles*
- *"Violet Food" or fertilizer specifically formulated for African violets*

overview

African violets have achieved cult status for their ability to flower year-round; their delicate petals (typically purple) and furry, heart-shaped leaves cheer up any room. But these compact houseplants show their blooms only under certain conditions. They need just the right amount of light—10 to 14 hours but not more of bright, indirect light per day, and at least 8 hours of darkness for a good rest. These plants bask in warmth, preferring temperatures between 70 and 75°F (21 to 24°C), and need soil that is moist but not wet with undistilled and unchlorinated water. As with all starlets, African violets love to be primped and groomed, so it's important to remove spent buds and leaves to create the perfect symmetry.

Today, there are more than 2,000 varieties of these houseplants under cultivation featuring blooms of many colors, including hot pink, blue, yellow, and white, some with frilly edges, all with a pop of yellow in the center.

history

Native to Tanzania and Kenya, African violets (which consist of the 20-odd species of the genus *Saintpaulia*, family Gesneriaceae) were first discovered in 1892 by German officer Baron Walter von Saint Paul-Illaire, who was stationed in Tanzania. The officer chanced upon the flowers in the East Usambara mountains and sent seeds to his father, a botanist, who propagated the plants and showed them throughout Western Europe. Though they are not related to European violets, the name African violet stuck, and the plants became an instant hit in the U.S. in 1926 when a California-based grower started importing them.

resources

African Violets: The Complete Guide, by Joan Hill and Gwen Goodship. (Trafalgar Square Publishing, 1998).

www.african-violet-brats.com: African Violet Brat Pack hosts an active forum, events calendar, and FAQs.

www.avsa.org: African Violet Society of America's portal to local clubs, national convention information, photos, and a library of resources.

www.theplantexpert.com: Detailed instructions for growing perfect African violets.

www.robsviolet.com: Vendor of African violets (including miniature varieties) and supplies.

getting started

Once you've selected your first African violet and brought it home from the nursery, you'll need to replant it. Here's how you can ensure that your plant will thrive.

- *PLANT YOUR AFRICAN VIOLET in a small flowerpot with rich fertilizer. Because these plants need to stay moist, first cover each drainage hole in the bottom of the pot with a pebble.*

- *FILL THE POT HALF FULL WITH SOIL, carefully place your plant in the center, then add more soil around the root ball—just enough to cover it.*

- *SET THE NEWLY POTTED PLANT in a saucer of tepid water and let it absorb the water for an hour. Then fill the bottom saucer with pebbles, too. To ensure a humid environment, always keep the pebbles slightly submerged in water.*

- *POSITION THE POT near an east- or north-facing window so it gets the indirect sunlight it requires. If the natural light in your home does not provide optimal conditions, you can purchase a grow light and timer, available at most nurseries. If your plant doesn't flower, it isn't getting enough light. If the leaves get brown edges or spots, it's getting too much light. Adjust accordingly.*

project: starting an african violet from a leaf

If you want to expand your African violet collection, purchasing an assortment from a nursery is not your only option. It's also a cinch to cultivate violets from leaf cuttings.

WHAT YOU'LL NEED:
African violet leaf cutting
Wax paper
Clean, empty jar
String

1) Cut a healthy-looking leaf from a friend's plant. If none of your friends grow African violets, consider joining a local club for access to leaf cuttings and advice about cultivating these plants *(see resources)*.

2) Wrap wax paper over the lid of the empty jar, then tie it with string to secure it. Poke two holes in the wax paper. Put the stem of the African violet leaf through one of the holes.

3) Use the second hole to nearly fill the jar with lukewarm water (make the hole larger if necessary). Use enough water so that it covers the stem but doesn't touch the leaf itself. For a shot of vitamins, you can add a drop of plant food.

4) Place in a sunny spot, and within six weeks a few roots should appear. Now you're ready to pot the plant.

other cult plants: *Consider trying your hand at other exotic houseplants.*

ORCHIDS. Tropical plants grown for their delicate blossoms. The orchid family, Orchidaceae, is one of the largest flowering-plant families on Earth, with about 24,000 documented species.

BROMELIADS. A family of tropical and subtropical plants. Many bromeliads grow in a pattern of overlapping leaves, forming "tanks" into which gardeners pour water directly. Though bromeliads flower, they're grown for the decorative nature of their leaves, which can be streaked with purples, yellows, and reds.

CARNIVOROUS PLANTS. Plants that derive most of their nutrition from consuming animals, usually in the form of insects. Three of the most popular varieties for cultivation are the Venus flytraps, pitcher plants, and sundews.

BONSAI. A tradition of using pruning and other techniques to contort small trees into specific shapes. *(See Bonsai.)*

ant farming

HOBBY PERSONALITY: adventurous • **animal-loving** • artistic • crafty • dexterous • epicurean • extroverted • history-loving • independent • **meditative** • meticulous • musical • **nature-loving** • **nurturing** • outdoorsy • **patient** • social • sporty • technical

ANTS COULD TEACH HUMANS A THING OR TWO about living in a community. These social creatures survive and proliferate based on a highly efficient system that depends on every member of their miniature world carrying its own weight. To watch these insects at work is to understand how constructive and productive a society can be. The industriousness of each member should be an inspiration to us all!

what you'll need

- Ants

- An ant farm or formicarium. You can make your own (see resources), or buy one from a retailer like Uncle Milton Industries.

- Sand or dirt (optional)

- Ant food (see project)

hobby hazard:

Like their relatives, the wasps, many ant species sting. The back end is the business end of an ant, so exercise appropriate caution until you know what kind of ant you're dealing with. For example, fire ants and harvester ants can deliver potent stings, while carpenter ants release a little formic acid, which hurts only if you rub it into your eyes or an open cut.

overview

Ant farms provide a fascinating theater for observing how the inhabitants coexist in a colony. Ant societies are based on the division of labor, with a queen as the ruler and several classes of workers that care for the young, dig tunnels, clean nests, find food, and defend the habitat. Observing the carefully calibrated equilibrium is the fun part. That, and watching an ant carry objects more than fifty times its own weight!

Scientists describe ants as "superorganisms" because at times the colony seems to function as a single creature. They communicate with each other using chemicals known as pheromones, which they secrete as they journey forth and use as a navigational tool to negotiate their way back. They also perceive and follow trails left by other ants. The queens (sometimes there's more than one in a colony) lay all the eggs—thousands of them per year—and can live for a few years.

history

Ants have been around, it seems, since the dawn of time; today there are almost 12,000 known species. Scientists believe they evolved after the disintegration of the supercontinent Gondwana more than 100 million years ago. The earliest ant discovered so far (fossilized and encased in amber in New Jersey—go figure) is 92 million years old. But ant farming as a hobby is a somewhat more recent phenomenon. The term "Ant Farm" is a registered trademark of Uncle Milton Industries, Inc., a toy manufacturer founded in 1946. As the story goes, Milton Levine came up with the idea in 1956 while attending a picnic that was infested with—you guessed it—ants.

getting started

- *FIRST YOU'LL NEED to choose a formicarium (a terrarium designed for the study of ant behavior). You can buy a plastic ant farm or build one out of wood, plaster, or plastic (see resources for websites that offer instructions). Ants are available by mail order, but of course you can also capture your own. They are most easily moved using an aspirator, which gently sucks them into a vial (see resources), but you can also get ants to crawl onto a piece of paper, then flick them into a container to transport them.*

- *IT'S ILLEGAL TO SELL QUEEN ANTS IN THE U.S.—the chance that a dangerous non-native species could be imported is too great. So if you want your colony to last more than a few months, you'll have to capture a queen. You can search an ant colony (the queen will be the largest one with a swollen stomach), but note that unless you take the whole colony with you, you'll destroy it when you kidnap its queen. You can also find an ant colony and wait for a "nuptial flight" during the spring and summer months, when a new queen leaves the colony where she was born. Or try luring a queen to your door with sweet goodies. Patience required.*

- *WHICHEVER TYPE OF formicarium you choose, it can have either dirt or sand for the ants to tunnel through or no medium at all. Most hobbyists prefer to provide sand for the ants to tunnel through. Water is a necessity in both types of farm (a water shortage can kill ants overnight), so either keep the dirt damp or make sure the ants have access to a test tube half filled with water and stoppered with a cotton ball. The colony also needs food to continue working. Different types of ants eat different things in the wild. Some are hunters and do best if they can catch insects. Others— such as leaf cutter ants—eat plant matter and fungus. (See the recipe for all-purpose ant food.)*

- *KEEP YOUR ANT FARM away from sun and in a spot where the temperature does not fluctuate much. If they have food, water, the right temperature, and a queen to lead them, the little critters can self-propagate indefinitely.*

project: make your own ant food

Now that you've got a full colony of ants, you need to feed them. Rather than buying generic ant food, make your own with this mix.

WHAT YOU'LL NEED:
1/2 cup (170 g) honey
1/2 cup (120 ml) water
1/4 multivitamin/multimineral pill, crushed

Mix these ingredients together and store them in the refrigerator. Feed your ants with an eye dropper, but be careful not to overfeed! Experiment with different amounts of food, observing the eating habits of your colony in order to figure out how much they require. You can also supplement their diet with little bits of fruit, vegetables, plants, and bugs.

resources

Ants at Work: How an Insect Society Is Organized, by Deborah M. Gordon (W. W. Norton, 2000).

Journey to the Ants: A Story of Scientific Exploration, by Bert Hölldobler and Edward O. Wilson (Belknap Press, 1995).

www.antcam.com: Offers step-by-step instructions to build several kinds of ant formicarium.

www.antcolony.org: The definitive source for ant enthusiasts.

www.antfarmcentral.com: Everything you need to know about ant farming, including links to suppliers.

www.unclemilton.com: Original retailer of Ant Farms, available in a variety of configurations.

astrological charting

WHAT'S YOUR SIGN? That old adage has weathered a few decades and, to some, is still as relevant a characteristic as a person's gender. Judging from the brisk business astrologists are doing—daily horoscopes can be found in every possible form of media, from radio and television to newspapers and the internet—the ability to predict the future, or at least to understand the present, is of utmost importance to a lot of folks. To them, where the planets rotate in relation to their rising sign can dictate when they'll find their dream job or meet their soul mate. The truth is out there!

what you'll need

- *Birth date and accurate birth time of the person whose chart you're making*
- *Place of birth (ideally, the exact latitude and longitude)*
- *A computer and printer*

resources

Astrology: Understanding the Birth Chart, by Kevin Burk (Llewellyn Publications, 2001).

What Time Were You Born? Creating Your Complete Astrological Chart, by Sasha Fenton (Sterling Publishing, 2005).

www.astrologers.com: Sponsored by the American Federation of Astrologers, this site offers many resources, including an astrology correspondence course.

www.astrology.com: Get a free horoscope and entry to a host of other astrological services.

www.chartplanet.com: Offers a free astrological chart with the date, time, and place of birth, and for a nominal fee, an interpretation.

overview

Astrology is the study of stars and planets in relation to the Earth and how their movements affect human actions. Those who study it use an astrological chart to try to tell a person's character traits, strengths and weaknesses, obstacles, compatible romantic partners and friends, and career direction. Charts are composed by graphing the position of the sun and other heavenly bodies at the exact date, time, and location of a person's birth. Charts are illustrated in a circle: The circle's exterior is divided into twelve 30-degree sections corresponding to the signs of the zodiac; the inner circle is divided into 12 houses. A chart pinpoints a person's sun sign (the zodiac sign that we refer to colloquially), as well as the rising sign, the one that was rising on the eastern horizon at the time and place of birth. The chart also shows the position of the moon and planets, each of which affects an individual's personality. Each planet rules over a different aspect of life. Venus, for example, governs love, art, and beauty, while Saturn dictates purpose and direction in life.

history

Western astrology can be traced back to ancient Mesopotamia (around 2300 B.C.E.). For thousands of years, astrological charts were used to predict seasons and weather patterns. The practice made its way to ancient Greece, then to Hellenized Egypt shortly after the country was conquered by Alexander the Great. (That probably could have been predicted, if they'd read the charts.) Interest in astrology waxed and waned through the centuries and was rekindled during the early Renaissance. Once scientists figured out that the Earth is not the center of the universe in the 1500s, astrology and astronomy officially separated into different camps.

getting started

Creating astrological charts is tricky business. Thankfully, there are a number of software programs available online (see resources) that translate your raw data into a comprehensive astrological chart. Creating one from scratch requires a great deal of special training (and interpreting one is no cinch, either), but if you're intent on going down that road, refer to the books in the resources section, which will guide you step by step. For most people, the best part of astrology is interpreting the signs and learning about a person, namely yourself.

project: customized astrological chart

Bestow the gift of prescience to a friend who's just given birth by creating a customized astrological chart for the baby.

1) Select a chart from one of the websites listed in the resources section; they come in a variety of designs and colors.

2) Enter the baby's birth date, time, and place and generate a personalized astrological chart.

3) Print out the chart. You can customize the chart by framing it or painting around the border or tracing it onto textured paper, then coloring or otherwise embellising it.

4) To complete the gift, considering adding something with the baby's birthstone, like a tiny charm, ring, or bracelet. If the chart predicts the baby will be a writer, add a leather journal and a fancy pen. There's no end to the paraphernalia you can include in an astrologically themed gift set!

profile: channeling the stars

ARLENE KRAMER was introduced to astrology like most other people: She read her horoscope in magazines. The more she read, the more Kramer became fascinated by astrology. Kramer became fascinated by it. She began cruising the library aisles for astrology books and combing through astrology magazines.

"I found out that there was much more to it than just your sun sign," she says. "There was mathematics involved, and it was much more complex. I was so taken with it, and everything it could do and everything it meant."

After taking a few classes, Kramer was hooked. "I wasn't looking for a second career," says the former schoolteacher, who lives in Woodland Hills, California. But 37 years later, she is a professional astrologer, specializing in a system called Uranian astrology. She has written a piece of soft-

ware called Planetary Hours, whereby a planet is assigned to a specific hour of the day, affecting what types of tasks should be done during specific hours. She's hired to choose wedding days, surgery days, and the timing of other important events that could benefit from the stars being correctly aligned.

> "Astrology is one of the most practical studies you can choose. It helps with every area of your life. You'll know when to zig and when to zag."

Kramer does not believe our lives are predetermined. "No Western astrologer would stand for that," she says. "I insist on free choice. But we are guided by planetary alignments."

autograph collecting

THE ALLURE OF FAME IS INTOXICATING. Whether it's a historical figure or the personality-of-the-month, connecting to a celebrity somehow brings the limelight closer to us. For those who are fascinated by luminaries, collecting autographs might be the only way to create that connection. Maybe you genuinely admire the celebrity and want to mark the occasion of meeting the person, or maybe you just want bragging rights. Either way, the spotlight edges ever closer to you.

what you'll need

- *Envelopes (standard business-size and large-format)*

- *Stamps or International Reply Coupons*

- *Unlined 3-by-5-inch index cards*

- *Pen and paper or a computer with printer*

- *Address of the celebrity*

- *Gift or personal item to send to the celebrity (optional). (Don't make it too personal. You don't want to seem like a nut.)*

- *Albums, binders, or frames for storing and protecting your autographs and signed photos*

overview

As with most hobbies, there's an easy way and there's a more challenging way. Buying autographs from a dealer is always an option, but for the true autograph collector, it doesn't count unless it comes straight from the source, either signed at a personal appearance or through the mail. Hobbyists usually focus on getting autographs from one category of public figure, such as sports luminaries, movie stars, teen idols, Nobel prize winners, or authors. Part of the challenge is finding celebrities who are agreeable to signing autographs (in the jargon of the hobby, they're called "good signers"). Naturally, the more minor the celebrity, the easier it is to get an autograph. Conversely, the bigger the name, the more tired and reluctant the hand of the signer.

history

During the 1920s, when sports stars like slugger Babe Ruth and boxer Jack Dempsey ruled the public consciousness, they gladly signed autographs at sporting events. Over the years, autograph signing became more widespread, and by the 1980s, memorabilia dealers were seeing this as an opportunity to make money. Now it's not uncommon for dealers to ask celebrities to sign dozens of autographs at a time, most or all of which will be sold to collectors. Some of the bigger personalities, like presidents and NASA astronauts, use an Autopen, a machine built in the 1940s for Harry Truman that simulates a convincing signature. Whether or not that autograph "counts" as an original is up to the collector.

getting started

- *DECIDE what type of celebrity you're most interested in: basketball players, musicians, poets, actors? Then find out when the subject of your devotion is going to make a personal appearance. Basketball players compete across the country, musicians go on tour, poets hold public readings, actors work on movie sets or in theaters. Chances are, if you attend one of these events, you'll score a signature.*

- *SERIOUS AUTOGRAPH collectors don't leave it up to chance; they write to their favorite stars and request autographs. The cardinal rule of autograph collecting by mail is to always include a self-addressed, stamped envelope with your letter. If you want to receive a photo of the celebrity, include a large-format stamped envelope, which you can fold into thirds and place inside a white business envelope. Be patient— your darling likely has many requests to fulfill, so it may be a while before you get a reply. Waiting for months is not uncommon; some have waited years. Also be prepared for the risk of forgery. For some collectors, the thrill of establishing an autograph's authenticity is part of the fun.*

project: writing a request for an autograph

Choose the celebrities to write to and find their address *(see resources)*. You stand the best chance of grabbing their attention if you invest in some nice stationery or a distinctive, handmade card—something that will stand apart from the avalanche of paper on the celebrity's desk. If your name is printed on the stationery, your star might even use it in the response. Handwritten letters are always appreciated, but either practice your cursive or make sure your print is legible; if it's not, go with a computer-printed letter.

Keep your letter short and sweet, and be sure it's personalized. Try the following three-paragraph format:

1) In the first paragraph, introduce yourself and describe why you know about and admire this person (most often, it's their profession).

2) Next, describe what specific example of their work has been most meaningful or inspiring to you. Mention a personal experience you've had—a reaction to a specific scene in a movie, for example.

3) To finish, politely ask your celebrity to sign the enclosed index card. Sign the letter in your best penmanship and send it—along with the self-addressed, stamped envelope and the index card—to the address. Hold your breath and wait for a response!

resources

The Standard Guide to Collecting Autographs: A Reference and Value Guide, by Mark Allen Baker (Krause Publications, 1999).

The Sanders Price Guide to Autographs: The World's Leading Autograph Pricing Authority, 6th ed., by Richard Saffro et al. (Alexander Books, 2003).

www.autographcollector.com: Provides celebrity addresses and articles on the joys of the hobby.

www.schulsonautographs.com: Autograph dealer who sells autographs of political and historical figures and luminaries in the fields of science, literature, entertainment, and music.

balloon twisting

KIDS HAVE AS MUCH FUN PLAYING WITH BALLOON ANIMALS as some adults do making them. Most often practiced by clowns and children's entertainers, the art of balloon sculpture is intrinsically tied to childhood, when the bubblegum colors, exaggerated shapes, and cartoonish faces were sure to elicit squeals of delight. Note of warning: Once you prove yourself as a master balloon twister, the birthday party invitations will flood your mailbox.

what you'll need

- *Pencil balloons*

- *Balloon pump (optional, but see getting started)*

resources

Twisting History: Lessons in Balloon Sculpting, by Larry Moss (Fooled Ya, 1995).

www.balloonhq.com: Instructions, history, and many games.

www.multihobbies.com/balloons: Step-by-step instructions with pictures.

www.tmyers.com: Instructions, video demonstrations, and equipment.

www.qualatex.com: Balloon supplier.

overview

Twisted balloon sculptures are made with pencil balloons, which are long and thin and come in a variety of sizes. Once inflated, they can vary in length from nearly 4 to 6 feet (1.2 to 1.8 m), and are usually between 1 and 6 inches (2.5 and 15 cm) wide. The most common size is 2 by 60 inches (5 by 152 cm), which is ideal for twisting and comes in the largest variety of colors. The whimsical little sculptures they can be made into capture the essence of everything from a basic four-legged animal—a dachshund, giraffe, elephant, monkey, and bear are the most common—to more "realistic" objects like a helmet or sword.

history

Though in ancient times balloons were made from dried animal bladders, the ones we use now—made of rubber, chloroprene, nylon, or latex—were invented by Michael Faraday in 1824 at the Royal Institution in London. (Faraday, incidentally, had bigger things on his mind than the creation of a toy. He developed balloons as part of an experiment with hydrogen. Among other lifetime accomplishments, he invented the electric motor.) The following year, rubber manufacturer Thomas Hancock began selling make-your-own-balloon kits that contained liquid rubber that were blown up with a syringe. In 1847, J. G. Ingram of London created the toy's next and final incarnation, in the form of vulcanized balloons, which could withstand varying temperatures. Balloon animals were first seen at the Pittsburgh Magicians' Convention in 1938, created by H. J. Bonnert. And in 1945, Wally Boag is said to have produced the first one-balloon animal.

getting started

Because pencil balloons are hard to inflate, twisters typically use a pump to blow them up. You'll probably want to do the same. Follow these steps to create a lock, the building block of every balloon animal.

1) *Pump up the balloon, leaving some of it uninflated to allow room for air movement.*

2) *Practice twisting the balloon and dividing it into different sections, starting at one end and moving to the other. In the illustrations opposite, the letters refer to the twists and the numbers refer to the bubbles.*

3) *To lock a twist into place, twist a second time a few inches away from the first, and a third time a few inches away from the second. Bend the balloon section between the second and third twist (next to the section between the first and second twist), then push the third and first twist together.*

4) *You've got yourself a lock! It's the first step to making heads, legs, and bodies. For a four-legged animal, you'll need three locking twists: nose, ears, and neck; front legs and body; and back legs and tail. A longer neck evokes a giraffe, while a long body creates a dachshund.*

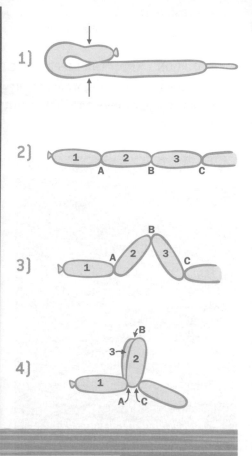

project: party favors

Make a balloon animal zoo as favors for the next kids' party you throw. Contort balloons into as many different animal shapes and sizes as possible, and display your menagerie on a tabletop. Include elephants, giraffes, rhinoceroses, flamingos, pigs, turtles, lions, and koala bears (*see resources* for instructions). You can add toy trees, barns, and feeding troughs for a barnyard setting. As guests leave the party, ask them to point to their favorite figure and guess what it is. If they are right, they get to take it home!

balsa wood sculpture

HOBBY PERSONALITY: adventurous • animal-loving • **artistic** • **crafty** • **dexterous** • epicurean • extroverted • history-loving • independent • meditative • **meticulous** • musical • nature-loving • nurturing • outdoorsy • **patient** • social • sporty • **technical**

IF YOU DON'T KNOW THE DIFFERENCE BETWEEN A BAND SAW AND A JIGSAW but you're fascinated by the idea of shaping and carving wood, try your hand at balsa wood sculptures as an introduction to woodworking. The wood's lightness and malleability make it the perfect medium for experimentation. BONUS: No power tools necessary.

what you'll need

- *X-Acto knives and fresh blades*
- *Balsa wood*
- *Utility knife*
- *Fine-grit sandpaper*
- *Sanding blocks*
- *Other wood-carving tools, such as a gouge, chisel, and auger (optional)*
- *Pencil (for marking patterns on the wood)*
- *Wax (optional)*

resources

Balsa Wood Projects, by Thorstein Kristinsson (Sterling Publishing, 1988).

www.guillow.com: Well-known maker of balsa wood model airplane kits.

www.solarbo.com and *www.nationalbalsa. com*: Retail outlets for balsa wood in all shapes and sizes.

www.woodcraft.com: Online store selling the gamut of wood-carving tools.

overview

Balsa's light weight (the cells of the wood itself are large and thin-walled) makes it ideal for small woodworking projects. Balsa trees grow quickly, reaching a height of about 90 feet (27.5 m) and a maximum diameter of 4 feet (1.25 m) in less than 10 years. The resulting wood is cheap and easy to manipulate, requiring only a few cutting and shaping tools. Because balsa absorbs shock and travels far, woodworking hobbyists typically use it to make model airplanes *(see Model Airplanes)* and animal sculptures.

history

Balsa trees grow in the rainforests of Central and South America, where they act almost like weeds, filling in empty spaces in the forest. And in the rainforests of the Amazon, where the trees grow abundantly, Indian tribes, the Piaroa, Piapoco, and Guahibo, have been using the wood to make animal sculptures for centuries. Jaguars, armadillos, tropical birds, and eagles are commonly carved from the wood, and may either be left to dry naturally or dyed with natural paints.

getting started

Balsa wood sculpture makes a great introduction to woodworking because even a beginner can achieve respectable results. Here are some pointers.

- *BECAUSE BALSA WOOD is so light and soft, it's very easy to cut, but you'll need sharp tools to avoid crushing or splintering the wood.*

- *IT'S POSSIBLE TO CARVE balsa wood with nothing more than an X-Acto knife; a fine-toothed coping saw can also be used to carve out larger segments.*

- *BALSA WOOD SCULPTURES can be left unfinished, or they can be sealed and shined to a satiny gloss with paste wax. They'll also accept almost any kind of spray paint if you choose to add color.*

- *IF YOU WANT TO PRACTICE before attempting an original sculpture, try putting together a model airplane or boat made of balsa wood (see resources). The kits are sold with all the necessary tools. Assembly, of course, is required, and is a large part of the fun.*

balsa wood alternatives:

Hobbyists also use basswood as an alternative to balsa wood for carving sculptures. Basswood comes from the *Tiliaceae Tilia Americana* tree and was used by Native Americans to make rope and mats. It's a soft, light hardwood that ranges in color from creamy white to a caramel color. It's quite easy to work with because it cuts easily across the soft, closed wood grain and clearly shows details. Though it's a bit more expensive than balsa wood, it's just as easy (or easier) to cut, sand, and finish, and takes well to painting and staining.

if you like this hobby, you might enjoy:

- Chair caning
- Dollhouse building *(see page 82)*
- Furniture making
- Model aircraft *(see page 142)*
- Model ships *(see page 146)*
- Whittling *(see page 216)*

project: relief carving

For your first original sculpting project, try a relief carving. You'll need a gouge, an X-Acto knife, fine sandpaper, and carbon paper for transferring the design onto the wood.

1) First, find a simple design you like—an asterisk, a silhouette, or even the letters of a name—and trace the pattern onto an 8-inch (20-cm) square piece of balsa wood of moderate thickness.

2) Cut a thin line around the edge of the pattern, then rough out the negative space around the pattern with your gouge, cutting shallowly at first, then going deeper. The effect you're going for is a raised design against a recessed surface.

3) Shave the background with the gouge to create a smooth finish.

4) Keep refining your pattern by crisping the corners and rounding off the tops of the shapes.

5) Lightly sand the sculpture before adding any final precise details.

baseball card trading

FOR THE TRUE BASEBALL FAN, spotting a talented rookie early in his career and nabbing the player's trading card is the equivalent of hitting a grand slam. Collecting trading cards not only adds another dimension to this all-American pastime, it could lead to the realization of another national obsession: a small fortune!

what you'll need

- Interest in baseball
- Baseball cards
- Internet access

resources

Trading Card Games for Dummies, by John Kaufeld and Jeremy Smith (John Wiley/For Dummies, 2006).

2006 Standard Catalog of Baseball Cards, by Bob Lemke (KP Books, 2005).

www.etopps.com: Topps, the major retailer of baseball cards.

www.thepit.com: Graded cards on this site allow traders to find cards in the best condition.

www.hhweb.com: Supplies for storing and displaying baseball cards.

overview

Baseball cards are collected and traded through a variety of methods. Trading is done mostly online these days. You simply go to a website with a trading forum *(see resources)* and post the cards you're willing to trade and what you're looking for.

If you're interested in buying baseball cards, look for a retail shop that specializes in this. These kinds of shops are often willing to trade or buy cards from customers. You'll also find many places to buy cards on the internet, including auction sites like eBay *(see resources)*, but verify whether they're reputable dealers before you proceed.

Another way of getting cards is to attend baseball card shows, where collectors and traders gather to check out one another's merchandise. Your hobby shop or trading magazine should have information about when the shows take place.

Lastly, baseball cards can also be purchased at large retail chain stores like Target and Kmart, though they're typically less valuable. (The most valuable cards are the vintage ones in mint condition that depict star players as rookies.)

Four companies are now authorized to sell Major League Baseball cards: Topps, Fleer, Donruss/Playoff, and Upper Deck. Each of them sells several different sets of cards: regular sets that come out early in the season and include most players; a premium set with a brand name, which are more expensive; super-premium sets; and "vintage" sets that look like antique cards. They also reprint cards from years past.

Rookie cards are those printed when a baseball player first enters the Major Leagues—these are the ones with the potential to become the most valuable. Other categories include "short prints," or limited quantities, which are more valuable than basic cards; errors, on which some type of mistake was made on the card; and commons, which are the least expensive cards of average players.

history

As baseball became popular in the 1860s, after the Civil War, the first type of baseball card was basically a photo glued onto cardboard. The photos portrayed famous players, as well as local teams and amateurs. At the time, they were used as souvenirs for fans. Late in that decade, a company called Peck and Snyder began printing baseball cards with ads promoting their sporting goods products on the backs and distributing them for free on the streets. For the next 20 years, these "trade cards," as they were called, advertised not just sports equipment, but all sorts of products. Tobacco companies began printing ads on the backs of baseball cards in the 1880s and tucked them inside packs of cigarettes. That all ended when the tobacco companies united to make one large corporation, which obviated the need for advertisements.

When the federal government broke up the tobacco monopoly in the early part of the century, the popularity of baseball cards with ads came back in full swing, and many people consider 1909 to 1915 to be the golden age of baseball cards. Players featured on the cards included Ty Cobb, Cy Young, and Shoeless Joe Jackson, among others. In the 1930s, candy companies entered the scene, specifically Boston-based Goudey Gum, which produced some of the most coveted cards in history. These cards portrayed Lou Gehrig, Babe Ruth, and Jimmi Foxx, while the company Gum, Inc., produced cards of Joe DiMaggio and Ted Williams.

In 1948, the first black-and-white baseball issue cards were distributed by Bowman Gum along with a stick of bubble gum, which turned out to be the advent of modern baseball cards. Topps Chewing Gum Company (which eventually evolved into Bazooka Bubble Gum) then joined the fray in the 1950s and offered sizable and colorful cards, and over the next 30 years they took over the industry, selling what are now some of the most significant trading cards known with packs of gum. These days, many baseball cards are still purchased with gum, but they can also be bought on their own.

getting started

It's easy to jump right into this hobby. You must simply decide what types of cards you're looking for: antique and valuable cards, themed cards, cards with just one baseball player or team, or new cards. Visit a hobby shop and ask the clerks about the type of card you're interested in. Ask them about baseball card shows and conventions, where hundreds of dealers gather to trade and sell, and ask them to alert you if a card you're looking for comes in. But be careful: Limit yourself to a budget so you don't go overboard. If you're collecting antiques, look for cards that are rare and in mint condition. Post your "wish list" on baseball card forums online, and check eBay frequently for cards you're looking for. Other places to look for valuable cards: moving sales, flea markets, garage sales, your childhood bedroom—you never know what might turn up.

project: storing baseball cards

If you're serious about collecting baseball cards, it's important to keep them in mint condition. Invest in plastic card protectors so the cards can be viewed without having to be touched. The top-loading variety is less malleable and prevents the cards from being bent. For your most prized possessions, go with cases that envelop the cards between two hard plastic sheets that are screwed or snapped together. Or mount them under UV-filtering glass and display them on your wall so you can enjoy them whenever you walk by.

basketry

WE'RE ALL FAMILIAR WITH THE BIBLICAL LEGEND of little baby Moses being sent down the Nile River in a basket. That famous voyage demonstrates the importance of a craft that has spanned the ages, bridging different cultures and eras through the simple notion of weaving. From Easter baskets to attractive storage units to museum-quality showpieces, basketry has a use and appeal for almost everyone.

what you'll need

- Basket-making material: rattan, willow, reed, or seagrass
- Basket pattern
- Cutting tools (scissors and pruning shears)
- Water and a bucket for soaking
- Wooden clothespins for holding woven rows in place
- Ice pick or awl to help widen holes to pass the fibers through
- Cloth or plastic tape measure
- Material for a handle, such as grapevine or other tough vine (optional)

overview

Basketry is the process of weaving natural fibers to make containers. Baskets can be made out of any number of materials: willow, honeysuckle, rattan, strips of wood, or pine boughs. Every basket is woven with a base, a rim, and side walls; some have lids or decorative handles. Round ones are made on a frame of radiating spokes, while those with flat bottoms or other shapes require stakes or staves. Some are based on a coiled-fiber frame. Basketry is a close cousin of wickerwork, in which flexible plant fibers are shaped into solid objects like furniture. It's also related to caning, a method for weaving chair seats out of rattan.

history

Baskets are among the oldest objects made by humans. Remnants of baskets have been found in Egypt that date back 10,000 to 12,000 years. Evidence of basket-making activity has been discovered all over the world, from Asia to North America. Some scholars believe that humans first conceived of weaving by watching birds interlace twigs to build nests. Baskets can be surprisingly strong, and even watertight—as demonstrated by baby Moses's story. Eventually, the skill was applied to weaving floor mats and roofs, and more sophisticated techniques led to netting that helped with catching fish and game and weaving hammocks, blankets, and clothes.

resources

The Complete Book of Basketry, by Dorothy Wright (Dover Publications, 2001).

www.basketmakers.org: A comprehensive web hub for all things basketry-related, including forums, chat rooms, patterns, and event listings.

www.basket-making.com: Instructions on how to make all sorts of baskets, including Indian stitch and oval baskets.

www.basketpatterns.com: Online purveyors of basket patterns and basket-making supplies.

www.wickerpedia.org: A fun spoof of the open-source encyclopedia website that focuses on all things wicker.

getting started

As with clothes, most baskets are made from patterns, which can be found in books or on the internet. Find a simple one that appeals to you (a pattern with photos or illustrations is best for your first project), then gather your tools and materials. Or consider investing in a kit. Most basket-making fibers need to be softened in water overnight or longer before they become supple enough to work with. You'll start by making a frame, which will vary in shape and construction according to the type of basket. When that's done, the weaving begins. The most basic weave—the true "basketweave"—is a simple over-under movement of the "weaver" (the fiber you're making the basket out of) around the pieces of the frame. The other stitches are variations on that idea, with varying degrees of complexity.

profile: dream weaver

The tallest basket JOYCE SHANNON has ever woven extends to the top of her head when she doesn't slouch—it's 5 feet, 5 inches tall. It took her nine months to weave and literally grew as she illustrated her first basket-weaving kit: "I used the basket as my go-to project when I needed to untangle my thoughts."

Shannon takes inspiration for her designs from the flora and fauna that surround her central Oregon home, especially the birds. "There are thousands of different varieties, and some of them have the brightest displays of color in nature."

A self-taught weaver, Shannon made her first basket for a high school project. The process fascinated her, and she became hooked. Through the years, she's won awards at state fairs and has shown her work at galleries in Oregon and California. She originally started selling baskets as a way to justify buying more basket-weaving materials. Fifteen years

"Don't be discouraged by mistakes. It's more than likely that some quirky little thing about the materials, shape, or construction [of a basket] is what will lead you to a distinctive style all your own."

later, she runs a successful business selling baskets, kits, and patterns online. What keeps her hooked? "The ever-widening possibilities of designs I can imagine is what keeps drawing me back," she says.

project: basket made of local ingredients

Every region of the world has its own basketry tradition based on materials that are locally available. Celebrate your surroundings by going on a basket scavenging hunt. Forage around your environs for natural fibers that lend themselves to the construction of a basket. Take along a pair of pruning shears and a canvas bag or bucket, and when you find something that looks like a worthy candidate for basket making, coil it up and tie it with twine to keep it from tangling with the other ingredients in your bag. Almost any plant supple enough to wrap around your finger a couple of times without break-ing will work. Tough materials like grapevine make good handles; small, long vines and berry canes work well for basket bodies; and textured elements like wheat, porcupine quills, and long pine needles make lovely decorative accents.

batiking

SEWING YOUR OWN CLOTHES IS ONE THING, but designing the fabric for the clothes you make takes the DIY ethos to another level. With the ancient art of batiking, you can infuse cloth with rich colors and graphic patterns, a process that's practiced around the world. Put your personal stamp on everything from the dresses you wear to the placemats that adorn your table.

what you'll need

- Fabric (natural fibers only)

- Fabric dyes (look for the words "fabric reactive" on the label)

- Batik wax (usually a mixture of beeswax and paraffin)

- A pan for melting the wax

- Rubber gloves

- Old pots and pans for dye

- An iron

- Newspapers

- Paintbrushes and/or a canting needle to apply wax

- Fabric transfer paper to copy a pattern onto your fabric (optional)

overview

Batiking is a technique for decorating fabric using wax and dye to create designs. Where wax is applied to the fabric, the dye cannot be absorbed. The wax is applied with a tool called a *tjanting*, or canting, needle (a wood-handled piece with a metal cup at the base from which the wax can flow), or with a paintbrush or metal stamp. Once the wax is applied and has cooled, the fabric is dyed (sometimes more than once for deeper hues) then hung to dry. The wax is then removed either by soaking it in a solvent, like hot, soapy water, or by ironing the fabric between paper towels or newspapers, which will absorb the wax as it melts. Traditionally, batik fabrics are used for sarongs, tablecloths, napkins, and decorative pieces like wall hangings.

history

Samples of batik that date back more than 2,000 years have been found in Southeast Asia. The technique has been practiced for millennia in Indonesia, Malaysia, India, Sri Lanka, China, Japan, and West Africa. *Batik* comes from the Malay word for "dot," and the Javanese word for "write." The invention of the copper block in Java revolutionized the process by making the application of wax quicker and more efficient. Of course, traditional batik was done with natural dyes, usually made from plants. Nowadays, synthetic dyes are readily available from art supply stores. Or you can try making your own natural colorants *(see project)*. Whereas traditional Indonesian batik patterns depict people and animals, Malaysian patterns are often purely decorative and abstract. Contemporary artists experiment with all types of designs.

getting started

Pick a natural fiber to dye, like cotton or silk (the dye won't set in synthetic fibers like polyester) and wash the fabric to remove any chemical treatment. Use "fabric-reactive" dye that will color the fabric even when the water is cool. (Water that's too warm will melt the wax.) Find a pattern to transfer onto the fabric. Melt the wax; it needs to be hot enough that it will soak through the fabric when you draw with it. Using a paintbrush or canting needle, draw the pattern with melted wax wherever you want the fabric to hold its original color. Wait for the wax to harden. If you want your piece to have the veiny look that's characteristic of some batiks, crumple it so the wax breaks in places. Dip the fabric in the dye bath and leave it in for the recommended amount of time. Rinse the dye out and let the fabric dry completely. Now press the fabric between two sheets of newspaper and run a hot iron over it so the wax flows out into the paper. Repeat with clean newspapers until as much of the wax as possible is gone. To launder batiks, hand wash or follow the instructions on the box of dye.

project: make your own dye

Fabric dyes are available at retail stores, but in the spirit of keeping to tradition, you can make colorants out of natural ingredients. First choose a color and dyeing agent to create the dye bath. Try raspberries for pinkish red, coffee or tea for shades of brown, yellow onion skins for a gold tone, blueberries for bluish purple, and beets for deep red. Make the dye solution by chopping the plant material into tiny pieces. Add the ingredients to a pot with twice as much water as you have plant material. Bring the pot to a boil and simmer it for about an hour, covered, to release the coloring. Strain out the solids, then add your fabric, leaving it overnight to let the color absorb. Treat the fabric to be dyed with a mordant, or fixative: For berry dyes, use ½ cup (120 ml) salt to 2 quarts (1.9 L) cold water; for plant dyes, use 2 cups (470 ml) vinegar to 2 quarts (1.9 L) cold water. Simmer your fabric in the fixative for an hour, then rinse it until the water runs clear.

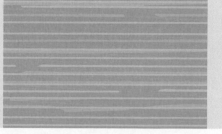

resources

Creative Batik, by Rosi Robinson (Search Press, 2001).

www.batikguild.com/main.php: A Malaysian batik site with information in English about the history of batik and different techniques.

www.batikguild.org.uk: The Batik Guild is a British-based group of batik artists offering workshops and a list of books and resources.

www.dharmatrading.com: Textile art supplies, clothing blanks, dyes, fabrics, kits, and books.

www.textilearts.net: A comprehensive site with links to textile-arts suppliers, practitioners, and other informational sites.

if you like this hobby, you might enjoy:

- Laser printing on T-shirts
- Silk-screening *(see page 186)*
- Tie-dying

beachcombing

SOMETIMES BURYING YOUR HEAD IN THE SAND can actually produce a reward. When you feel like disengaging from the hassles of daily duties, grab your metal detector and sifter and head to the beach. Hours will fly by as you search for a coveted trove embedded in the sand. You'll find that all sorts of bonanzas are lying just below the surface.

what you'll need

- Metal detector (the pricey ones are waterproof)
- Headphones
- Sand scoop
- Sifter
- Probe, a long screwdriver-like device that can be stuck in the ground to locate a target
- Pail
- Garden trowel
- Magnifying glass

overview

There are two categories of beachcomber: (1) the casual stroller who ambles along the shore looking for seashells and pretty rocks and (2) the more enterprising treasure hunter, who braves wind and storm to scour the ocean's edge with a waterproof metal detector in hand. Whichever approach you choose, you'll most likely stumble upon some sort of treasure, even if it's valuable only to you.

If you don't live near the coast, you can still enjoy beachcombing while vacationing in coastal towns. In Hilton Head Island, for example, a cruise takes visitors to the shores of Daufuskie Island, where they can disembark and search for shells and sharks' teeth; and in China Beach, near Quincy, Massachusetts, guides take explorers in search of treasures that might date back more than 100 years, such as china, sea glass, or pottery.

history

Historians believe that beachcombing originally helped unemployed coastal residents supplement their income. They'd use found driftwood for building fires and for shelter, and sell it to businesses that used wood for manufacturing consumer goods. Buoys found on the beach were used to build makeshift stoves and as chairs and stools. And to lure passing ships to shore, cunning beachcombers would light fires on the beach. The ships would invariably run aground, launching more valuables into the water and into the hands of the beachcombers. Mutinied and shipwrecked sailors also became expert beachcombers in order to survive on deserted islands.

It's hard to pinpoint exactly when people first started beachcombing as a hobby, but there was a time in history when the hobby turned into a lifestyle choice. In the 18th and 19th centuries, when wealthy Europeans started traveling to the South Pacific Islands for holidays, some decided to abandon their Continental existence and embrace island life. They ended up espousing all the cultural ideals that came with their new home, including living off the land—and whatever happened to wash ashore. Paul Gauguin was one such notable figure, a French artist who fled Western civilized life for the idyllic shores of Tahiti in the 1890s.

getting started

The best time to do serious beachcombing is right after a storm, after an extraordinarily high tide, or when a large surf swell has just come to an end. Objects usually wash up onto—or, in some cases, into—the sand when they're caught in a storm that pushes them toward the shore. Try to arrive after the crowds have left the beach for the afternoon. It will be easier to scavenge treasures that have washed up without having to work around towels and umbrellas, and you might run into a few worthy items the beachgoers left behind. (Only you can be the moral arbiter of what you keep and what you attempt to return.) Slowly and methodically, swing your metal detector over small spots of sand, listening for the signal on your headphones. When you hear it, use the sand scoop to shovel loose sand into the shaker, and see if anything turns up. For damp sand, use the trowel in the same way.

If you don't live near a beach, you can still go treasure hunting in other spots, like in parking lots, picnic areas, and campgrounds; under large, shady trees and bushes; and around man-made lakes and public swimming pools.

resources

Seaside Naturalist: A Guide to Study at the Seashore, by Deborah Coulombe (Simon & Schuster/Fireside, 1990).

Blue Planet, by Alastair Fothergill, et al (DK Publishing, 2002). A photographic introduction to the world's seas for readers with a beginner's knowledge of science.

Treasure Hunting: Seek and You Shall Find, by Eddie Okonowicz (Myst & Lace Publishers, 2001).

Beachcombing the Pacific, by Amos L. Wood (Schiffer Publishing, 1997).

www.beachcombers.org: Website depicting objects—from rubber duckies to bottled messages to lost containers of Nike shoes on their way to the U.S. from Indonesia—found as a result of beachcombing.

www.kellycodetectors.com: A metal detector supplier.

www.losttreasure.com: The online home of *Lost Treasure* magazine, as well as access to a Prospectors' Club or similar group in your area.

project: keep a treasure log

Once you start finding shiny metal objects or different types of marine life during your beachcombing excursions, you'll want to keep a record of the found items. Do some research and learn about the history of the area you're going to beachcomb so you'll have an idea of what you might find and the best way of recovering it. You'll find all this information in treasure hunting magazines and books, as well as hobbyist sites (see resources).

For sea-life expeditions, take along a guide to help you identify what you discover, then jot it down in your log.

if you like this hobby, you might enjoy:

- Collecting driftwood
- Dumpster diving (see page 88)
- Oyster farming
- Panning for gold
- Sand sculpture
- Treasure hunting (see page 208)

beading

DANGLING ALONE ON A DELICATE NECKLACE, a single bead makes a lovely enough decorative accent. But amassed with hundreds—or even thousands—of other beads, impressive feats of art can be created. Technically speaking, beading takes a keen eye and a steady hand, but from a creative standpoint your own inclination is all you need.

what you'll need

- Beads
- Loom (optional)
- Bead box
- Bead board
- Beading tweezers
- Beading awl
- Pliers of various sizes and tip types, like round-nose, needle-nose, and crimping pliers
- Thread scissors
- Beading needles
- Wire-cutters
- Beading wire or beading thread
- Jewelry findings, like chain or string

overview

Beadwork typically takes the form of jewelry—mostly necklaces and bracelets—but beads can also be used to embellish sculptures, bags, blankets, wall hangings, you name it. There are several different types of beading techniques: loom and off-loom weaving, stringing, bead embroidery, bead crochet, and bead knitting, among others. Beads come in a broad range of materials. Crystal (such as Swarovski), plastic, wood, bone, precious metals, glass (such as Venetian), horn, ceramic, fiber, and ivory are common types. Like many forms of art, different beading techniques and looks reflect different parts of the world.

Beading can vary widely in terms of intricacy, too. For elaborate patterns that require more than a single strand of string, a loom provides more versatility. You can start with a small, inexpensive loom made of either wood or metal, which can be found at most craft stores. Bead looms are like fabric looms, but are much smaller and are used on a table. They are mostly used for seed beads, the smallest type of bead, though the bigger looms can accommodate larger beads.

history

Beads appear to have been used throughout human history. Based on shell beads found in the Blombos Cave in South Africa, some archaeologists believe beading goes back 75,000 years. Beads made of animal teeth and bone in France date to 38,000 B.C.E. Beads made of coral have been found in Çatalhöyük, a central trading spot in Anatolia that was inhabited around 6000 B.C.E. From a social perspective, they have often been a symbol of wealth, as in ancient Cyprus, where carnelian beads were all the rage, and in southern Mesopotamia, where lapis lazuli beads from Afghanistan were worn by the well-heeled. Beads were also worn to ward off the evil eye, and figure prominently in prayer rituals such as those involving Roman Catholic rosaries and the prayer beads used in China, Tibet, Korea, and Japan.

getting started

First, you need to decide what type of beading appeals to you: embroidering beads onto fabric, stringing bead necklaces, or making seed-bead creations on a loom are a few projects to consider. Then stock up on your required supplies and find a pattern you like. Patterns can be found online, in magazines, and in craft stores. After doing some research, you'll get a sense of your aesthetic and level of attention to detail. Most beginners prefer to start with a simple pattern and work their way up to more elaborate ones.

resources

Beadwork: A World Guide, by Carolyn Crab-tree and Pam Stallebrass (Rizzoli, 2002).

The Art of Beadwork: Historic Inspiration, Contemporary Design, by Valeria Hector and Louis Sherr Dubin (Watson-Guptill Publications, 2005).

www.allaboutbeading.com: A comprehensive website maintained by an avid hobbyist beader, featuring tutorials and free patterns.

www.genbead.com: Online retailer of all sorts of beads.

www.interweave.com/bead/beadwork_magazine/default.asp: Online version of *Beadwork Magazine.*

project: make a bead necklace

A basic beaded necklace requires nothing but beads, a string, and some clasps. Beads come in an endless variety of sizes, shapes, and colors, and part of the fun is rifling through the bins at the bead store to find just the right combination. To make a necklace, borrow a bead tray from the store, then go through each bead bin and choose the assortment you like best. The key to achieving a harmonious design is to keep the variety of beads to a minimum. Go with a few shades of the same color, or choose different colors of the same style and size of bead. If you pack in too many disparate elements, you'll end up with an incongruous jumble.

Once you've chosen your beads, find a set of clasps that complement them. There are many different designs and metallic finishes to choose from. Now, slip your beads onto an 18-inch (or desired length) wire or thread. (Tigertail, a strong, flexible, nylon-covered wire that's stiff enough to thread beads without a needle, is a good choice.) You can add a bit of texture and set the beads off from one another by placing crimp beads between each of your other beads.

When you think you've finished, hold up the necklace carefully to your neck and decide whether you need to add or subtract any beads. Now's the time to do it—before you add your clasps. Once you've finalized your design, you can finish by asking the beading clerk to add your clasps. Then you can adorn yourself with your one-of-a-kind piece of handmade jewelry!

beekeeping

HOBBY PERSONALITY: adventurous · **animal-loving** · artistic · crafty · dexterous · **epicurean** · extroverted · history-loving · independent · meditative · meticulous · musical · **nature-loving** · **nurturing** · outdoorsy · patient · social · sporty · technical

THE SIMPLE PLEASURES OF BEEKEEPING are not just for country folk. You can raise honeybees almost anywhere—even urbanites are catching the buzz. Get to know these fuzzy little creatures and you'll become captivated by the way they dance around flowers, the sophistication of their courtship rituals, and the meticulous organization of their hive. And did we mention the joy of having your own supply of fresh, organic honey?

what you'll need

- Protective gear (bee veil, hat, gloves, long-sleeved heavy shirt, ankle-length thick pants, high-top shoes or boots)

- Hive—a wooden box filled with frames called supers (you can buy or make one; see resources)

- Feeder cans

- Sugar syrup

- Bee smoker

- Hive tool

- Frame grips

- Storage jars

- A "package" of bees—this will contain a full colony (you can order one online; see resources)

- A secluded, sheltered, mostly sunny outdoor location for the hive

overview

A honeybee colony behaves as a single unit. In a strong one, there may be as many as 50,000 honeybees headed by a queen (who may lay 2,000 eggs per day), several hundred drones (male bees whose major function is to mate with the young queens), and female worker bees. Workers tend and feed larvae, then construct and clean the wax comb cells. After serving as guards at the hive entrance, they forage for water and for nectar, pollen, and natural resins (propolis) from plants. They turn the nectar into honey, store and use pollen to feed their larvae, and employ the propolis to strengthen and waterproof the hive.

history

Beekeeping has been depicted in cave drawings dating back to 7000 B.C.E. It was practiced by the ancient Egyptians and is discussed in some detail by the ancient Roman writer Virgil. It wasn't until the late 1500s that the life cycle of bees was documented and understood, leading to the development of techniques for bee propagation—and beekeeping as we know it was born. The European honeybee was brought to North America in the early 1600s. It flourished in the New World, and today we have more than 200,000 beekeepers tending more than 3 million hives.

resources

Beekeeping for Dummies, by Howland Blackiston (Hungry Minds Inc., 2002).

The New Complete Guide to Beekeeping, by Roger A. Morse (Countryman Press, 1994).

www.bee-commerce.com: Online superstore for backyard beekeepers.

www.gobeekeeping.com: Offers free online beekeeping classes.

www.honey.com: Recipes and scientific information about honey.

getting started

It may seem counterintuitive, but bees are pretty harmless—unless, of course, you're allergic to bee stings, in which case you shouldn't tempt fate: Choose another hobby from the many profiled in this book. The rest of you, listen up and fear no more: A bee stings only when it's provoked, frightened, or crushed, or its colony is threatened. As long as you learn to handle your bees with gentle firmness, you will succeed. So don your protective gear and let's get started.

1) *ASSEMBLE THE HIVE according to instructions. Fill the feeders with sugar water.*

2) *TIME TO INSTALL the bees: Smoke them so they will be docile.*

3) *UNCORK THE QUEEN first and place her in a combless foundation. Shake out the frames to free the workers. They will enter the hive on their own.*

4) *INSPECT THE BEES regularly to be sure they are taking to their hive. Refill the feeders with sugar water when necessary.*

5) *HARVEST THE HONEY according to the directions contained in your kit. Bon appétit!*

project: ginger-infused honey gift

Homemade flavored honeys are a great way to share the sweet rewards of your new hobby. A recipe for ginger-infused honey follows, but you can infuse your honey with other flavorings, from allspice to rosemary to citrus, following the same method.

INGREDIENTS:
1 cup (340 g) freshly harvested honey
1 tablespoon fresh ginger root,
  peeled and julienned

Fill the bottom of a double boiler with water and place the honey in the top pan. Stir in the ginger, bring the water to a boil, and heat the honey mixture for 10 minutes at about 185°F (85°C). Remove from the heat and let stand for 10 minutes. While the honey is still warm, strain it into sterilized jars and cap.

profile: the bee's knees

STUART SUSSMAN AND HANNAH FROST'S home on the outskirts of San Francisco is a tribute to their love of collecting. You'll find everything from toy police cars and wooden robots to objects featuring the number eight, the state of Texas, and, you guessed it, bees.

While browsing in their local bookstore, they bought a book on beekeeping because they liked the imagery on the cover. But once they cracked open the book, they became intrigued by the practice of beekeeping, too. A conversation with the owner of the store led to an invitation to a beekeeping club meeting, which led to their enrollment in a beekeeping class.

"Beekeeping is a very simple process once you know the parts. There's a certain harmony with nature, and the more you learn, the more interesting it becomes."

"One day in class, we opened up a hive and all these bees came flying out," Sussman recalls. "And just to be in the midst of the bees was an amazing feeling. It was like being underwater on a beautiful, sunny day. We were hooked."

Armed with information from their class, they soon set up hives in their backyard. "We have chairs set up, so we can go out and watch [the bees] whenever we want."

beer brewing

THE SATISFACTION THAT COMES WITH DRINKING A GREAT BOTTLE OF BEER is all the sweeter when it's your own brew. Better than a Bud or even a Beck's, the flavor of your concoction is calibrated to your own particular taste. And when a party calls for a BYOB invitation, you can take the request literally and give them a taste of your private label.

what you'll need

- Brewpot (a huge pot made of stainless steel, with at least a 5-gallon [19 L] capacity)

- Primary fermenter (a huge, airtight plastic vessel, with at least a 7-gallon [26.5 L] capacity)

- Airlock and stopper (allows carbon dioxide to escape from your beer without letting air in)

- Plastic hose

- Bottling bucket (a big, food-grade plastic bucket with a spigot at the bottom)

- Sanitized bottles

- Bottlebrush (thin, curvy brush for cleaning bottles before reuse)

- Bottle capper and caps (if glass bottles are used)

- Stick-on thermometer

- Household items (bowl, saucepan, rubber spatula, oven mitts)

overview

Brewing beer at home takes patience, and knowing that there will be a mountain of dishes to wash when it's all over. At its essence, home brewing is done by boiling water, malt extract, and hops in a kettle; letting the mixture cool; then adding yeast for fermentation. To keep it manageable, home brews are usually done in 5-gallon (19 L) batches. The process is infinitely easier if you use a kit, but you have more control over the flavor of your beer when you experiment with the chemical processes of fermentation on your own.

history

If chemical tests of ancient pottery jars found in Iran are to be believed, beer dates back to more than 7,000 years ago. As far back as 1900 B.C.E., beer brewing recipes were being passed around in Sumerian writings (specifically, in a poem that honors Ninkasi, the patron goddess of brewing).

The earliest beers were usually made with barley. Hops were first added to the brewing process during the Middle Ages, as early as 800 C.E. in Europe. By about the 15th century, industrious brewers had started selling beer in pubs and monasteries in what became a bustling commercial industry in Europe.

resources

Complete Joy of Homebrewing, 3rd ed., by Charles Papazian (Harper Collins, 2003).

www.beertown.org/homebrewing: The American Homebrewers Association, which organizes conferences, festivals, and competitions to foster a home-brewing community.

www.byo.com: The online home of *Brew Your Own* magazine, and all of its available resources.

www.howtobrew.com: An extremely thorough, step-by-step guide by author John Palme.

www.midwestsupplies.com: A large mail-order supply house for the home brewer.

getting started

The most important part of home brewing is preparation. Be sure you understand all the steps and set all your ingredients and equipment out in the order in which they will be used. Take note of the amount of each ingredient you use for future reference.

- *FOR THE PURPOSES OF THIS BOOK (that is, in a small amount of space), we'll get you started with instructions for using a home-brewing kit. First, fill your primary fermenter with 4 gallons (15 L) of water (each kit will specify the volume of ingredients, but this is a general guideline). In your brewpot, boil 2 quarts (1.9 L) of water, then add the contents of the beer mix, which should include malts and other fermentable ingredients, like sugar or malt extract. Stir it well. Then add this to the primary fermenter. Mix it well, then add the yeast. Let it ferment for about five days.*

- *NOW IT'S TIME to bottle your beer, a process that will allow it to go through a second fermentation, which makes the beer carbonated. The fermentation part takes at least two weeks, so you might want to buy a six-pack from the store while you wait.*

profile: gift of the grog

CHARLIE PAPAZIAN got his first sampling of beer when he was five years old—a sip of Ballantine from his Uncle Paul at a family Christmas party. But it was not until his early twenties that he tasted a homemade brew, which Papazian recalls as a "fizzy, cidery, and alcoholic-tasting Prohibition-style home brew."

He thought he should give this home brewing a whirl, and after feeding the sewer rats with his first batch of "undrinkable" beer, he kept practicing. His day job was working as a schoolteacher in Boulder, Colorado, but in his free time he figured out how to improve his results using different brewing techniques, and over the next 10 years, he taught more than 1,000 people in the Boulder-Denver area how to make beer. The next logical step was to form the American Homebrewers Association and its magazine, Zymurgy.

His job as the founder and president of the association has allowed him to meet some of "the most fantastic people in the world, from all walks of life," he says. "There's something about knowing how to make great beer that is a ticket into the world of beer and brewing wherever you roam."

project: cook with beer—amber cayenne-citrus marinade

Making your own beer is endlessly satisfying, but the cookery doesn't have to end there. Add beer to marinades, stews, and a batch of other recipes, like this one, which you can try on beef or lamb.

INGREDIENTS:

Two 12-ounce (350 ml) bottles amber ale
1 tablespoon red wine vinegar
2 tablespoons fresh orange juice
1 teaspoon grated orange zest
1/2 cup (120 ml) canola oil
1 tablespoon grated horseradish
1/2 cup (80 g) minced onion
2 tablespoons minced garlic
2 teaspoons salt
1 teaspoon cayenne pepper (or more, to taste)

Mix all the ingredients together in a blender, puréeing until smooth. Reserve 1 cup (240 ml) for basting as you grill. Marinate the meat for at least 2 hours for best flavor. (Makes enough marinade for 2 pounds of meat.)

See www.grillingwithbeer.com for more recipes that use beer.

"There's nothing that spoils the flavor and character of a home brew more than worrying, so relax."

bell ringing (aka change ringing)

YOU DON'T HAVE TO BE A CHURCH PARISHIONER to enjoy bell ringing. All you need is an appreciation for music and math, and a predilection to preserve a charming, provincial pastime.

what you'll need

Depending on how involved you want to get, you need either a set of two handbells, or access to a church with change bells. Whether you're playing on a large or small scale, you also need a group of change ringers to play with.

overview

Most of us know bell ringers as those who pull the ropes of church bells to summon parishioners for weddings or funerals. Those bells, known as carillons or chimes, don't swing and are generally controlled by one person. Change ringing is a completely different form of the art. It's done by a group of people, each ringing a tuned bell in a series of patterns called "changes." Change ringers usually stand in a circle and ring these bells, which range in weight from a few hundred pounds to several tons, not to a traditional melody, but to an elaborate mathematical algorithm. The idea is to ring the bells in every possible order (or "change") without repeating any patterns. For example, if a tower has eight bells, ringers will have 40,320 permutations of rings. A ring of bells usually consists of 4 to 12 bronze bells that are attached to large wooden wheels hung in large frames so the bells can swing 360 degrees. The wheels are turned by means of a handmade rope. Because it takes a few seconds for a bell to rotate, the art of this hobby comes in ringing the bells at just the right time.

history

Though bell ringing dates as far back as the early Chinese dynasties in 200 B.C.E., bells have played a part in the religious rituals of many civilizations. Bells have been used in the churches and cathedrals of the West since the Middle Ages, but the scope of bell ringing changed with the development of the full wheel in the 17th century, which allowed ringers to control the chimes. In 1668, Fabian Stedman published *Tintinnalogia,* or *The Art of Change Ringing*, detailing everything there was to know about systematic ringing. Though some of the techniques have varied over the years, the premise remains very much the same. Change ringing was brought to the U.S. by British colonists, who installed bells in Boston, New York, Philadelphia, and Charleston in the 1700s. Though the popularity of the hobby began to wane in the 19th century, the installation of the 10-bell ring at Washington, D.C.'s National Cathedral in 1963 helped rekindle people's interest. In 1997, the Cathedral Church of St. James in Toronto, Canada, installed a 12-bell ring—the only one in North America.

getting started

Like learning any instrument, bell ringing requires a lot of practice and, if possible, some tutelage from an experienced teacher. If you live near a church tower that has bells, find out if a bell ringing group is associated with it (the answer is probably yes). You can find groups in the U.S. on the North American Guild of Change Ringers (NAGCR) website *(see resources)*, which also offers courses from time to time.

If a church tower can't be found in your general vicinity, you can join a handbell-ringing group *(see handbell choirs)*. Each ringer controls two bells, simulating those in church towers, and follows the same process as change ringers.

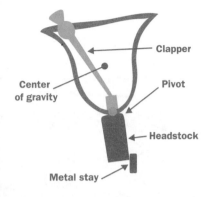

Clapper

Center of gravity

Pivot

Headstock

Metal stay

handbell choirs

In contrast to the heft of church bells, handbells are lighter bells with flexible handles, designed to be rung by individuals, one in each hand. The bells are held against the ringer's shoulder, bell upwards, then swung down and forward. A wrist-snapping action is involved that takes some practice to master.

Originally tuned sets of handbells were assembled to give change ringers a way of rehearsing outside drafty church towers. The handbells came in tuned sets that typically represented the number of bells in a particular tower (often six or twelve tuned to a diatonic scale) to provide an accurate simulation of the change ringing experience.

Handbell choirs, however, often gather to practice and perform for the sheer joy of making music together. Because their goal is to perform recognizable melodies, they are outfitted with a fuller set of bells that allows them to play complete songs. Each bell ringer is responsible for sounding a particular note, so staying alert is critical. Contact the American Guild of English Handbell Ringers (www.agehr. org) to locate a handbell ensemble near you.

project: visit church towers

Like architectural jewels, there are a finite number of church towers with bells in the U.S., and many of them are located on the East Coast. (Or broaden your horizons and head across the border to Canada or overseas to England, where it all began.) Plan a vacation to these cities and the surrounding areas, and make arrangements to meet the change ringers. They might invite you to watch, or even play. The trip will give you insight into this fascinating hobby, demonstrate the range of practices in different churches, and introduce you to a band of brethren you'll always be able to ring up.

resources

www.cccbr.org.uk: The website for *Ringing World*, a weekly newspaper published by the Central Council of Church Bell Ringers in Great Britain.

www.handbellservices.com: Retailer for handbell information and supplies, sheet music, and related accessories.

www.jhsbell.com: A supplier of bells, sheet music, and instructional videos.

www.nagcr.org: The North American Guild of Change Ringers site features a list of working bells in church towers, change-ringing group contact information, and submitted "peals."

www.ringing.info: Change-ringing resources with links to dozens of other ringer organizations.

bike customizing

FOR THOSE WHO LIKE TO PUT THEIR STAMP OF INDIVIDUALITY on every available medium, the bicycle is the perfect canvas for expression. Whether it's your 1970s cruiser or your state-of-the-art, light-as-a-feather off-roader, customizing your wheels takes bike riding to an altogether higher plane.

what you'll need

. . . .

FOR DECORATIVE CUSTOMIZING:

- *Electrical tape*

- *Superglue*

- *Adornments of your choice, including: Spray paint, stickers, streamers, fake flowers or birds, Astroturf, hood ornaments, noisemakers, beads*

- *New seat, wheels, crank (optional)*

resources

Atomic Zombie's Bicycle Builder's Bonanza, by Brad Graham and Kathy McGowan (McGraw-Hill/TAB Electronics, 2003).

Bicycling Science: Third Edition, by David Wison (MIT Press, 2004).

www.critical-mass.org: Organized monthly bike rides through urban downtown areas with links to bike events near you.

http://fossilfool.com/burners: Neon safety lights that emanate light underneath bicycles.

www.hokeyspokes.com: LED-lit psyche-delic lights for your wheels.

overview

With bicycle customization, almost anything goes. You can go the classic route, outfitting your bike with upgraded essentials like carbon seat posts, or add accessories like a basket, a bell, and vintage decals. Or go postmodern and artsy with splattered paint and glued-on sculptural objects. Nocturnal rides require the use of lights, another excuse for embellishments, such as neon bulbs and LED-lit spokes. Others enjoy listening to tunes as they ride and install a handlebar-mounted boom box to that end. The choices are infinite.

history

Depending on the source, top contenders for the honor of having invented the bicycle include (1) Leonardo DaVinci, who drew—or had one of his students draw—a sketch of a modern-looking bicycle in 1490 that was never realized (a drawing some scholars contend was forged in the 1960s), (2) German inventor Baron Karl von Drais de Sauerbrun, who in 1817 introduced a vehicle with two in-line wheels connected to a wood frame that was pushed with feet, Flintstones-style, and (3) father-and-son team Pierre and Ernest Michaux, who introduced pedals to the vehicle in the 1860s. Styles have evolved and changed through-out the years, with lighter materials and aerodynamic designs giving riders an immense variety of souped-up options to choose from.

Experimenting with artistic design on bikes goes back to about the mid-1970s, when the Deko-Chari (which literally means "decorating bike") phenomenon sprung up in Japan. It was a response from kids who were fascinated by the "Truck Yaro" phenomenon, a series of movies about giant tricked-out trucks. The younger generation applied the ideas to their bikes and decked them out with chrome plating, lights, and hi-fi audio systems. In the U.S., bike customization has become almost compulsory at such events as the Burning Man Festival, an annual gathering of performance artists and observers in the Black Rock Desert in Nevada, a venue for the artsy set to exhibit their creative prowess.

getting started

First, come up with an overall plan of what you'd like your bike to look like. Look closely at bicycles you admire and figure out what exactly you like about them. Do you want the fastest, lightest bike on the market, or do you prefer to make an artful statement? For the former, take it one part at a time: Swap your ordinary seat for a racier version or change your rims for a snazzier set. For the latter, add accessories like handlebar coverings, baskets, and plastic spoke adornments. Or spray paint the bike different colors, using masking tape to define straight lines and shapes. You can also splatter paint onto it for a more randomly artistic take. You may want to experiment on a cheap thrift-store bike as you establish what kind of look you're going for. There are no hard-and-fast rules when it comes to this hobby.

"When someone rides a bike long enough, they naturally gravitate toward customizing parts to suit themselves. But the true Zen moment comes from riding the bike."

project: rattly spokes

Add a little color to your spokes with this easy project. Take a fistful of colored or patterned drinking straws and, using scissors or an X-Acto knife, cut a slit lengthwise in each straw. Slide the straw sections onto your spokes. You can cut the straws into smaller 3-inch (7.5 cm) lengths and stack them or leave them as they are. Alternate colors for an overall pattern, adding as many as you deem fit, but leave enough room for them to slide up and down so they make that hypnotic "flt flt flt" sound.

profile: custom king

FOR PURISTS LIKE JASON MONTANO, who owns a bike shop in Piedmont, California, a wealthy suburb of San Francisco, where bicyclists take their gear seriously, the goal of bike customization is optimum efficacy. "The whole point of the upgrade is about performance," Montano says. "You can add a bike part that's blue in color, but what counts is how it operates. It should never be at the cost of the performance."

That's unlike the many "art bikes" Montano has seen at festivals and around town: bikes stacked on top of each other with the cyclist riding the top one; a bike hinged in the middle, where the cyclist rides beside another set of wheels; or one that turns right when you turn the wheel to the left. "They have all sorts of those crazy bikes," he says.

Most of his clients focus on things like customizing the wheels of their bikes. They look for different-colored rims and hubs and generally "add jewelry when they can." Montano's customers come to him for rare parts that can't be found at other shops. "We tend not to just take a bike out of the box and assemble it," he says. "We do custom paint jobs and 'pimp-your-ride' kinds of customization that make the bike perform better, look better, the whole nine yards." The most expensive bike for the mass consumer costs about $9,000. What makes it worth that much? "It's got the nicest, lightest parts out there," Montano says. "Carbon fiber everything: seat posts, crank, wheels."

For himself, the perfectionist has scored a single-speed road bike handmade by a bicycle maker named Nagasawa, a one-man shop in Japan. The waiting list for a Nagasawa bike is two or three years. "It's like a Samurai sword," Montano says. His 14-pound beauty is covered with three different layers of translucent paint, making it black indoors and the color of blood in the sun.

birding

FOR BIRD LOVERS, spotting a scarlet tanager twittering around in its natural habitat is the equivalent of Catholics seeing the pope: a wondrous and rare event. Birders, who are passionate about our feathered friends, enjoy being outdoors, learning about and communing with nature, and being a part of the birding community, a vast and enthusiastic group of like-minded folks.

what you'll need

- *Binoculars or a spotting scope*
- *Field guide*
- *Pad and pencil for making sketches and taking notes*
- *Comfortable outdoor clothing and shoes*
- *Camera*

overview

Though birding is a relatively quiet and serene hobby, birders are an excitable bunch. They travel far and wide to add to the catalogue of their findings, known as a "life list," and keep copious and detailed records of birds they've spotted. They stay active in birding groups, trading stories and keeping abreast of each other's sightings. Local groups and clubs even keep blogs and hotlines that birders can contact when they sight rare birds, so others can follow their trails. They also organize "Big Days," during which they gather at a designated spot and compete to find the most species of birds in one day.

history

John James Audubon is the most notable historical figure associated with bird-watching. Born in what is now called Haiti in 1785, Audubon moved to the Philadelphia area when he was 18 years old. There, he observed birds' nesting patterns and habitats, and noticed that birds return to the same site every year. Traveling across the U.S., Audubon created detailed paintings of the birds he'd observed. Audubon's seminal work, *The Birds of America*, is the effort of decades of research, and includes his paintings and catalogued field notes on nearly 500 of the 700 birds that existed in North America at that time. After the book was published, bird-watching entered the public consciousness. The hobby grew in popularity when ornithologist and bird artist Roger Tory Peterson published his 1934 *A Field Guide to the Birds*, known in the birding world as "the first modern field guide."

getting started

Birding can be done in any natural setting—from your backyard to the local park or the beach. Each habitat has its own distinguishing characteristic that draws certain types of birds. Fall and spring are important times of year to watch for birds in migration. (Some will sport bright breeding plumage during the spring.) During warm weather, get started early in the day, as dawn to mid-morning is the best time to find birds. In the winter, the warmest time of day is best. You'll have better luck finding different varieties of birds in wetlands and at the edges of streams, woods, and lakes. If you can, try going with an experienced birder who can give you pointers on how to spot birds and how to assess what you find.

Look for the following characteristics in a bird's appearance and behavior to help you recognize its species.

- *LOOK FOR COLOR AND MARKINGS. Though most are brown, there are spots of color to look for as well. Even seemingly drab-colored birds often have streaks or speckles. Also note if the bird has a distinctive cap or underbelly, or if it has dark or light bars on its tail or wings.*

- *NOTE HOW BIG the bird is. It's an important point of its identity. Observe the bird's body characteristics, too, such as the shape of the bill, wings, and tail.*

- *WATCH the bird's actions: whether it flits among the branches, creeps along the tree trunk, pecks at the grass, or soars and hovers in the sky.*

- *RESEARCH what types of birds live in the habitat you're observing, and you'll likely see those very birds there. While some birds prefer evergreen trees, others flock to deciduous ones.*

- *LISTEN FOR their calls. Experts can tell in just a few notes what type of bird they're listening to.*

project: build a birdfeeder

To invite birds to your backyard (or window ledge), make a birdfeeder for your personal viewing pleasure. Here's a super-simple version. Rinse an empty plastic jug, such as a gallon milk bottle. Draw a 3-inch (7.6 cm) square on a piece of paper, then round off the two top corners of the square. Two inches (5 cm) above the bottom of the jug, trace the pattern, then cut out what will be the door. Use a nail to make two small holes at the top of the jug, just below the cap, then glue the cap on top. Place a large rock inside the jug to keep it from moving too much in the wind. Thread some strong twine through the holes and hang the feeder from a post or tree branch. Add bird seed and watch the birds flock to their new eatery.

resources

How to Be a (Bad) Birdwatcher, by Simon Barnes (Pantheon, 2005).

National Geographic Field Guide to the Birds of North America, 4th ed., by The National Geographic Society (National Geographic, 2002).

Sibley's Birding Basics (Knopf, 2002). Pocket-sized birding guide by the author of *The Sibley Guide to Birds,* by David Allen Sibley (Knopf, 2000).

www.americanbirding.org: The American Birding Association represents a range of interests, from identification and education to listing and conservation.

www.audubon.org: The Audubon Society is a national conservation group with an emphasis on birds.

www.birdwatchersdigest.com: The website for *Bird Watcher's Digest*, a magazine about bird-watching.

bonsai

HOW CAN A FULL-SIZE LIVING TREE BE TRANSFORMED into a tiny potted plant? Standing regally in their petite pots, mimicking their giant counterparts, bonsai are a marvel of the botanical world. Caring for a bonsai is an all-consuming hobby in its own right, but training one from its early beginnings is the true art.

what you'll need

- *Tree*
- *Pot*
- *Pencil and chalk*
- *Two types of scissors: a long pair with sharp tips to trim the small branches, and a heavy pair with thick blades for trimming roots*
- *Knob cutters, which make spherical cuts and are helpful in removing chunks of wood*
- *Concave branch cutters*
- *Woodburning tool (optional)*
- *Wire cutters with strong tips to remove wire*
- *Folding saw, for removing thick branches*
- *Soil (see project)*
- *Fertilizer*
- *Tools for general maintenance, such as scoop, sieve, and rake*

overview

A bonsai plant or tree is one that has been intentionally kept diminutive by root and crown pruning. Bonsai are not grown from special seeds, and in fact have the exact same genes as their life-sized counterparts. Plants with naturally smaller leaves and twigs can be easily trained to be bonsai, although, technically, pretty much any species can also be trained. If they're cared for properly, bonsai can live as long as their full-sized brethren, but they demand a lot of attention. Just the right amounts of water and light are crucial to their survival. They must also be pruned with painstaking care, and each variety requires a different regimen. Bonsai are shaped using copper or aluminum wire, which is wrapped around the branches and trunks to hold them in place. The most common forms of bonsai are juniper, cherry, pine, maple, and apricot trees.

history

Bonsai originated during the Tang Dynasty (from 618 to 907 C.E.) in China. Referred to as *penjing*, which means "tray scenery," the art was brought to Japan during the Heian era, from about 800 to 1200 C.E., and was at first practiced only by the wealthy classes. By around 1300, however, the art of bonsai had become as commonplace in Japanese culture as the tea ceremony, and it grew in popularity as a hobby over the next several centuries. The West was first introduced to bonsai at the Paris Exhibition in 1878. As interest flourished in Europe, Japanese nurseries began offering the plants by way of catalogues. Today, fine bonsai collections can be found in both the East and the West, many of which include specimens that are more than a century old.

getting started

The best way to become familiar with this specialized art is to join a bonsai club. You'll have a venue for asking questions and learning from those with more experience (and you might be allowed to practice on real trees). Decide where you want to keep your bonsai, indoors or outdoors. Then find a plant you're interested in, ideally one that is resilient and fast-growing for your first attempt. Start by researching the plant to learn which season is best for pruning. (Some plants can be pruned year-round, but many will be damaged if pruned at the wrong time.) Prune gently and carefully, keeping in mind both your vision of how you want the plant to look in its final form and how its existing shape contributes to that vision. At the same session, trim the plant's roots, too; this is an important part of the miniaturizing process.

After your first pruning, observe the tree over the next few days, making sure you like the shape it is taking, then start the final trimming, keeping in mind that it's better to leave some bushiness than to hack away too much. Give the tree time to heal from a severe pruning before you start again. Focus on the trunk, which adds heft to the appearance of a bonsai. Remove problematic branches early in the process—specifically, those that grow across each other, back toward the trunk, or underneath the primary branches. Use wire to gently and gradually bend the branches into your chosen positions, and keep it as natural looking as possible.

resources

Beginning Bonsai: The Gentle Art of Miniature Tree Growing, by Shirley Student and Larry Student (Tuttle Publishing, 1993).

The Complete Book of Bonsai, by Harry Tomlinson (Abbeville Press, 1991).

www.american-bonsai.com: Bonsai trees and supplies for sale.

www.bonsaibasics.com: A resourceful site for beginners, with answers to the fundamental questions of caring for bonsai.

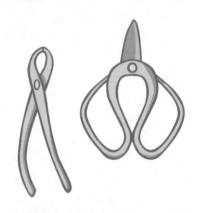

project: make your own bonsai soil

For the ideal root-growing environment, the best combination of soil ingredients is 75 percent inert aggregate material and 25 percent organic material. Combine 1 part Haydite (a porous rock also known as "expanded shale"), 1 part granite or river rock, 1 part Turface (a clay product used for aerating grass), and 1 part pine bark. Pass the mixture through two sets of screens to sift out particles that are between $1/8$ and $1/4$ inch (3 and 6 mm) in diameter and discard the remaining dust.

book arts

THE ART OF MAKING BOOKS IS A PROFOUNDLY PERSONAL ONE. You can't wear the product of this hobby, eat it, hang it on a wall, or ride it around. Book artists create these delicate pieces with painstaking care as a way of marking a moment or representing an idea that can only be expressed in this most precious medium.

what you'll need

- *Bone folder, a paper-folding tool*

- *Paper*

- *Sharp paper-cutting knife, such as an X-Acto, and a cutting mat*

- *Boards for hardcovers and bookboard covering cloth*

- *Archival glue and glue brush*

- *Awl or paper-punch tool*

- *Sewing needles and strong thread*

- *Boards for spines*

resources

The Essential Guide to Making Handmade Books, by Gabrielle Fox (North Light Books, 2000).

Hand-Made Books: An Introduction to Bookbinding, by Rob Shepherd (Search Press, 1995).

www.centerforbookarts.org: The New York–based Center for Book Arts offers events, classes, exhibits, and resources for those who don't live in the area.

www.flaxart.com: Comprehensive source for paper and bookmaking projects.

www.philobiblon.com: The Book Arts website.

overview

Hand bookbinding is an ancient art form that has been revived in the past few decades. Bookbinders use a variety of techniques, from simple accordion-fold bindings, to sewn bindings, to hardcover bindings, each requiring a different type of skill. Book covers can be made with various materials, from leather and vellum to fabric, cardboard, and paper. Made for both functional and artistic purposes, a handmade book can be used as a scrapbook, journal, photo album, guest book, or just a unique work of art.

history

Before there was the book as we know it—printed pages folded and sewn together into a form called a codex—people scratched their writings into clay, or wrote them in scrolls or on wax tablets. But those forms were cumbersome and limited the space available for writing. What was needed was a more expandable medium, and the book, with its variable number of pages, was the answer. The Romans were the first to think of it. They folded vellum or parchment sheets, then sewed them along the fold. By the end of the 1st century C.E., the codex was on the rise. Paper, invented in China as early as the 1st century, had made its way to Europe by the 14th century; it provided a less expensive, lighter-weight alternative to parchment and vellum. The success of Johannes Gutenberg's printing press in the mid-1400s meant texts no longer had to be written out longhand, and thus were available to a wider public. However, the printed pages still had to be bound by hand. Wealthy bibliophiles commissioned gorgeous bindings for their books—many can be seen in museums today. It wasn't until the 19th century that machine binding became possible, making books affordable for the masses.

> "Expand your idea of what a book can be. Go to book arts exhibitions in galleries or museums. Start a book arts club in your community. If you're good at following directions, it will be easy to teach yourself."

getting started

For your first book, consider trying a Japanese stab binding. All you will need is a bookbinding awl, a stack of paper for pages, decorative paper for the cover, and a needle and thread. Consult books or the internet for instructions about how to punch holes through the paper and stitch the book together. If you like, you can fill the pages with art and writings before you compile the book. This is especially helpful if you plan to paste pictures onto your pages, because adding them to an already bound book tends to make the book swell open from the spine rather than closing flat. From the Japanese stab binding, your imagination will guide you to ever more complicated book projects. To broaden your horizons, consider enrolling in a bookbinding class at a local art school or community college.

profile: treasure box

WHEN LESLEY PATTERSON-MARX was a child, she liked to cut out the funny pages from the newspaper, glue them back together out of sequence, and bind them with staples. In college, she would salvage old scrapbooks or blank journals and insert her own writings and sketches in the pages. So it was only natural that bookmaking eventually became the focus of her art and her profession as a teacher at Watkins College of Art and Design in Nashville, Tennessee, where she taught for several years.

Patterson-Marx uses old photos and found objects like buttons, antique paper, and even plant matter—anything that lies flat—in her art. "The objects I use have to have the right 'mojo,'" she says. "They have to help convey the overall concept of the book, and transcend their original function." Her books range from small, three-dimensional sculptures that house images to traditional tomes with sequential pages. "I love the qualities of bookmaking, especially the sewing. I love that books are a bridge between two- and three-dimensional mediums," she says. "I love that the book is meant to be held by its viewer and that the viewer is meant to have an intimate, tactile, and visual experience with the book. And I love that books are sequential. They reveal themselves gradually with every turn of the page."

If you're a beginning binder, Patterson-Marx advises, "Learn some basic binding techniques from books or classes just so you understand the fundamental structure of books, and look at examples. From there, take your own approach. Make up your own bindings, incorporate your own drawings, paintings, prints, or collages."

project: make your own marbelized paper

For your bookmaking project, try making a book cover with marbelized paper. The swirls will add a lovely texture to your book.

WHAT YOU'LL NEED:
2 or 3 colors of acrylic paint and an equal number of disposable mixing containers
1/2 cup (120 ml) liquid fabric starch
Sheet pan (the kind with four shallow sides)
Paintbrushes

For each color, mix 1 tablespoon acrylic paint with 2 tablespoons water; set the containers aside. Pour all of the liquid fabric starch into the sheet pan, then use a paintbrush to drizzle the paint mixtures onto the surface of the starch. Use only a couple of colors at a time for best results. Using a clean paintbrush, gently swirl the colors across the top of the liquid starch. Don't mix them too thoroughly; you want a marbled effect. Lay a sheet of paper on top of the colors, then carefully lift the paper. The swirling colors will transfer to the page. Let the paper dry paint side up. For each new page, add more paint and repeat the steps. You should be able to decorate several sheets of paper before the paints are all used up.

calligraphy (western and eastern)

THESE DAYS, THE ART OF CALLIGRAPHY is used only in wedding invitations or other such prodigious event announcements. The ancient art form has been relegated to vitrines in dark museum rooms. Sure, one could argue that the thousands of different typographic fonts on a computer, easily accessible and usable, are worthy substitutes. But calligraphy stands apart. With a quill in hand, the romance of letter-writing can be resurrected, the brush of each stroke bringing dignity to every word.

what you'll need

FOR WESTERN CALLIGRAPHY:

- *Writing utensils appropriate for the alphabets you choose (dip pen with metal nibs, calligraphy fountain pen, reed, quill, or double pencil; see project)*

- *Inks or pigments*

- *Smooth bond paper that won't bleed*

- *Writing board (optional)*

- *Tape or binder clips (optional)*

FOR EASTERN CALLIGRAPHY:

- *Calligraphy brush*

- *Xuan paper (for practice, use mao-bian paper or newsprint)*

- *Ink*

overview

You don't need to understand Chinese characters to appreciate the beauty of Eastern calligraphy, which for many Westerners serves as abstract art, and is a highly esteemed form of art in East Asia. The artist controls each stroke according to his interpretation by varying the concentration of ink, the flexibility of the brush, and the thickness of the paper, much like painting. Western calligraphy, on the other hand, is written more like fonts than images. The uniformity of the characters is an important part of the craft. Some Western calligraphic letter styles include black letter (or gothic script), uncial, italic, roundhand, and copperplate.

history

The word *calligraphy* comes from the Greek words *kali* (beautiful), and *graphia* (writing). In the East, the ancient civilizations of China, Japan, Korea, and Vietnam used calligraphy as both an art form and for written communication for thousands of years. In China, the first culture to develop the art, calligraphy has evolved a great deal from the inception of the dazhuan script, or large seal characters, which were an early form of writing used during the 12th century B.C.E. Over the centuries, the script progressed to a more regular form—*xiaozhuan*, or small script—and has stayed consistent since the Han Dynasty, beginning in 206 B.C.E.; it is still used in some formal contexts.

Western calligraphy essentially derives from the Latin script, a descendant of the Greek and Cyrillic writing systems—alphabets that had been developed by around 3000 B.C.E. Since so much writing of the time was devoted to copying the Bible, the church became a driving force behind this art. Calligraphy prospered in medieval Europe within the context of monastic scriptoriums. The most lavishly decorated illuminated manuscripts were created in northern Europe between the 7th and 9th centuries. After the invention of the printing press in the 1450s, handwritten books became rare.

getting started

- *WESTERN: Choose the style of lettering you're going to learn; uncial and italic are good for beginners. Determine the height of the letters, then choose your nib size accordingly. Holding the nib at an angle (30 degrees for uncials, for example), write the letters in smooth strokes using a calligraphic written page as your guide. After each letter, dip your pen in the ink. You can also try tracing over calligraphy letters to become familiar with the script.*

- *EASTERN: It is key to learn how to hold the brush correctly; consult books and the internet or enroll in a class. There are three basic forms to each character—the circle, the triangle, and the square—and a specific number of strokes and appointed positions. Following a Chinese character chart that shows the order of the strokes, practice strokes and lines by tracing them. When you're ready, try them freehand on graph paper.*

profile: scripting with spirit

At the age of nine, JOSHUA HOUGH embarked upon an indoor activity that blossomed into his profession: Chinese calligraphy. Soon enough, Hough was winning awards in his small Taiwanese town and was apprenticed by a master calligrapher who was the cousin of the last emperor of China, Pu Yi. Even after 30 years of practicing the technique, Hough, who now lives in Dallas, Texas, is still "obsessed" with the way the characters are formed. He recounts with not a little pride that great works of calligraphy have been preserved with care, and that the best calligraphers held important positions in ancient Chinese and Japanese governments. "The Asian people regard calligraphy as representing one's personality, capabilities, and spirit," he says. Though Chinese calligraphy can be appreciated for its aesthetic beauty, Hough says the practice also has physical benefits, including promoting correct posture, improved breathing control, memory, relaxation, concentration, and coordination.

project: make a double pencil

Practicing with a double pencil, which mimics a calligraphy pen, can help you learn the technique. Take two short pencils and cut a flat side along the length of each one. Face the flat sides together, then tape the pencils so their points are about 0.8 inch (20 mm) apart. Once that's done, draw a straight line on a piece of paper with a regular pencil and ruler. Then hold the double pencil in your hand at a 30-degree angle to the line you drew and write a letter. You can use a protractor to make sure the angle is accurate. The thickest stroke is the diagonal one going from the top left to the bottom right, and the thinnest stroke is the one going from the bottom left to top right. Practice making patterns based on letters in preparation for using a calligraphy pen. Or write the letters and then fill in the outlines with ink.

"We regard calligraphy as representing one's pesonality, capabilities, and spirit."

resources

The Calligrapher's Bible: 100 Complete Alphabets and How to Draw Them, by David Harris (Barron's Educational Series, 2003).

Chinese Calligraphy Made Easy: A Structured Course in Creating Beautiful Brush Lettering, by Rebecca Yue (Watson-Guptill, 2005).

www.calligraphicarts.org: The Association for the Calligraphic Arts, open to professional and novice calligraphers.

www.calligraphycentre.com: The Calligraphy Centre, in Winston-Salem, North Carolina, offers workshops and retreats.

www.johnnealbooks.com: Source of supplies for calligraphers.

www.studioarts.net/calligraphy: Calligraphy for Everyone: a helpful online resource that provides specific instructions, stroke by stroke.

www.societyofscribes.org: Helpful site for learning about the history of calligraphy and finding current information about workshops and lectures.

candle making

THERE'S SOMETHING ABOUT A LIT CANDLE that instantly changes a setting, evoking a certain mood. Candles complete a dinner table, add a warm glow to nighttime parties, and can fill a room with a wonderful aroma—and, of course, everybody looks gorgeous by candlelight. Experimenting with different colors and fragrances makes this hobby all the more enjoyable.

what you'll need

- Stove or hotplate
- Double boiler
- Thermometer
- Pretabbed wicks (with metal tabs attached to one end)
- Wax
- Additives (scents and colors)
- Mold (optional)
- Mold release such as cooking spray or silicone

overview

Candles are prized for their warm, decorative light and ambrosial scent. They're made from paraffin, vegetable waxes, beeswax, and gel wax, and come in every size, shape, color, and fragrance imaginable. You can make pillars, votives, container candles, scented candles, and even ice candles (by pouring the hot wax into a mold filled with ice). Candles are made by either using a mold or dipping them. After a bit of practice, you can begin experimenting with more complex shapes and sculptural pieces.

history

Candles have been lighting the way for humans for more than 5,000 years. Egyptians began making them around 3000 B.C.E. by soaking bundles of rushes in beeswax or tallow, animal fat extracted from cattle and sheep. In the Roman Empire, the candle-making process was improved by pouring melted tallow over a single piece of rush, which formed the wick. By the Middle Ages, candles for the lower classes were typically made from tallow, which smelled unpleasant and burned poorly. But the upper classes could afford the fragrant—and expensive—all-beeswax variety.

The first patented candle-making machines were developed in the mid-19th century, making candles available to every class. It was then that candle makers also perfected the braided wick, a further improvement upon wicks that are made of simple twisted cotton strands, which needed to be maintained constantly. The tight braid made the wick burn more slowly, thus extending the life of the candles. After paraffin, petroleum arrived on the scene in the 1830s, and candles became even more affordable. Of course, the advent of gaslight in the early 1800s and then electricity at the end of the century relegated them to decorative uses.

getting started

The steps for basic candle making are fairly straightforward, especially if you buy a kit for molded candles. Many of them include easy-to-follow instructions and all the equipment you need, including the double boiler, a thermometer, a mold, and a starter supply of wax and wicks. You don't have to limit yourself to the mold in the kit, of course. You can make one out of household items like metal coffee cans, cupcake containers, toilet paper rolls, muffin tins, or anything that can stand the heat of melted wax. You might also choose to start by making dipped candles. There are numerous websites that offer instructions for doing this and the result is almost instant gratification.

resources

Basic Candle Making: All the Skills and Tools You Need to Get Started, by Eric Ebeling (Stackpole Books, 2002).

The Candlemaker's Companion: A Comprehensive Guide to Rolling, Pouring, Dipping, and Decorating Your Own Candles, by Betty Oppenheimer (Storey Publishing, 1997).

Candle Making in a Weekend, by Sue Spear (North Light Books, 1999).

www.candlesupply.com: All the materials you'll need to make candles.

www.candletech.com: A candle- and soap-making site.

www.igca.net: The International Guild of Candle Artisans' site, with resources aplenty, including a list of candle-making supply houses, safety tips, workshops, and conventions.

www.peakcandle.com: Inexpensive starter kits.

project: make a votive candle

To make a simple votive candle, you don't need a special mold. Those tiny paper cups do the job just as well. Start by melting your wax in a double boiler, keeping the temperature at about 175°F (80°C). Once the wax has completely melted, pour in any additives you choose—first dyes, then scents—and mix the ingredients thoroughly, being careful not to make any air bubbles. Before pouring the wax into the cups, lightly spray them with the release agent. Tie the end of each wick around a short stick or straw and lay the stick across the top of a cup so the tab just touches the bottom and the wick is straight. Fill your votive molds to the lip without overflowing, pouring slowly to prevent air bubbles from forming. Save some wax for repouring later in the process.

After the wax has cooled completely, a process that takes three to four hours, it will have shrunk, leaving a small hole in the center. Remelt the wax you saved earlier, making it hotter than before—about 185 to 190°F (85 to 88°C)—and fill each cup right to the lip. Once the candles have cooled completely, slide or peel them out of the molds. Then light them up and bask in the glow!

candy making

FOR MOST OF US, BITING INTO A PIECE OF CANDY—whether taffy, licorice, or a jelly bean—fulfills an almost primordial craving. Bring that childlike rush of excitement home by making your own sugary treats. And don't spoil it with any residual guilt: Enjoy every last morsel!

what you'll need

- *Candy thermometer*

- *Medium-sized saucepan with a heavy bottom and straight sides to prevent boil-overs*

- *Bowl large enough to hold the saucepan for cooling candy*

- *Long-handled wooden spoon*

- *Pastry brush (for certain recipes)*

overview

There is a great variety of sweet stuff available for your tasting pleasure. There's hard candy like lollipops, jawbreakers, lemon drops, and candy canes; chewy candy like fudge, taffy, and licorice; and, of course, the mother of them all—chocolate. Most are made by dissolving sugar in water or milk to form a syrup, then boiling the mixture until it starts to caramelize. By varying the temperature, cooking time, and ingredients, the texture of the candy can be made hard or soft, chewy or brittle. A "soft-ball" candy should not be cooked higher than 240°F (116°C), while "hard-crack" varieties top out at 310°F (154°C). The boiling of the syrup causes the sugar concentration to increase as the water evaporates, which consequently raises the boiling point. Because the boiling temperature at each of these stages is fixed, you can know exactly how hot to make the syrup to achieve the kind of candy you want. The general rule: The higher the temperature, the harder the candy.

history

Sugar was first made by evaporating cane juice around 500 B.C.E. in India. The ingredient gradually spread with increases in trade and reached Persia by 600 C.E. Before long, it was being produced throughout the Old World. Christopher Columbus himself brought it to the New World in 1493. Not, of course, that life was sugar-free before sugarcane—honey (arguably sweeter than sugar) has been available for as long as people have been keeping bees *(see Beekeeping)*. Honey-sweetened confections were abundant at elaborate Greek banquets and at Roman feasts. Savvy physicians during the Middle Ages learned how to disguise the nasty taste of medicines by dipping them in something sweet. In the New World, sugar was a precious commodity kept under lock and key. Colonists enjoyed candied fruits, brittles, and toffee, as well as liquorices and ice cream in the mid-1700s. In the latter half of the 19th century, as part of the Industrial Revolution, commercial candy exploded onto the scene, with marketers like Stephen F. Whitman, founder of Whitman's chocolates, cashing in on the candy craze. Soon thereafter came candy corn (1880s), Tootsie Rolls (1896), and, in 1906, Hershey's Chocolate Kisses. In 1930, M&M Mars rolled out the Snickers Bar, which has been America's best-selling candy ever since.

getting started

Since one or two degrees can drastically change the outcome of your recipe, test your thermometer for accuracy. Insert it in a pan of water and bring the water to a boil. (Be sure not to thrust the thermometer into already boiling water, which can break it.) When the water is boiling, the temperature should read 212°F (100°C). If it's off by a few degrees, you'll need to adjust accordingly. Measure all ingredients before you get started. This will help you act quickly once the water has boiled.

For most candies, you'll dissolve sugar in liquid ingredients over low heat, then bring the mixture to a boil. Either attach the thermometer to the side of the pan, or regularly check the temperature. Either way, the bulb of the thermometer should not touch the sides or bottom of the pan, which can give an inaccurate reading. Clean the thermometer after every reading and keep it in a glass of warm water nearby. Cook the syrup until you reach the specified temperature—for example, saltwater taffy needs to be cooked to 258°F (126°C)—and stir as instructed.

For those who like to take the names "soft-ball stage," "hard-crack stage," and so on literally and who want to wing it without a thermometer, you can test the candy by dropping a small amount of the mixture into a glass of cold water. Look for more instructions about this online and in cookbooks. Be sure to remove the pan from the heat while you test so that the candy doesn't overcook.

A final bit of advice: Try not to make candy on a humid or rainy day, as the candy might not set as well.

if you like this hobby, you might enjoy:

- Beer brewing (see page 38)
- Cake decorating
- Coffee roasting (see page 60)
- Cookie baking
- Deep-frying (see page 74)
- Ice sculpture (see page 120)
- Making preserves (see page 136)

project: easy maple candy

. . . .

Serves 6

Bring 2 cups (480 ml) maple syrup to a boil in a 4-quart (3.5 L) pot, stirring constantly so the syrup doesn't boil over, and when it reaches 235°F (122°C) (measure the temperature with a candy thermometer) remove the pot from the heat. Stop stirring and let the syrup cool to 175°F (91°C), which should take about 10 minutes.

With a wooden spoon, briskly blend the syrup for a few minutes until you see the color turn lighter, the consistency thicken, and the syrup become creamier. Now it's ready to be poured into either a buttered baking pan (quickly sliced into squares for easy removal later) or into rubber molds. Let the candy cool for 10 to 30 minutes, depending on the humidity. When it's cooled and hardened, just turn over the pan or molds and pop out the candy. Enjoy!

resources

Truffles, Candies, and Confections: Techniques and Recipes for Candymaking, by Carole Bloom (Ten Speed Press, 2005).

Candymaking, by Ruth Kendrick (HP Trade, 1987).

www.candymaking.net: Facts about candy making and recipes galore.

www.candyusa.org: The National Confectioners' Association presents recipes, games, quizzes, and references about everything candy-related.

www.sugarcraft.com: Candy-making and cake-decorating products.

car modding

WHAT DOES YOUR CAR SAY ABOUT YOU? Do you have tricked-out fenders, tinted windows, spinning rims, or racing stripes? No? Then maybe it's time to propel your set of wheels to the next level. With a little bit of imagination and some cues from the experts, you'll be the belle of the boulevard.

what you'll need

- Car
- Customization kit
- Car tools

resources

How to Build the Cars of the Fast and the Furious, by Eddie Paul (Motorbooks, 2004).

Car Hacks and Mods for Dummies, by David Vespremi (Dummies, 2004).

www.autosportz.com: Articles, photos, and simplified explanations of all different kinds of car mods.

www.importmodifications.com: Page after page of images of car mods.

overview

Car modding (or modifying you car) can be as elaborate or as simple as you envision. You can customize the exterior or the interior of the car, or both. Exterior changes can include adding fiberglass fender flares, spinner rims (the kind that continue to revolve even when the car is stopped), wings, spoilers, decorative lighting, grills, racing stripes, and other designs—just about anything to make the car stand apart from the others gridlocked on the asphalt.

Beyond making your car into a public spectacle, you can also trick out the interior for your own private pleasure. Racing seats can be added, windows can be tinted, and a booming audio system can be installed, with subwoofers and bass speakers that will blow away the next nearest unwitting driver.

Modders can increase their car's horsepower with a sporty exhaust system, improve steering and handling by installing antiroll bars, springs, and shocks, and improve anything on the car that was not included in the standard-issue model. You can buy customization kits from auto body shops and do the installation yourself, or add the parts bit by bit. Each model and type of car comes with its own kit and adaptable gear.

history

The MTV show *Pimp My Ride* debuted in 2004 with a fairly straightforward premise: Take a rattletrap and restore it (in ways that are anything but straight-forward). But people had been engaged in this hobby long before the show hit the small screen. Ever since the first gasoline-powered automobile, produced by Ransom E. Olds, rolled out in the U.S. in 1902, cars have been bought and customized to their owners' specifications. Hot rods in the 1930s were modified by removing and replacing existing running boards and fenders, which made the cars lighter and faster. Car customization became increasingly popular in the 1950s, when car owners started experimenting with bright colors, painting on flames, and applying acrylic for a glossy effect.

In more recent pop culture history, we saw cousins Bo and Luke Duke of Hazzard County evading the rascally county commissioner Boss Hogg in their souped-up hot rod "The General Lee" in the TV show *The Dukes of Hazzard*. Superhero Batman's wheels, the legendary Batmobile, represents the fantasy of customized cars with the ability to fly, tread water, deflect bullets from bad guys, and other amazing feats. Before embarking upon each of his missions, British spy James Bond is handed the keys to an automobile that features, among other handy devices, retractable tire slashers, a passenger ejector seat, a retractable roof panel for jettisoning the enemy, rear smoke screen releases, and oil-slick ejectors. Nice ride!

getting started

- *THE FIRST THING to consider with this hobby is how much money you can invest. If you've got unlimited funds, then the hardest part will be deciding where to start. For the rest of us, it's a matter of prioritizing. Decide whether you're more interested in your car's performance or its image. If it's more zoom you're looking for, go to your local car customization dealer and talk to the clerk about your options. Look into things like hacking the engine control unit and making engine and exhaust system modifications, which add horsepower and give the car a more aggressive feel; upgrading the air intake system, which adds more horsepower by improving the filtration system; and modifying the suspension for a smoother ride.*

- *IF YOUR GOAL is to turn heads, focus on your car's image. Inside, you can add racing seats, tinted windows, racing pedals and gear shift, aluminum or carbon dashboard gauge covers, multicolored fire extinguishers, racing floor mats, even a pair of fuzzy dice. For the exterior, make an instant upgrade with decals—small flames, racing stripes, 5-foot dragons, or any image that strikes you. Apply them to the hood, the driver's door, the back window, or the trunk. Then keep adding features: bigger wheels, a set of strobe lights to the hood for a police effect or underneath to help light the way, wings, a sunroof, or even Batmobile-style lambo doors that open upward instead of out to the side. You'll feel every bit like the superhero you are.*

project: tint your windows

Shield yourself from the sun and the paparazzi by tinting your windows. First, check out the laws in your state regulating visible light transmission: see *www.autowindowtintings.com/lawsexplained.ihtml*.

1] Collect the following tools: window washing solution, sponges, X-Acto knife, tinting film, squeegee, blow dryer, and bone tool. Measure your windows and cut the film to their precise measurements and shape. You can draw the shape of the window on tracing paper and use that as a guide.

2] Clean your windows thoroughly with a glass cleaner and scrape off every last trace of gunk, then wipe down the remaining residue from the glass cleaner with a squeegee.

3] Starting with one of the side windows, carefully apply the tinting film, leaving about 1/4 inch (64 mm) at the top of the window clear. With your bone tool, press the film down underneath the window seals. Blast your blow dryer onto the tint while smoothing out the bubbles with your squeegee. Repeat these steps with the other windows.

caving

HOBBY PERSONALITY: **adventurous** · animal-loving · artistic · crafty · dexterous · epicurean · extroverted · **history-loving** · **independent** · meditative · meticulous · musical · **nature-loving** · nurturing · **outdoorsy** · patient · social · **sporty** · technical

PERHAPS THE IMAGE OF INDIANA JONES BEING CHASED BY A MAMMOTH STONE barreling behind him is how you envision a caving expedition. Although most cavers aren't routinely pursued by a rogue rock, there is a certain amount of risk associated with the sport. Still, for those who don't mind—and who even relish the thought of getting dirty, crawling on hands and knees, and discovering previously uncharted paths and species—this sport is for you!

what you'll need

- *Helmet with mounted light source, such as a halogen lamp or LED*
- *Backup light source, in case something happens to your helmet light*
- *Backup batteries for the lights*
- *Appropriate clothing, such as a wetsuit or easy-to-layer clothing made of fabric that stays warm when damp*
- *Hiking boots and water-absorbent socks*
- *Gloves*
- *Climbing ropes and related accessories (such as bolts, slings, carabiners)*
- *Food and water*
- *First aid kit*

overview

Caving is the recreational sport of exploring caves, a hobby that requires quite a bit of physical exertion. It involves climbing, crawling, and using ropes to gain access to deep recesses, all the while negotiating pitches, squeezes, and waterways. Most cavers consider the sport a challenging form of exercise as well as a way to commune with nature and learn about history and science. For the adventurers of the world, the potential of unearthing undiscovered caves and exploring the unknown, which requires digging and even diving, is reason enough to get dirty. But there are other rewards, like coming across spectacular rock formations, gravity-defying stalactites, and underground waterfalls and lakes.

history

Caves have served as dwellings since prehistoric times, but they have also been explored for water, sources of medicine, and, more recently, valuable treasures and historic artifacts. Caving gained national prominence in the U.S. with the publication of Mark Twain's *The Adventures of Tom Sawyer*, in which Tom and Becky Thatcher get lost in a cave. *Speleology*, the word for the scientific exploration of caves, gave rise to the slang terms *spelunking* and *spelunker* for amateur cave exploration and cavers. Accessibility to modern tools like helmets, headlights, high-tech ropes, and ladders have since rendered the sport safer and more sophisticated than it was in its early days.

resources

Caving (Essential Guides), by Peter K. Swart (Stackpole Books, 2002).
Caves: Exploring Hidden Realms, by Michael Ray Taylor and Roman C. Kerbo (National Geographic, 2001).
www.caves.org: The National Speleological Society, an American group with local chapters that explores and conserves caves.
www.cave-research.org: The Cave Research Foundation is a nonprofit group that studies and protects caves.
www.caving.uk.com: A British-based resource with a link to *Descent*, a magazine for cavers, as well as a listing of great caving spots in the U.K.

getting started

Caving can be a dangerous pursuit, so the first thing to do is get yourself the appropriate gear. Sturdy clothing and footwear and a helmet are compulsory. Choose layers of synthetic fibers and woolens, which don't absorb water like cotton does. If you know you're going into a wet cave, wear a wetsuit to reduce the chance of hypothermia. Carry easily metabolized food, like fruit or sweets, and warm foods like vegetable soup in a thermos. Don't forget to take at least two sources of long-lasting light with backup batteries.

When you're ready to start your expedition, first try joining a guided group (see resources for nearby organizations). After a few organized treks, ask a few of the more experienced cavers if they'd be interested in going out in a smaller group.

When going out on your own with your caving group, it's important to take a few precautions: Be sure someone aboveground knows where you are and when you'll return. Rainwater can flood a cave quickly, so look at the weather forecast for the day, and find out if it has rained in that spot on previous days. Try to memorize landmarks as you traverse passages. In some caves, you can leave behind small stacks of rocks or flagging tape to mark your path. If you find yourself going down a steeper slope than you think you'll be able to climb in the other direction, turn back.

Caves have a fragile ecosystem and must be carefully preserved during exploration. Be cautious of damaging or removing any cave formations and pick up all your trash before you go. Never build fires inside a cave or paint graffiti on cave walls.

profile: delving into the depths

JOEL DESPAIN has seen everything from elephants to orangutans in caves while on spelunking expeditions. But the discoveries that intrigue him the most are on a much smaller scale. He's fascinated by the unusual minerals that turn up in caves—like 6-inch-long pieces of green crystal, azure cave formations, and marble. As with most experienced cavers, Despain knows to admire these natural wonders from a respectful distance. "You don't touch these things because they're so delicate, they would break," he says.

Despain works as a cave management specialist for Sequoia and Kings Canyon National Parks, but he's traveled the world exploring caves. "You never know where a cave is going to go," he says. "It's the question of the unknown. It's intriguing to not know what's around the corner, to see something that you may have never seen before." Because of their odd habitats, caves are home to unfamiliar living things, which Despain

> **"If you're a beginner, join a local caving club, let them show you the ropes, and keep going back."**

loves to learn about. In fact, Despain and his colleagues recently discovered 27 new species in the California caves where they work: invertebrates like silverfish, isopods, millipedes, crickets, and spiders.

project: make a bat house

You can't always be in a cave, but maybe you can bring a little bit of cave wildlife to you—with a bat house. You can purchase bat house kits, which are easily assembled and can be mounted on a tree, building, or pole. They look vaguely like wooden mailboxes, and, depending on their size, can house 300 bats or more. Some have multiple chambers, but all have ventilation gaps for circulating air and maintaining the right temperature. At the right time in the evening, you can watch these mystical creatures come home. A bonus for those who live in humid climates: Bats eat lots of mosquitoes!

coffee roasting

FOR MOST AMERICANS, enjoying a cup of coffee has become an essential morning ritual. Although for some, the primary appeal is the immediate boost that comes with the first cup of joe, many people relish the rich taste. For those who are curious about concocting their own ideal blend—and for those who resent paying more than a dollar for a simple cup of coffee—home roasting is a compelling idea. It's simple, clean, and requires few accoutrements.

what you'll need

- Roaster—you can use your oven, an air popcorn popper, or one of the several commercially available home coffee roasters

- Green coffee beans

- Airtight storage jar

- Kitchen thermometer

- Notebook or journal to record your work

- Digital scale and timer (optional)

overview

When they're picked, coffee beans are green and hard. During the roasting process, they swell to more than double their size, cracking open two different times. They also change color, gradually going from yellow to light brown, then to dark glossy brown—the sheen comes from oils expelled from the inside of the beans. The oils give off their own flavor that's distinct from the flavor of the beans; the more oil released, the more robust the taste. Lighter roasts accentuate the flavor of the particular bean. For example, Hawaiian Kona and Java are roasted lighter to maintain their distinctive flavor. Home roasting is an easy process, especially with a computerized drum roaster. But many people roast coffee right in the oven or in air popcorn poppers. After they're roasted, the beans are ready to grind and brew right away.

history

In around 850 C.E., legend has it, Ethiopians noticed their goats were more energetic after chewing on a certain kind of berry, which turned out to be the coffee bean. Traders from Arab countries traveling through the region to buy and sell spices became intrigued by this wonder bean. They brought the plant home and began cultivating it. They also started boiling the beans, which resulted in a drink called qahwa—literally, "that which prevents sleep." Word spread, and by 1475 the world's first coffee shop, Kiva Han, opened in Constantinople. We owe thanks to Captain John Smith, who founded the Jamestown Colony of Virginia in 1607, for introducing this captivating little bean to the Americas.

In the 1800s, coffee beans were typically bought green and roasted at home in a frying pan. This remained a common habit until the 1930s, although as early as the 1850s, a San Francisco company later known as Folgers offered customers the option of buying it already roasted and ground. World War II brought about the introduction of instant coffee. Today, coffee is the world's most popular drink, with more than 400 billion cups consumed each year.

getting started

Coffee roasting happens fast—it takes between 10 and 20 minutes for a dark roast, so be prepared to stand near the oven for the duration.

Preheat your oven to between 460 and 530°F (238° and 277°C). Pour a small batch of green coffee beans (about ½ pound, or 230 g) into a baking pan with holes punched in the bottom or a large wire-mesh sieve and place them in the oven. They'll begin to change color, and the oils inside will evaporate, which is when you'll start to smell that telltale aroma. You'll hear the first round of loud cracks as the moisture bursts from the beans and the sugars start to caramelize. Your coffee is officially roasted—but very lightly—at this stage.

For a richer, fuller flavor, keep on roasting. Most people achieve their favored coffee roast just before they hear the second crack. If you wait much past the second crack, you'll be drinking some pretty bitter brew. Also keep in mind that the beans' internal temperature keeps them roasting even after you remove them from the heat, so pull them out just before they reach the color you want. You can also toss them in a colander or spray water on them while they're on the baking pan to cool them more quickly. Allow them to sit uncovered for about 12 hours before sealing them in the storage jar.

You will likely need to experiment a few times before determining your ideal brew. It's also a good idea to take notes on how long you roast each batch of beans and your impressions of how they turn out in order to adjust the procedure on your next attempt. Save samples of the roasted beans you like best to compare to future roasts.

resources

Home Coffee Roasting: Romance and Revival, by Kenneth Davids (St. Martin's Griffin, 2003).

www.coffeeproject.com: An online source for green coffee beans and home-roasting supplies, including roasters and other accessories.

www.ineedcoffee.com/99/04/homeroast: "Roast Your Own," a tutorial on the website describes how to roast coffee at home using an air popcorn popper.

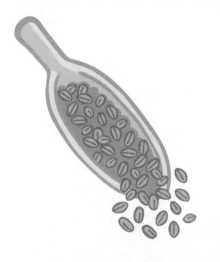

project: chocolate-covered roasted coffee beans

Line a baking sheet with wax paper. Melt about ½ cup (85 g) chocolate chips (your choice of milk or bittersweet) in a double boiler. Add a handful of roasted beans and stir. Take out the beans with a slotted spoon and place them on the prepared baking sheet, separating each one from the other. You can wait until they harden at room temperature (about 12 hours), or pop them in the freezer for about 30 minutes. Store them in an airtight container and enjoy when you need a sweet pick-me-up.

collecting

EVERYONE'S GOT ONE TYPE OF OBSESSION OR ANOTHER. For those predisposed to fixating on material things, collecting is a hobby that can quickly turn into an obsession. Though it can be easy to sit back and throw money at dealers who are more than happy to do the foraging for you, it's far more rewarding to embark on the hunt yourself. The thrill of outbidding another collector on eBay, of searching out a priceless coin at a flea market, or snagging a valuable painting at a garage sale can't be matched by having items hand-delivered to your door. Whatever your personal passion is, get out there and collect it.

what you'll need

- *An item you're infatuated with to collect*

- *Research tools such as access to the internet and a telephone*

resources

To Have and to Hold: An Intimate History of Collectors and Collecting, by Philipp Blom (Overlook Press, 2003).

Collectibles Price Guide 2005, by Judith Miller (DK Adult, 2004).

www.avdm.com/Collectibles.html: Display cases for every type of collection, including modular pieces for DIY displays.

eBay.com: Online auction site for every type of collectible imaginable.

overview

Collecting encompasses an extremely broad range of other hobbies and preoccupations. Starting a collection simply entails amassing multiple objects of the same kind. These can range from postage stamps to wine bottle labels to thimbles to figurines *(see things to collect, pages 63–65).* Collectors can search for specific items within a category, such as dolls from the Civil War era, or much broader categories, such as dolls of all types. They might choose to collect every album by a certain band or singer, or every book by an author. Collectors can search for their items of choice on their own time or buy them through a professional dealer connected to a vast network of people and institutions searching for rare items. Working with a dealer, however, typically costs much more than scoring a find yourself. Auction sites such as eBay can cut out the middleman (though dealers also advertise their wares on the sites), but it's a riskier proposition—the item might not be authentic, and occasionally the unscrupulous seller defaults on the promise to send an item. Original items of value typically come with either a certificate of authenticity or are signed or marked in a way that verifies their authenticity. Collectors also trawl flea markets, conventions, and other publicly held sales and events where they might stumble upon prize finds.

history

Coins were one of the first items to be collected—at least since the Roman era. According to a book called *Lives of the Caesars,* written in 75 C.E. by Suetonius, Emperor Augustus collected old foreign coins and gifted them to friends and acquaintances. Famous collectors throughout history include Sir Thomas Phillips of England, who during the 19th century attempted to own a copy of every single book published in the world (he came close: 77,000 titles at the time of his death), and Franz Gall, an Austrian who got a kick out of decorating his walls with rows of human skulls he collected from gallows and asylums.

getting started

Getting started can be the most challenging part of this hobby simply because the choices are infinite. So your first priority is to choose something you're fascinated by, or obsessed with, or simply something you want to own in multiples because of its aesthetic value. A good way to start is by checking around your own house. You might discover you already have a small collection of tea tins, for example, which you've been keeping because you like the way they look. That counts as a collection.

Then start researching. Visit auction and dealer websites to familiarize yourself with your collectible of choice and its market value, and subscribe to magazines and newsletters that contain information about sales and classified ads. Take copious notes during your research and keep important phone numbers and websites on file. Tell everyone you know about the item you're collecting and see how quickly your home fills up with your chosen collectibles.

SPOTS TO RUMMAGE FOR COLLECTIBLES:

- *FLEA MARKETS. Depending on where you live and how energetically you search, flea markets can yield big scores. Don't be afraid to haggle for a better price—the seller doesn't have to know how important the piece is to you.*
- *YARD, TAG, ESTATE, OR RUMMAGE SALES. When homes are cleared out in preparation for being sold, all kinds of priceless items—antique clocks, furniture, jewelry, china, and the homeowners' own collections—come up for grabs. Beat the dealers to the punch by showing up early and scavenging for the best goods.*
- *COLLECTORS' CONVENTIONS. These are typically populated by professional antique dealers, so they might not save you money, but for that coveted item you can't find anywhere else, this might be the place to go.*

If you're interested in collecting rare or extremely valuable items, be sure to check them carefully for authenticity before buying. Is it a limited edition? If so, what is its number in the series? Is there any obvious damage or wear and tear that would diminish the value of the piece?

To validate the authenticity of china, pottery, glassware, or furniture, refer to manuals and books about what signs to look for. Research how furniture of that particular time period was made, what types of wood were used, how the pieces were assembled, and the period's distinctive flourishes. Artists, designers, and manufacturing companies usually sign or stamp their logos or signatures on the back or bottom of their work.

things to collect

Aluminum foil balls
Americana (Canadiana, etc.)
Animal-themed collectibles
Aprons
Arrowheads
Art
Bakelite
Baskets
Books
Bottles
Breweriana
Buttons
Cameras
Cans
Cards
Chia pets
China
Christmas stuff
Clocks
Coins (and currency)
Comic books
Cookie jars
Costumes
Crystals
Dice
Dolls
Ephemera
Fans
Firearms and weaponry
Fishing lures
Food/candy packaging
Found photos/postcards
Furniture
Glassware
Hats
Jewelry

(continued on page 64)

collecting (continued)

[continued from page 63]
things to collect

Jigsaw puzzles
Jukeboxes
Kaleidoscopes
Keys/hotel room keys
Knives
License plates
Lighters/smoking paraphernalia
Lint
Lunch boxes
Magazines
Maps
Marbles
Matchbooks
Military uniforms/medals
Miniatures
Movie props
Music boxes
Newspapers
Paperweights
Patches
Pencil sharpeners
Pens
Pez dispensers
Phonographs
Pinball machines
Pins
Playing cards
Political stuff
Posters
Quotes
Radios
Rocks
Rugs

[continued on page 65]

project: display your goods

Once you start to accumulate your collectibles, you'll want to store them in a safe place. You can find a custom-made display case for almost every collectible item *(see resources)*. But since you've gone to the trouble of personally finding each one of your cherished pieces, you can create a unique way of displaying them.

The key things to remember are: Keep them away from direct or bright light if that could damage them; keep them cleaned and dusted; keep them away from smoke or humidity; and keep them out of the reach of kids and pets.

Here are a few ideas for displays you can build:

- Attach a piece of crown molding to the wall and place a shelf on top of it. You can put up five or six of these shelves, depending on what you're displaying, all lined up underneath each other, or in another pleasing pattern.

- Affix a shelf to the wall and attach a ¹/₂-inch (1.3 cm) strip of wood along the edge as a protective lip to prevent fragile items from falling. It's a clean and simple look that focuses on the collectibles instead of the display itself.

- Attach a chair rail or other display railing about three-quarters of the way up your wall and prop your collectible pieces on it, either framed or not.

- Find a vintage medicine cabinet and hang it on the wall. You can either remove the door or, if it has a glass door, just place your collectibles inside.

- Affix a narrow shelf in your window (preferably one that doesn't open). Cut two small pieces of 1-by-3-inch (2.5 by 7.6 cm) wood and screw them into the sides of the window to serve as shelf supports. Then cut a piece of the wood as long as the window is wide and place it on top of the supports. Arrange your collection on the shelf—translucent objects like glass vases and crystal look great with light shining through them, but make sure that your collectibles are not light-sensitive.

profile: cabinet of (morbid) curiosities

NIC RATNER has squeezed a veritable taxidermy zoo into his 300-square-foot (90 m) apartment in downtown Manhattan: a 4-foot-tall (1.2 m) standing baby bear, ducklings, a lamb, a house cat, three or four rabbits, penguins, and a monkey's head, among many other former denizens of the wild. "I consider them art," Ratner says. "I derive pleasure from looking at them."

Also scattered throughout the house are a brain imprisoned in a jar of formal-dehyde; a human skull; a two-headed cow bust (a tragic case of Siamese-twin calves); a collection of turn-of-the-previous-century medical supplies; and small bottles that used to contain strychnine and chocolate-coated arsenic. You get the picture. "I am morbidly fascinated by the grotesque," he says. "If Morticia Addams walked into my apartment, she'd say, 'I love what you've done with the place.'"

He also collects cigarette lighters to fuel his obsessive smoking habit; not just the plastic Bic variety found at the local drugstore, but ornate, antique affairs that, if given the chance to speak, could spin some colorful yarns. The lighter collection started when Ratner was a 14-year-old working as a busboy in a restaurant. A customer left what turned out to be a 1940 silver Dunhill on the table—"something Bogart would have in his pocket"—and after waiting patiently for the owner to return and claim it, he ended up keeping it. "It's one of the nicest I have," he says.

Then there are the dice. Ratner has lost count of how many he's amassed over the years, but says they number in the hundreds. This collection was inspired by a book called The Dice Man by Luke Rheinhart, about a bored psychiatrist who decides to use dice to make all the major decisions of his life. The book profoundly moved Ratner when he read it in his mid-20s, and since then he has carried a die in his pocket at all times.

Why the obsession with clinging to objects? His shrink would tell you it was obvious. After watching his scholarly father chuck all the family belongings before moving to a new city every three years (reasoning that they'd "buy new things"), Ratner believes he's trying to create a semblance of stability. "[My personal history] has made me a packrat," he says. "It's my bizarre way of having a sense of permanence, because the rest of my life is rife with impermanence."

But Ratner doesn't pack his house just for the sake of collecting random items, like Beanie Babies (though he might consider those if they were somehow mutilated). The collections grow organically, as with the accumulation of the morose, death-related objects. How would the shrink explain that one? That's another story.

(continued from page 64)

things to collect

- Salt and pepper shakers
- Seashells
- Snow globes
- Sheet music
- Spoons
- Sports cards
- Stamps
- Stickers
- String
- Stuffed animals
- Swords
- Telephones
- Televisions
- Thimbles
- Ties
- Toys
- Tractors
- Trains (or any other toy vehicle)
- T-shirts
- Typewriters
- Vintage textiles
- Vinyl records
- Watches
- Wine (and wine labels)
- Yardsticks and rulers

> "You'll get a sense of what you want to collect by noticing your own buying patterns. First you get one of something, then you'll buy another. By the time you've got a half dozen [of any single item], you've got yourself a collection."

composting

"ASHES TO ASHES, DUST TO DUST" applies not just to the human life process, but to gardens, too. Nutritious soil and, in turn, thriving plants and vegetables, need rich, organic fertilizer, and the best way of providing this shot of vitamins is to give your garden soil exactly what you took from it: your food!

what you'll need

- Kitchen waste such as coffee grounds, egg shells, fruit, and vegetable scraps

- Garden and yard waste such as small twigs, leaves, grass clippings, straw and hay, pine needles and cones, cow or horse manure

- Miscellaneous items that can be composted include cotton or felt wastes, shredded newspapers, sawdust, and wood chips

- A compost bin or designated area

- Rake, shovel, or spading fork for turning the compost

overview

Compost is the accumulation of decomposed scraps of food and plant matter used in gardening and agriculture. Mixing compost into soil improves its quality, adding organic materials that provide nutrients to the plants you grow. Home composting is done by collecting "brown" and "green" waste in a pile and, in some cases, adding microbes or other creatures like earthworms, ants, and nematodes. Composting requires a controlled environment, with the proper amount of carbon, nitrogen, oxygen, and water, in order to encourage the growth of active microbes. You can start a compost in your backyard in a contained bin like an old garbage can or in an open pile—but the latter might be a bit smelly if not turned on a regular basis to aerate the mixture.

history

The first evidence we have of composting, or at least the idea of returning organic scraps to the soil, is in clay tablets from about 2350 B.C.E., in the Akkadian empire in Mesopotamia. The Romans, Greeks, and early Hebrews are also said to have added rotted manure to soil. By the Middle Ages, composting was the rule rather than the exception in agricultural practice. American president James Madison touted the benefits of it in an 1818 speech to an agricultural society in Virginia. Many of the composting methods most familiar to us now were developed in the first half of the 20th century by Sir Albert Howard, a British botanist and organic farming pioneer who worked in Indore, India. Composting today—in a world where landfills are taxed to their limits—is an important method of waste reduction, as well as a good way to maintain healthy, organic gardens.

getting started

You can choose from a variety of composting methods: container composting, indoor composting, composting with worms, and mound composting, among others. Container composting is quite common and relatively easy. First, find a place for your container—ideally, a spot in your backyard that's out of plain sight but close to the kitchen. You can either buy a composting bin or build one with wood or recycled pallets, leaving the bin open on one side for easy access. Not only will you be adding compost, but you'll also need to turn it regularly and be able to scoop out finished compost from the bottom of the pile.

Before you begin adding kitchen scraps, let the process get a head start using yard waste only. Try mixing together one part grass clippings and old annuals ("green" waste) with two parts dry leaves and soil ("brown" waste) until the mixture is damp but not wet. Start with a 4-inch (10 cm) layer of leaves (brown waste) at the bottom of the pile, then 1 inch (2.5 cm) of good garden soil. Layer on 2 inches (5 cm) of grass clippings or old plants, and keep alternating brown and green waste. After a week, turn the pile with a spading fork, then start adding your food scraps, and turn the compost weekly. When you can no longer recognize the individual items you threw in and all the material looks uniformly like soil (dark color, small particles, and an earthy odor), the compost is ready. (This should happen within two months.) Dig it out with a shovel and use it to add the best kind of nutrients to your garden soil. Remember to mix the pile to ventilate it—oxygen keeps foul odors away.

project: build a wire mesh container

If you don't want to pay for a composting bin, make one out of wire mesh. You can easily turn the composting materials in this convenient container.

WHAT YOU'LL NEED:

10 feet (3 m) of 36-inch-wide (.9 m), 1-inch (2.5 cm) galvanized chicken wire
Three or four 4-foot-tall (1.2 m) wooden or metal posts
Heavy wire to tie the chicken wire to the posts and together
Tools such as heavy-duty wire or tin snips, pliers, hammer
Work gloves

Wearing work gloves for protection, fold back about 4 inches (10 cm) of wire at each cut end of the chicken wire. Join the two folded ends of the wire together to make a cylinder shape with open ends by inserting and twisting together several short pieces of heavy wire with pliers. Place the cylinder of wire, with one open end facing up, where you want your compost pile. Evenly space the posts around the cylinder, pounding them into the ground, then bind the posts to the chicken wire with more pieces of heavy wire. After piling in your yard waste and kitchen scraps, the best way to turn the contents is to lift the wire bin off and away from the composting material, set it on a new spot next to the old, and shovel the compost back into the wire bin. Be sure to harvest compost from the bottom of the pile.

resources

Worms Eat My Garbage: How to Set Up and Maintain a Worm Composting System, by Mary Appelhof (Flower Press, 1997).

Let It Rot! The Gardener's Guide to Composting, 3rd ed., by Stu Campbell (Storey Publishing, 1998).

www.compost-bin.org: An educational and news site about composting, featuring articles, news, and events.

www.compostinfo.com: Florida's online composting resource provides a wealth of information for beginners from any state.

www.4backyards.com: Supplier of tools and equipment for backyard composting.

www.mastercomposter.com: A subscriber site offering detailed instructions, diagrams, and tele-classes.

crochet

TO THE UNTRAINED EYE, CROCHET IS A MIRACLE OF ENGINEERING: thousands of links of thread looped together to create a whole piece. To crocheters, it's a rewarding hobby that results in beautiful clothing, table covers, and any number of decorative home accessories. Whichever way you look at it, crocheting can be a source of delight for just about anyone.

what you'll need

- *Worsted-weight yarn*
- *Size G crochet hook*
- *Yarn needle with a big eye*
- *Small scissors*

resources

The Crochet Answer Book: Solutions to Every Problem You'll Ever Face; Answers to Every Question You'll Ever Ask, by Edie Eckman (Storey Publishing, 2005).

www.craftyarncouncil.com: The Craft Yarn Council of America offers free instruction and an outline of basics for beginners. It's also a good source for free projects, patterns, and discussion groups.

www.crochet.org: The Crochet Guild of America's website features events, information on local chapters, and lessons.

www.crochetpartners.org: Crochet Partners is a membership-based resource that connects crocheters around the country.

overview

Crochet comes from the French word *crocher*, which means "to hook." The process involves creating fabric from cord, yarn, or thread with a specialized hook. First you place a slipknot loop on the hook, then you pull another loop through the first one, then another through that, and so on, to create a chain. After a row is completed, the chain is either turned and remade into another row, or is joined end-to-end and worked in rounds. Rounds can also be created by working many stitches into a single loop.

history

The technique of crocheting seems to have originated around the 1800s. As a less-expensive alternative to lace, crochet soon began to play a role in class differentiations around the world. Those who could afford it chose delicate and intricate lace and disparaged crocheted items. But with the endorsement of Queen Victoria, who wore Irish-made crochet (also called "Irish lace") and learned the technique herself, crocheting was given the royal nod. In Europe, handmade hooks of ivory, brass, or wood—some ornately carved or inlaid with mother-of-pearl—were used to work natural-fiber thread. By 1845, published patterns and instructions for reproducing bobbin lace and needle lace with crochet were being circulated courtesy of a Frenchwoman named Riego del Branchardiere. Until 1950, crochet was done only with thread, but by the mid-1950s, crocheters started using heavier yarns for heartier clothes and home accessories. And during the next decade, what was once relegated mostly to homemakers began making the rounds among the younger generation. Looking back at the fashions of the 1960s—particularly all the granny-square ponchos and afghans—shows us just how popular this technique became.

getting started

The best way of learning how to crochet is by taking a class. That way, you'll have close instructional help from an expert who can guide those first crucial steps. Many yarn and craft stores offer classes. They're also available at recreation centers, through adult-education programs, and at design centers.

To make the foundation row for crocheting, hold the hook in your right hand (if you're right handed— otherwise, hold it in the left) and make a slipknot on the hook. Bring the yarn over the hook from back to front and grab it with the hook. Draw the hooked yarn through the slipknot and onto the hook. You've got one chain stitch! Bring the yarn over the hook again and draw it through the loop to make the second stitch; repeat the sequence as many times as you like to create a longer chain.

project: stiffen a crocheted piece

To straighten out those lovely doilies or inherited tablecloths that have begun to curl at the edges, lightly spray each piece with spray starch, then shape it the way you want it to "freeze." You can do this by covering the piece with a handkerchief and pressing it with an iron set on cool. Alternatively, you can stretch it out on a piece of cardboard or bulletin board and fix it in place using rust-proof pins. If extreme flatness isn't critical, you can just stretch it out on a terry-cloth towel and let it dry.

profile: off the hook

ERICA MULHERIN has creative energy to spare, both in and out of the workplace. "I'm an illustrator [based in Olympia, Washington] and I have way, way too many hobbies. I like to try a bit of everything, but my favorites are sewing, felting, embroidery, papier-mâché, woodworking, and, of course, crocheting."

She's a third-generation crocheter—her mother and both grandmothers crocheted—and she has fond summertime memories of crocheting Barbie doll clothes with her grandma. She continues to enjoy the simplicity of this craft. "It's easy, portable, soothing, and fairly unstructured. You only need a hook and some yarn," she says. Her most ambitious project to date? "I once made a crocheted quilt. It ended up being gigantic and really, really heavy. I tend to stick to smaller things these days." Her little crocheted critters, especially the sea monkey, are truly irresistible.

Mulherin doesn't believe that you

> "Remember that it is OKAY to rip stitches out and start over. Practice makes perfect."

have to follow a crochet pattern, or even set out to make a specific item. "Just crochet. It doesn't have to "be" anything yet. Sit in front of the TV and practice single crochet, then double crochet; then try a different stitch for a while. This will help you get used to handling the yarn and making nice, neat stitches," she advises.

decoupage

A BLANK, FLAT SURFACE IS A TERRIBLE THING TO WASTE. Find your favorite photos and images and fill in that blank! The process is absurdly easy and instantly gratifying.

what you'll need

- *Clear-drying white glue (diluted— 3 parts glue to 1 part water), Mod Podge, or varnish*

- *Paper cutouts, tissue paper, bits of gilding or metal foil, and the like*

- *Paintbrush or other implement for spreading the glue or varnish*

- *Popsicle stick or brayer (a miniature roller) to smooth out wrinkles and remove excess glue*

- *Damp rag to wipe up excess glue and other cleanup*

- *Fine steel wool or sanding sponge (optional)*

- *Paint (optional)*

overview

Decoupage is the art of decorating an object by gluing bits of paper onto it, embellishing it with different painting techniques, and covering it with multiple coats of varnishes or products like Mod Podge, which work as both adhesive and polished finish. The end result looks as if the cutouts—which usually come from magazines or photos—have been inlaid or painted onto the surface. It is typically done to small boxes, furniture, and dishware, among other household items.

history

The roots of decoupage can be traced to 12th-century Chinese peasant art that made use of paper cutouts for decoration. The idea of adding layers of varnish over the paper cutouts was introduced by Venetian craftsmen in the 17th century; they were trying to make a more affordable substitute for the elaborate lacquered furniture being imported from Asia. For that reason, decoupage became known as "poor man's art," but it quickly caught on with the not-so-poor. Decoupage captivated aristocrats like Marie Antoinette and Madame de Pompadour and, in the 20th century, artists like Pablo Picasso and Henri Matisse. The word derives from the French term *découper*, which means "to cut out."

getting started

- *FIRST, FIND A FLAT SURFACE you want to cover with art. Anything works: a side table, photo album, shelves, picture frames, boxes, even mirrors. Wipe off dust and dirt, and if you want a background color, paint it. Then it's time to find images you want to see on the surface. Consider using wrapping paper, wallpaper, magazine clippings, fabric, or photos (photocopies may be easier to work with). Cut out the the images you want to use, then arrange them on the surface to see what shapes and colors look best together. Don't be afraid to overlap images—that's a common technique in decoupage.*

- *WHEN YOU'VE PLANNED THE DESIGN, coat the back of each image with glue or whatever decoupage medium you have. Also spread a thin layer of glue on the background surface. Gently position the cutout, taking care not to let it wrinkle or bubble. Use your finger, a Popsicle stick, or a brayer to press the image down on the surface, and to wipe off any excess glue. Repeat with the other images and let the glue dry.*

- *ONCE THE GLUE IS completely dry, coat the entire surface with your decoupage medium. Wait until that dries, then continue adding coats of the medium, taking care each time that the previous coat has thoroughly dried before you spread on a new one. You can stop layering when the edges of the images have been completely smoothed down. You might find that using fine steel wool or a sanding sponge on the later coats helps to create a smoother surface.*

resources

Absolute Beginner's Decoupage: The Simple Step-by-Step Guide to Creating Beautiful Decoupage, by Alison Jenkins (Watson-Guptill Publications, 1999).

New Decoupage, by Durwin Rice (Potter Craft, 1998).

www.decoupage.org: The National Guild of Decoupagers.

www.decoupage-online.com: All about decoupage.

project: decoupage a coffee table

Add a bit of personality to a bland old coffee table using decoupage. First, decide on a theme, such as travel. Then start collecting pieces that could work as part of a collage: magazine clippings, postage stamps, vintage postcards, travel ads, old plane or train tickets, admission stubs, even photocopies of your own photos will work. Lay out the pieces on the top of the coffee table, moving them around until you find a pleasing arrangement. Now apply some Mod Podge or another decoupage medium to the surface of the table where you want each piece to go. Add the same type of adhesive to the back of the cutout pieces and place them on the glued areas on the table. Carefully smooth out any bubbles or creases with your fingers. After each of the pieces has dried, apply three coats of the decoupage medium over the entire table, waiting for each application to dry before applying the next.

deejaying

THERE'S NOTHING LIKE THE THRILL OF MOTIVATING a group of people to groove to one rocking song after another. It's a little-known fact that deejaying is one of the healing professions: bringing music (and therefore dance) to a crowd is the best medicine of all.

what you'll need

- *A solid sound system, including good speakers and amplifiers*

- *A broad range of music in any medium—vinyl records, CDs, or MP3s*

- *At least two music-playing devices*

- *Microphone*

- *Headphones, to cue up the next song without playing it to the audience*

- *A mixer to combine songs from two players (optional)*

- *Sound effects such as drum machines, samplers, and the like (optional)*

overview

Deejaying encompasses a broad range of activities, from choosing a lineup of songs and playing them in order, to adding beats and other special effects to the music. The deejays we hear at parties play a big role in getting dancers onto the floor by choosing the right rhythms; mixing songs; and cutting, scratching, phrasing, and beat-matching to keep the rhythm going. Some people like deejaying for friends at home and do it for the pure pleasure, while others are hired for events and arrive with a full set of equipment, including hundreds of records or CDs and a sound system.

history

The first record player that used grooved, flat discs was invented in 1887 by Emil Berliner, but spinning records for a public audience didn't hit happen until the mid-1940s, on the radio. Facts are fuzzy in the field of deejaying at live events. David Mancuso, founder of New York City's first underground party, was one of the first deejays (or "disc jockeys") in the modern sense of the term. But as early as 1920, at a Dada gathering, the German composer Stefan Wolpe lined up eight phonographs and used them to play snippets of Beethoven's Fifth Symphony at different speeds. Many popular techniques, such as beat-matching (synchronizing the beats of two different pieces in order to fade from one to the other), were devised by deejay greats like Francis Grasso and remixer Larry Levan. DJ Kool Herc, known to many as the "father of hip-hop," is credited with inventing the backbeat technique (playing a continuous background beat on a second record player while changing the foreground sounds on a primary record player). Grandmaster Flash added scratching and cutting (moving the record back and forth under the needle with one hand while operating the fader with the other to bring in or mute the resulting sounds) to the bag of tricks in the late 1970s. By the 1980s, people were squaring off at deejay battles, vying to show who was faster and more creative while keeping a rhythm.

getting started

- *DEFINITELY TRY THIS AT HOME before going public. As with any performance art, deejaying takes plenty of practice. Start by collecting one category of music—let's say it's techno dance. Listen to a variety of songs and choose ones that flow together organically. One simple way of fulfilling your first deejay duties is to prerecord a CD and play it straight. Observe how people respond to your picks, then think about the next occasion.*

- *TO PLAN YOUR LINEUP, load your first CD or record into the player and play the song with the crossfader all the way up. Then load the next song into the second player with the crossfader down, and listen to the song on your headphones. You can wear the headphones on one ear and leave the other ear uncovered so you can hear both pieces—this'll help to keep your rhythm straight. Try to match the rhythm of the second song with the song that's playing on the first deck. If it doesn't work, find another, keeping in mind the length of time the first song has left. When you find a tune that's a perfect follow-up to the first song, cue it to the beginning, then just as the other ends or fades, play the second song and move the crossfader to the middle position. Gradually move the crossfader over completely to the second deck and down on the first one. Then begin the process again.*

resources

How to DJ Right: The Art and Science of Playing Records, by Frank Broughton and Bill Brewster (Grove, 2003).

Last Night a DJ Saved My Life: The History of the Disc Jockey, by Frank Broughton and Bill Brewster (Grove, 2000).

www.djforums.com: Forums, tutorials, and downloads.

www.djtimes.com: Online magazine for deejays with features about the pros, music charts, and forums.

www.panasonic-europe.com/technics: Supplier of the industry-standard turntables for deejays.

www.rockandsoul.com: Online supplier of deejay gear.

project: make a mix cd

For the one you love, or the one you want to woo, music can maneuver the way to the heart. Consider the kind of songs your beloved likes. Then think about the message you want to convey and find songs that carry the general theme of that message. For those with eclectic tastes, do some research to find the newest music by bands they like. Check out the websites of college radio stations or those that focus on independent labels and look at their playlists. After you compile a set of songs, arrange them in an order that works in its entirety, rather than throwing them together randomly. Start with a bold, catchy tune that will immediately set the tone. You can slow down the pace later on, then build up momentum again. Burn the tracks onto a CD. If you want to make a customized cover, you can download software from any number of websites, then come up with graphics, liner notes, and even a name for the CD.

deep-frying

THERE'S GOOD REASON for that deeply satisfied feeling you get after eating French fries or fried chicken. The taste sates an innate craving—that's why it's called "comfort food." But not all fried foods are created equal, and they're not all necessarily unhealthful. Frying at the proper temperature makes foods not just delectable, but also guilt-free.

what you'll need

- Cooking oil (a neutral-flavored oil with a high smoking point, like canola or peanut)

- Deep-fryer or other vessel to heat the oil in

- Cooking thermometer

- Tongs, long slotted spoon, or spatula

resources

The Frequent Fryers Cookbook: How to Deep-Fry Just about Anything That Walks, Crawls, Flies, or Vegetates, by Rick Browne (Regan Books, 2003).

www.allrecipes.com: Offers recipes—including deep-frying ones—from the general public.

www.crisco.com: The website for the best-known shortening brand has a number of deep-fried recipes.

www.epicurious.com: From deep-fried baby artichokes to zucchini, you'll find recipes in their searchable database.

overview

Doughnuts, french fries, fried chicken, fish and chips, fried calamari, and tempura all fall under the broad and sinfully delicious category of deep-fried foods. The technique calls for immersing food in hot oil, a quick process that swiftly fries the foods. Contrary to what we associate with deep-fried foods, slippery fingers shouldn't necessarily result from eating them. Because the moisture in the food actually repels the oil, only a small amount of it should remain, confined to the exterior layer of the food. Often, though, as at most fast-food restaurants, the frying temperature is not high enough and the food stays in the oil too long, resulting in the dreaded post-grease gloom. For authentic deep-frying without the oily residue, foods should be fried between 345 and 375°F (174 and 190°C) or higher, depending on the type of the food.

Nearly any deep-fried food develops a crisp, golden exterior. But breading it, or dipping it in batter—milk, flour, eggs, and crumbs—creates another kind of crispiness, which makes for a flaky coating around a soft, warm interior.

history

As a cooking technique, deep-frying has a long history in a multitude of cultures. Recipes from Apicius, an epicure during the Roman Empire, mentions various fritters, deep-fried cakes made with fruit, vegetables, or fish. Although there's good reason to assume that many people thought of the idea of deep-frying blobs of bread dough, the Dutch are generally given credit for gifting civilization with the first doughnuts, called *olykoeks*, which, incidentally, did not yet have holes.

Images of dropping food into boiling oil have been found in early Chinese art. In Japan, the tempura method was introduced by missionaries from Spain and Portugal, who taught the locals the wonders of deep-frying battered foods in the late 1500s. The Japanese perfected the tempura we now know in the 18th century. Deep-fried chicken, typical fare of the American South, actually came from Scotland. Fish and chips has been typical British takeout food since the first chip shop opened in London in 1860. The idea of deep-frying fish was apparently carried to the U.K. by Portuguese Jews, who immigrated to England in the 1500s.

getting started

If you have a deep-fryer, follow the manufacturer's instructions for using it. To deep-fry on the stovetop, pour in as much oil as it takes to cover your ingredients completely. Turn up the heat on your stove and use a cooking thermometer to gauge when your oil gets to about 365°F (185°C). If it gets past 400°F (204°C), the oil will burn. Place ingredients carefully into the oil using tongs, a long slotted spoon, or a spatula (you don't want to get splashed). Battered foods will turn a golden brown. Take out one of your cooked pieces carefully and slice it open to see if it's cooked inside. If it's still crunchy or raw, lower the temperature to about 325°F (163°C), and start again. As each piece finishes frying, take it out and place it on paper towels, paper bags, or cooling racks to drain.

Extremely high temperatures are employed in deep-frying, so make sure you have a fire extinguisher designed for grease fires. Never throw water on this type of fire (known as a class B fire); instead cut off the air supply by covering the pot or throwing baking soda on the flames.

profile: deeply satisfying

"Fat tastes good," says RICK BROWNE, cookbook author and host of the PBS television show Barbecue America, *to explain why humans of all creeds, cultures, and classes are drawn to deep-fried foods. "Fat adds a nice, sweet flavor and moisture to food." Hence our insatiable craving for doughnuts, fried chicken, and french fries. The word "deep" added to* fried *is what gives it a bad rap, he says. "But if you think about it, everything cooked on the stove is fried: eggs, pancakes, vegetables. Every culture in the world fries food, from the Eskimos to the people in the Sahara."*

Browne, who lives in Vancouver, Washington, notes that if deep-frying is done right—oil is heated to the right temperature and the food is taken out in time and drained—the fat content is comparable to foods roasted in the oven. "The fat sears the meat, it doesn't go into the meat," Browne says of the technique. "The extremely hot temperature seals in all the juices of the meat or fish you're frying." Deep-frying begs for experimentation. Try deep-frying steak, Oreos, corn on the cob, even fruit like the Eastern Europeans do, Browne suggests.

"Stay away from safflower oil and palm oil, which are high in triglyceride; use the right temperature; and drain the oil from the food."

project: scottish deep-fried mars bar

First, don't spend any time searching for Mars bars in American stores—here they're called Milky Way bars. (Incidentally, you can try deep-frying pretty much any type of nougat-filled, chocolate-covered bar.) Chill the candy bar by leaving it in the refrigerator for a while (not the freezer). Mix together 1 cup (125 g) all-purpose flour, 1/2 cup (65 g) cornstarch, and a pinch of baking soda in a bowl. Pour in a splash of milk and stir until you get a creamy texture, then set aside. Now start heating your frying oil in a pan. When the oil reaches the right temperature, remove the Mars bar from the refrigerator and dip it in the batter. Lower the chocolate bar into the oil using tongs and fry until the exterior turns golden brown. Bring it out, drain it briefly, and enjoy this scrumptious treat while it's hot. For an over-the-top splurge, serve it à la mode, with vanilla ice cream.

docenting

IF YOU FIND YOURSELF SPENDING HOUR AFTER LEISURELY HOUR at museums reading every last placard, wondering how you can get more information, and love explaining points of fact to friends, you should consider docenting. Sure it doesn't pay much (if at all), and you have to go through some rigorous training, but for docents, their job is more a calling than a hobby, a true point of pride.

what you'll need

For this hobby, you need a lot of free time, an interest in a particular cultural institution or subject, and a natural inclination to absorb and communicate information. You'll also need some "people skills."

overview

Docents provide instructional guided tours of museums, zoos, historic sites, parks, landmarks, and other public attractions. They are considered educators and are trained extensively in their specific field to answer questions and provide basic information about the institutions they represent. They undergo a training process following experienced docents and eventually work up to offering their own tours. They must attend seminars to keep up with the changes at the institution they represent. Some docents receive a small fee for their work, while others work on a volunteer basis.

history

It's hard to pinpoint exactly when docenting began. It is said in docenting circles that the first museum to institute such a program was the Museum of Fine Arts in Boston. It is also believed that the Rhode Island School of Design has had docents for about a century.

resources

The Professional Guide: Dynamics of Tour Guiding, by Kathleen Lingle Pond (Wiley, 1992).

www.docents.net: The National Docent Symposium Council's website offers information about sponsored activities and recruitment opportunities, plus a handbook on docenting.

www.idealist.org: Find docenting and other volunteer opportunities.

www.volunteermatch.org: Volunteer Match: listings of hundreds of volunteer opportunities.

getting started

Find a local institution, like an art museum, historical site, library, or other institution in your area that is looking for volunteer docents. Get in touch with the person in charge and ask about docenting opportunities. Chances are, they are looking for volunteers.

project: offer a tour of your own neighborhood

To get a feel for this kind of work, start by offering a tour of your own neighborhood. Research all the pertinent facts about the history of the region: when your house and the houses around you were built, who the architects were, the demographics of the people who first moved to the area, and how it evolved over the years both in cultural and in geographical ways. Find out if any fires, floods, or other natural occurrences changed the way the streets looked. Also look into what types of businesses were first established in that region, how long they lasted, and what accounted for their closure. Go to the library and look for old photos of the neighborhood or business plans. Many cities keep these records on file and might allow you to photocopy them.

Talk to old-timers in the area to add colorful anecdotes to your tour. They've probably witnessed many of the changes you're reading about and can give you firsthand accounts of how they were affected. When you've accumulated all the information, put together a comprehensive time line of the neighborhood. Plan a walking tour with stops at the significant sites you've learned about. Try to make the time line correspond to the stops in the tour, to give context to the information. Keep the tour to between 30 and 45 minutes. Practice on your family and see if it holds their interest. When you've got the green light, put together a flyer and pass it around to your neighbors. Schedule a time and date for your premiere tour and watch them line up!

profile: porter to the past

BETSY THOMAS has a penchant for learning, a trait that has led her to some fascinating experiences. As a history buff, she learned about long-gone eras that provide context for the present. When obtaining her master's degree in American history at the University of Southern Illinois, she wrote her thesis on the history of the 19th-century house she lived in and the many generations who had lived there before. She first became a docent at the historic Deacon John Grave House in Madison, Connecticut, and eventually served on its board of directors. Built in the late 1600s, this beautifully preserved structure housed seven generations of the same family—dressmakers, innkeepers, soldiers, and farmers—up until the early 20th century. Meticulously kept records and accounting books detailed the long and textured lifeline of the families who lived in the house. Documents like receipts for goods from London, letters from soldiers who stayed at the home during the Revolutionary War, and even written charges of kicking and "other tumultuous and offensive behavior" provided colorful accounts of life in the coastal New England

town over the past 400 years. "I loved teaching people about the house, and learned most of what I knew by following other docents on their tours," Thomas says.

Once she got a taste of the docenting life, Thomas followed her interest in art and architecture to the Colorado Springs Fine Arts Center, where she now gives tours. Her training took five months and gave her an extensive knowl-

> **"Talk to someone at a history museum, an art museum, or even a zoo and inquire about their docent training and when it starts."**

edge about the museum's collection. "The best part is that I get to learn," she says. "And every time we host a new traveling exhibit I continue to learn more." Thomas gives tours once a week and sometimes serves as a mentor to new docents. It turns out that many of the docents she's met so far have worked as teachers in the past. After six years of docenting, Thomas says she plans to continue as long as she enjoys it.

dog breeding

IMAGINE HOLDING A NEWBORN PUPPY, playing with it, and letting it slumber away contentedly in your arms. Helping to bring that adorable creature into the world is the heart-warming part of dog breeding. But this hobby also involves several weeks of sleepless nights (puppies cry just like human babies), veterinarian bills, and the responsibility of finding good homes for the little tykes. Why go through all the trouble? Have you held a newborn pup lately?

what you'll need

- Female dog, or bitch

- Male dog, or stud

- Quiet spot for the female to whelp (or give birth to) the puppies where they can be swaddled in warmth; also known as a "whelping box"

- Towels for delivering and drying the puppies

- String or dental floss to cut the umbilical cords and iodine to clean them

- Syringe to absorb excess fluids from the puppies' mouths and noses

- Clean cardboard boxes to house the puppies

- Thermometer

- Food scale

- All additional supplies (food, water, grooming tools) necessary for the health and well-being of your dogs

overview

Dog breeding is the propagation of a specific breed of dog by mating a bitch and a stud of the same breed. After the mating is complete, gestation takes between 61 and 63 days (about nine weeks, as compared to 38 weeks for humans). Most purebred (not mixed with other breeds) puppies are recorded on a breed registry that's kept by a kennel or breeder. Like children, newborn puppies require a tremendous amount of attention and care, and helping bitches through the birthing process can be an intense experience. Don't underestimate the effort and expertise involved: Breeding dogs is an ambitious undertaking.

history

There's evidence that ancient dog breeds originated all over the world, from Siberia to Africa. Of the 14 ancient breeds that have been officially identified, one of the oldest is the basenji, images of which have been found on stone slabs in the tombs of ancient Egyptian pharaohs. People have been reproducing breeds of dog throughout the ages for different purposes. In the scorching heat, desert dwellers needed their dogs to withstand days of travel without food and water, while snowbound owners in northern countries needed heavy-coated working dogs that could run through snow and swim in icy waters. Dogs have been instrumental for hunting, guiding, and, of course, keeping their owners company. As a pastime, dog breeding became popular in the mid-1800s, when wealthy Europeans busied themselves by organizing dog shows, the first of which was held in England in 1859.

> "There are many puppies that families think they want until they grow out of the cute stage and are abandoned. These dogs need rescuing and that can be every bit as gratifying as breeding dogs."

getting started

A breeder must have thorough knowledge of the breed of choice. Compare your purebred to the standard and see if it's got any major "faults," such as skeletal problems, or any other health issues that would impede breeding. If you find none, then it's time to find a mate—either a bitch of breeding age or a stud.

When it's time for the birth, you'll need to find a warm and quiet spot—preferably a box you've constructed for this purpose, known as the whelping box, where the bitch can deliver her puppies. When they're born, the puppies will need to stay in the whelping box, and you'll probably need to stay nearby day and night for the first two weeks to ensure that the mother doesn't crush the pups and that the puppies are thriving. You'll measure their weight on the food scale twice a day, and take their temperatures once in the morning and once at night. You'll cut their toenails and clean their ears, supply the mom with something to eat three times a day, and basically make sure they have everything they need. As with newborn babies, puppies need to be fed every couple of hours. Don't count on getting much sleep, as you may need to help them find the mother's teats. If the puppies don't appear to be gaining weight, you'll have to supplement with formula. Once the puppies are weaned (in about eight weeks), decide whether you'll be selling or keeping them. If some will stay, it's time to start doing your research on dog training.

profile: puppy love

CYNTHIA KELLY, who breeds Rhodesian Ridgebacks, spends hours a day watching the puppies she's helped breed and birth. "They are wonderful," she says. "I love to watch them as they learn to walk, to play, as they eat and sleep, and as they begin to learn about the world and their place in it."

That's the fun part. But Kelly is also pragmatic enough to caution potential breeders about the challenging aspects of this hobby. "If a puppy becomes very ill, I'm fighting with the mother to keep that puppy alive," she says. "If a pup doesn't make it for some other reason, you feel the loss yourself and share the intense grief the mother feels." Breeders must also contend with the expenses incurred, the doctors' visits, the shots, and finding the right homes for the new pups. "It is hard, hard, hard work!"

But for her, it's obviously a labor of love. "They are so cute," she says about the puppies. "You have to cuddle each puppy several times a day, handle and talk to the little tykes. My goal is that no puppy leaves my home without a thousand kisses to remember me by."

project: instant whelping box

Building a whelping box from scratch takes time, energy, and power tools. If you'd prefer to skip that step altogether, do what some breeders do and opt for using an inflatable pool. It can be cleaned much more easily than wood, and if lined with a soft blanket, mom and puppies will be kept warm and snug in the confines of their new circular home. An inflatable pool is roomy enough for the lot, but cozy enough to make them feel safe and comfortable.

resources

Breeding Better Dogs, by Carmelo L Battaglia (Battaglia Enterprises, 1990).

The Complete Book of Dog Breeding, by Dan Rice (Barron's Educational, 1996).

www.akc.org: American Kennel Club's official site with links to breeders, different kinds of breeds, and clubs.

www.denmothers.net: The website for a documentary by the same name about Rhodesian Ridgebacks "and the humans who love them," directed by filmmaker Keegan Walden.

www.learntobreed.com: Breeder Jane Anderson's site for the beginning breeder, including a checklist of criteria, books to read, and advice on screening your dog for hip dysplasia.

dog show training

EVERYBODY DESERVES HIS 15 MINUTES OF FAME—EVEN YOUR PET. If you know you've got yourself a top-notch purebred and want to show the world, maybe it's time to give him a whirl in the presence of his pedigreed peers. Just promise to love him whether or not he takes "Best in Show."

what you'll need

- *Show-quality pet*
- *Leash (for dogs)*
- *Obedience training classes (for dogs)*
- *Grooming tools*
- *Show clothes*

cat shows: Like their canine counterparts, cats have shows in which pedigreed felines are judged by conformation points and awarded titles. But the structure of the show is a bit different: Cat owners bring their cats to each judge's cage for appraisal rather than prancing them in a circle in front of the judges. Judges are looking for cats in prime physical condition (no fat cats need apply), with a calm and even temperament, shining eyes and coat, and an attentive look about them. They will also feel the shape and size of the cat's bone structure, as well as its muscle tone. For information on how to prepare and enter your feline friend in a cat show, visit the American Cat Fanciers' Association website at www.acfacats.com.

overview

Dog shows (also known as "conformation shows") are in some ways similar to human beauty pageants. Organized by kennel clubs, they are a vehicle for breeders and proud dog owners to strut their dogs' best stuff. Judges who are proficient in all the characteristics of each breed rate the dogs on how well they conform to breed standards. The idea is not so much to compare breeds to each other as to compare dogs to the ideal of the specific breed—a list of "conformation points."

The majority of breeds have separate classes, and the highest level of showing is the championships. For each show level that a dog wins, it earns points toward winning the prized title of "champion." Points won depend on the level, how many dogs are competing, and whether the show is considered major or minor, just like in sports leagues. Winners are gradually narrowed down until the last round, in which judges bestow the coveted title "Best in Show."

history

British aristocrats were the first to organize a dog show, back in 1859. A year later, the first dog society was formed in Birmingham, England, followed by the Acclimation Société dog show in Paris in 1863. What started as a small gathering of dog lovers in a tiny London flat in 1873 quickly grew into the Kennel Club of Great Britain, a sprawling organization. Just a few months after its first meeting, almost 1,000 participants attended the club's first show at the Crystal Palace, trotting proudly along with their canine protégés. Soon afterward, dog showing became an American hobby, when in 1884 12 delegates of smaller dog clubs met at the Philadelphia Kennel Club and decided to create a larger entity, which became the American Kennel Club.

getting started

First, be sure your dog's papers are in order. Before you sign up for a show, you must possess credentials that indicate yours is a show-quality dog.

If your dog has completed obedience training, you're well on your way. If he hasn't, you must set aside at least a few months to train him before his first show. Each breed has its own set of instructions, so contact clubs that offer handling classes or buy videos that go into details about showing your breed. No matter the breed, your dog should learn how to walk on either side of you on a loose leash. He should stop when you do and be able to cross over from your left to your right. Slowly speed up the walk to a brisk trot and practice turns on both sides. The dog's head should be held up high and proud. Correct him along the way with a sharp tug of the leash. Remember, positive reinforcement always works. Praise your dog for each accomplishment and give him a biscuit. Repeat every newly learned trick until it becomes second nature.

Talk to a dog groomer about grooming techniques, or take your pup for the professional once-over. Grooming at home, which requires grooming tools and a rubber mat, will familiarize your dog with being handled and teach him to sit still during the process. This will help prepare him for the "posing" part of the show, when the judge will check his teeth, pick up his feet, feel his fur, and check under the tail.

If they're offered locally, take your dog to conformation training classes, which will help acquaint both of you with the show environs and teach you all the skills the judges will be looking for. You should also attend some dog shows (or at least watch them on TV) so you know exactly what to expect. On show day, go equipped with a grooming table, dog food, water, show clothes, and a first-aid kit.

other canine competitions:

Even if you don't own a purebred pup, there are other competitions—beyond the traditional conformation show—to choose from, including:

Agility: Handlers guide dogs through an obstacle course
Disc Dog: Frisbee for dogs
Musical Freestyle: A chance to prance with your pooch

project: stop your dog from pulling on the leash

One of the best indications of a well-trained dog is how it handles a leash. Most dogs will try to pull on the leash to indicate what direction they want to go (and some will drag you along with them), but in a conformation show, that is strictly frowned upon. Discouraging your dog from pulling on the leash is a surprisingly quick and relatively painless process. Each time you feel a tug on the leash, stop, go back a couple of steps, and say "heel." Keep the dog in a sitting position for a few seconds, then continue walking. Each time he pulls, repeat the sequence. In a few days, he should have kicked the habit.

resources

Raising a Champion: A Beginner's Guide to Showing Dogs, by Meredith A. John and Carole L. Richards (The Well Trained Dog, 2001).

The Absolute Beginner's Guide to Showing Your Dog, by Cheryl S. Smith (Three Rivers Press, 2001).

www.akc.org: The American Kennel Club's official site provides links and information about breeders and shows.

www.dogpatch.org/dogs/shows.cfm: Offers pointers on how to prepare and show your dog.

www.onofrio.com: Show details and a discussion board from the premier dog show organizers in the U.S.

www.showdog-magazine.com: Show Dog magazine's website offers training, grooming, and travel tips and articles of interest to anyone interested in this hobby.

dollhouse building

KIDS AREN'T THE ONLY ONES WHO ENJOY PLAYING make-believe house. For many adults, it's almost as much fun to design, build, and decorate a small-scale house as it is for kids to play with it. A few woodworking tools are required, but even for the novice builder, there's immense pleasure in creating one of these enchanting miniature realms.

what you'll need

FOR A KIT:

- *Kit and whatever additional supplies are called for in the instructions*

FROM SCRATCH:

- *Design plan (see resources or create your own)*
- *Wood, like mahogany plywood*
- *Small hammer*
- *4d nails (smallest size)*
- *Needle-nose pliers*
- *X-Acto knives*
- *Cutting mat*
- *Sandpaper and steel wool*
- *Straightedge*
- *Latex paint*
- *Wood finishing varnish*
- *Paintbrushes*
- *Clamps and weights*
- *Wood glue*
- *Syringe and toothpicks for gluing*

overview

Though we're supposed to have passed the age of playing with dollhouses, adults are still fascinated by the idea of constructing them. You can create a house from a kit or design one and build it from scratch. Kits, which range in price from $40 up to $5,000, come in a variety of styles, including Victorian, English Tudor, farmhouse, log cabin, and modern. Most are designed on a 1-inch, or 1:12, scale to life-size homes. That means an inch on the dollhouse is equivalent to a foot in a real house. All types of materials can be used to build dollhouses, from rich mahogany to lighter woods more conducive to detailed carvings. To build one from scratch, you can buy a pattern from any hobby store or an online retailer, or design one—maybe a miniature replica of your own home.

history

One of the oldest dolls to have been found is an alabaster doll with movable arms that dates back to Babylonian times. Egyptian graves dating back to 2000 B.C.E. have turned up dolls buried with their owners. Most likely, though, the first dollhouses weren't built until the 1600s to house the exquisite doll collections of wealthy Europeans. By the 1800s, Germany had become a major source for the manufacture of dollhouses made of both wood and paper. During the Industrial Revolution in the late 18th century, manufacturers started to copy German and English styles of dollhouses and made them available to middle-class consumers.

getting started

Kits are easy enough to put together—just follow the directions on the box. If you prefer to build from scratch, the most important decision to make before you start is its intended use. Are you building it for a kid to use and play with, or as a piece of art to be observed but not touched? This will help you determine what design and materials you'll use. Next, choose the scale of the house in relation to its life-size counterpart. Then decide what architectural style you want to emulate, keeping in mind the additional work that elaborate styles require.

1] *DRAW THE DESIGN of the house you want to build. Keep your scale in mind so elements will be proportionate to each other—and the right size for the doll inhabitants.*

2] *BEGIN BY CUTTING out the walls, the base, and the roof, marking spots for windows and doors. For the base, use 3/4-inch (19 mm) plywood, and for walls and the roof, use 3/8-inch (9.4 mm) plywood.*

3] *PAINT THE INTERIORS of the walls, floors, and roof before you join the pieces together. For a soft, smooth edge, sand down all the corners of the cut pieces, then, with wood glue and 4d nails, attach the walls to the base and to the roof.*

4] *PAINT THE EXTERIOR of the house.*

5] *NOW, DECORATE your house, either with store-bought furniture and fittings or miniatures of your own design. (See resources for inspiration and suppliers.)*

project: make a roombox

For a quick introduction to dollhouse making, start by creating a roombox, a 12-by-16-inch (30.5 by 40.5 cm) box with an open front that's used to display miniature collections, or which can be completely outfitted as a room of its own.

1] Use the instructions outlined in the overview to build the base, walls, and roof. You can even buy precut plywood pieces from hobby stores that come in 12-inch squares or 12-by-24-inch dimensions.

2] Paint and decorate the walls, then attach the pieces of your roombox together with 4d nails and wood glue. You can glue decorative wrapping paper on the walls and use scraps of fabric for rugs and bedspreads.

3] Arrange your miniature diorama inside the box. Your furniture should be arranged in a warm and inviting way, with the backs of chairs and sofas against the wall. To add a touch of authenticity, paint the street address of your house on the outside wall. Consider it a guesthouse to the dollhouse you'll build next!

resources

The Complete Dollhouse Building Book, by Kathryn Falk and Edlcycoe Greik (Macmillan Publishing, 1982).

The Art of Miniature, by Jane Freeman (Watson-Guptill, 2002). Practical techniques, tips, and inspiration for creating miniature rooms, structures, or landscapes.

www.dollhousecollectables.com: Online retailer of every imaginable accessory, from curtains to electrical supplies.

www.dhminiature.com: Dollhouse Miniatures magazine, a monthly periodical featuring projects, artist profiles, and plans.

www.micromark.com: Retailer of precision miniature tools for hobbyists.

www.miniatures.org: National Association of Miniatures Enthusiasts' site with links to events, retailers, and a lending library.

www.redsword.com/dollhouse: Tips, how-tos, and links to miniature associations.

drawing (pencil, charcoal, pastel, pen & ink, crayon)

HOBBY PERSONALITY: adventurous • animal-loving • **artistic** • crafty • dexterous • epicurean • extroverted • history-loving • independent • **meditative** • **meticulous** • musical • nature-loving • nurturing • outdoorsy • patient • social • sporty • technical

CAN'T DRAW A STRAIGHT LINE TO SAVE YOUR LIFE? Don't despair. Learning to draw takes at least as much instruction and practice as it does natural talent. Drawing can open up an entire realm of creative expression—a way to capture a moment, an object, or a person from a personal perspective unlike that of anyone else. Even if your drawings will never be exhibited in the Metropolitan Museum of Art, they will always have a place in your home.

what you'll need

- Sketchbook or other good-quality drawing paper

- Drawing pencils. Leads are graded, hardest to softest, 4H, 2H, H, HB, F, B, B2, and B4. The softest ones make the darkest, thickest lines.

- Vine, stick, or compressed charcoal

- Artists' crayons or pastels

- Kneaded eraser

- India inks and a pen or brush

resources

The New Drawing on the Right Side of the Brain, by Betty Edwards (Tarcher, 1999).

Ed Emberley's Complete Funprint Drawing Book, by Ed Emberly (Little, Brown, 2002).

The Natural Way to Draw: A Working Plan for Art Study, by Kimon Nicolaides (Houghton Mifflin, 1990).

http://myamericanartist.com: American Artist Drawing magazine, featuring contemporary and historic artists.

www.pearlpaint.com: Online source for every imaginable drawing tool.

www.portrait-artist.org: A tutorial website with lessons on sketching and drawing faces, an overview of art and drawing techniques, and resource guides.

overview

Drawing can be as simple as putting pencil to paper or as elaborate as using paints, charcoals, pastels, markers, crayons, wax color pencils, or a combination of media. Artists use a variety of techniques to create different effects, including line drawing, scribbling, stippling, blending, hatching, and crosshatching. Subjects can be anything the artist wants to depict—portraits of people or animals, landscapes or seascapes, architectural renderings of buildings, or botanical illustrations of plants and flowers. The depictions can be realistic, abstract, or stylized, as with caricatures.

history

Some of the earliest known drawings are found in the Lascaux caves in southwestern France and date back 40,000 years. But since the invention of writing *(see Calligraphy)*, drawing has been elevated to an art form. It blossomed in popularity in Renaissance Europe, when artists like Leonardo da Vinci, Michelangelo, and Raphael created elaborate drawings, called "cartoons," as preparatory studies for paintings and frescoes. In the 20th century, drawing, once considered a "lesser" art, was practiced for its own sake by artists like Matisse and Picasso. The art of drawing took a completely different turn with the advent of comic books in the 1930s, which led to cartoon drawings and animation. Now many graphic artists use computer programs to "draw" figures.

> "Draw, draw, draw! Carry a sketchbook around with you and draw in it constantly. It sounds so simple, but practice really is the only way to get better."

getting started

The most important tool for a beginner is your eyes. Take a close look at what you're drawing, note shapes, angles, and shadows. The stronger the light source, whether it's natural or from a lamp, the more defined the edges will appear.

1) *FIRST, PRACTICE SCRIBBLING with your drawing tools—pencils, crayons, charcoals, ink—to get a feel for how they work.*

2) *THEN START THE SKETCH with contour drawing, or drawing the general outline of an object. Choose something simple, with defined shapes and angles. Keep the object at a consistent perspective while you're drawing, so you're observing it from the same distance and angle from start to finish. Vary the thickness of the line to give the illusion of a three-dimensional object. Thinner lines make objects appear flat, as if they're sinking into the paper. You can play around with this technique to make the objects appear close or far away.*

3) *NOW BEGIN SHADING the object, starting with the darkest parts. You can use dark pencils for shadowed areas. Don't worry about making mistakes at first. You can erase them later.*

4) *STEP BACK AND COMPARE your rendering to the object, adding any details you think are needed.*

project: blind drawing

Test your drawing abilities by playing an old parlor game. Set a kitchen timer to one minute, then start drawing or sketching an object without looking down at the paper. It helps if you draw one contiguous line, but you can experiment with other techniques. The results of this exercise might be more interesting than drawings you make with your eyes open!

profile: practice makes perfect

JARED CHAPMAN'S drawings look deceptively easy. His cartoonish, exaggerated characters are sketched with simple lines and shadows, but somehow each manages to convey a complete portrait of a person. Chapman has been drawing as long as he can remember (his first effort, at three years old: an abstract portrait of Darth Vader). And he's had plenty of training, including a degree in animation from the Savannah College of Art and Design in Savannah, Georgia. Now based in Austin, Texas, and working as an animator, he still says practicing is the only way to get ahead.

"I think talent will only get you so far," he says. "It will make it easier in the beginning, but if a person with talent doesn't make an effort to develop and refine their skills, then it's going to be hard for them to get better as an artist. On the other hand, a person who may not be the strongest draftsman in the room can really work hard, learn all they can, and draw constantly, and, a lot of times, can transform into a stronger artist than the person with the initial talent."

Wise words from a young artist who's influenced by everything around him—from a tree outside his window to the work of other artists. "My inspirational sources tend to be all over the place, and I like that," he says. "This way the well will never run dry." The best part, and coincidentally the most challenging part, about drawing for Chapman is the freedom. "The only limits in drawing are those of my own imagination," he says. "All you need is something to draw with, something to draw on, and you. How simple is that?"

drying flowers

ALTHOUGH WE CAN'T FORCE THE EPHEMERAL BEAUTY of garden-fresh flowers to last, we can preserve their appearance and sometimes even their lovely aroma without resorting to buying silk ones. If created with skill, dried flowers can look surprisingly alive, boasting bright, vivid colors that last for months, or longer. Once you get the hang of it, you might even prefer these over the fresh-cut variety.

what you'll need

- *Fresh flowers*

- *Containers for storage and display*

FOR PRESSING:

- *Flower press or heavy book and a weight*

- *Cardboard, tissue paper, and newspaper (optional)*

FOR AIR DRYING:

- *Wire or string and rubber bands for hanging flowers*

- *Dry, dark place in which to dry them*

FOR USING A DRYING AGENT:

- *Desiccating agent, such as silica gel*

overview

There are three ways to dry flowers: pressing, air drying, and using dehydrating agents, or desiccants. Pressing involves placing plants or flowers between two heavy objects. Air drying entails hanging a bunch of tied flowers upside down in a warm, dark, and dry room and obviously results in a fuller look. You can also use desiccating agents to help dry and preserve flowers, or substances such as talcum powder, alcohol, borax, or sawdust—each agent works differently with different flowers.

history

Over the ages, dried flowers have been used for everything from food and medicine to décor. The earliest identified remains of dried flowers were found in a 4,000-year-old Egyptian tomb; reportedly the colors of the blossoms were still surprisingly bright and vivid. During the Middle Ages, superstitious types used to carry around dried herbs and flowers to fend off stinky smells and diseases. By the 1500s, dried blooms were being used to adorn the wealthy classes and became an important accessory in fashionable circles. As bosoms were thrust up against scooped necklines, flowers offered an enticing invitation to look. Flowers were first pressed about 500 years ago, when botanists and scientists discovered this useful method for keeping track of specimens they collected. They were glued onto index cards specifying the plant's name and species. By the Victorian era, the practice had evolved into an art form.

resources

Book of Dried Flowers: A Complete Guide to Growing, Drying, and Arranging, by Malcolm Hillier and Colin Hiton (Simon & Schuster, 1987).

Harvesting, Preserving, and Arranging Dried Flowers, by Cathy Miller and Rob Gray (Artisan, 1997).

www.gardenguides.com/tips and technique/drying.htm: Recommends the best flowers for pressing and offers tips for displaying pressed flowers.

www.preservedgardens.com: Preserved Gardens Pressed Flowers site features a forum, arts and crafts ideas, and resources.

www.pressed-flowers.com: Kate Chu's comprehensive site includes beautiful examples of vivid-hued pressed flowers.

getting started

- *FOR THE PRESSING TECHNIQUE, small, dainty flowers like violets, pansies, and larkspur are the best kinds to use (ferns and leaves also work nicely). Carefully place the entire flower within the pages of a heavy book, close the book, and weigh it down with something heavy. For a more precise technique, you can place flowers on top of tissue paper covering a piece of cardboard, making sure none of the flowers are touching each other. Use another piece of tissue paper to cover the flowers, then cover that with newspaper, then cardboard. Once you've got all your flowers covered, place a heavy book, brick, or stone on top, and let it sit for a few weeks. Once they're dried, the flowers will come out flat, almost like paper, and can be framed.*

- *FOR AIR-DRYING, use baby's breath, goldenrod, pussy willow, or heather. Just tie a bunch tightly together using wire or string and hang upside down in a warm, dark, and dry room. The dark keeps the color of the flowers from fading, while the dryness repels rot. The complete process takes a couple of weeks. A few things to note: Yellow and blue flowers are more likely to keep their colors, while pink flowers fade, and some types of flowers shrink more than others.*

- *TO USE A DRYING AGENT (daisies and pansies work beautifully with this method), add about an inch (2.5 cm) of desiccating material to the bottom of a 6-inch deep (15 cm) box, then cut off all but about 1/2 inch (1.5 cm) of the flower stem. Place the flower in the container so the stub of the stem sticks into the desiccating agent. With a spoon, sprinkle desiccating agent around the edge of the container and then gently shake it so that it begins to cover the flower. Repeat this process until all the petals are covered. Place the container in a cool, dry place, and after a day or two the petals should be dry and papery. Commonly used desiccants include borax, silica gel, oolitic sand, and common sand, all of which are available at hobby stores.*

project: make a pressed-flower picture or card

Cut a piece of wax paper the size of a store-bought frame. Arrange your dried, pressed flowers on the wax paper in a design you like—a sun, a starburst, a circle, or heart—then add a bit of glue to the back of each flower to hold it in place. After the glue dries, cover the flowers and wax paper with a piece of clear contact paper. Press the contact paper to the flowers, and place the whole thing inside the frame. You can also make a card or a book cover using the same technique.

if you like this hobby, you might enjoy:

- African violet cultivation [see page 14]
- Basketry [see page 28]
- Bonsai [see page 46]
- Gourd crafting [see page 112]
- Ikebana [see page 122]
- Topiary [see page 204]
- Vegetable and herb gardening [see page 212]

dumpster diving

HOW MANY TIMES HAVE YOU WALKED by a piece of furniture or other perfectly functional item on the curb and thought about taking it home? Don't be ashamed—you're not the only one who believes that one man's trash is another man's treasure. Though it can be a somewhat grubby hobby, it's no longer relegated to the desperate. In fact, we live in an age of such absurd material excess that it seems almost wrong not to find a use for these discarded pieces. So go ahead and snoop around. You never know what you'll discover!

what you'll need

- *Clothes you can get dirty*

- *Dumpsters, trash bags, or trash-loaded curbsides to search*

- *Flashlight or headlamp*

- *Knapsack*

- *Grabber stick*

- *Heavy-duty work gloves*

- *Sanitary wipes and antibacterial gel for quick cleanup*

- *First-aid kit*

resources

The Encyclopedia of Garbage, by Steve Coffel and William L. Rathje (Facts on File, 1996).

The Art and Science of Dumpster Diving, by John Hoffman (Breakout Productions, 1999).

www.dumpsterworld.com: Dumpster diving discussion forums, including recent finds for sale or swap.

www.freecycle.org: Sign up on this free listing service and connect with all those who want to discard of potentially useful items.

overview

Dumpster diving is the practice of rummaging through trash, be it residential or commercial, in search of valuable or useful goods and collectibles. Though food is a commodity typically reserved for the homeless, there are actually hobbyists who dive for the fun of it—seeking nonperishables, of course. When it involves crossing property lines, Dumpster diving is technically illegal, but a lot of items can be retrieved from trash left outside on the curb—a perfectly legal act in most areas. Department stores, offices, factories, and other businesses dispose of goods that are worthless to them but of great value to others. But be warned: There is a criminal element sometimes associated with Dumpster diving, especially when it's carried out by those in search of personal information to exploit. We want to be clear that this is not the wholesome hobby we're proposing. Dive for tchotchkes, not classified information.

history

It's difficult to pinpoint the exact time when Dumpster diving began, but it's a safe bet to assume that as long as people have been dumping trash, other people have been sifting through it. Certain eras in history, however, do refer specifically to this practice. The term *ragpicking* was used in the late 1800s and early 1900s, when European immigrants, who arrived in the U.S. en masse, took jobs as rackpickers, salvaging and selling discarded books (when books were still made of rags).

The term *garbology* was coined in the early 1970s, when University of Arizona head William Rathje began to study trash as an academic discipline, following the patterns of how trash is created and disposed. In the mid-1980s, a subculture of Dumpster divers was defined when "phone phreaks"—people fixated by phones and telephone companies—organized dives to sort through large telephone companies' internal manuals.

getting started

First, find out whether Dumpster diving is legal in your general vicinity. This is easy to do: Just call your police station to find out. Now go and scope out some Dumpsters (those that are freestanding rather than compactors attached to buildings). Don't go near locked Dumpsters or even park your car next to one, and stay far away from hazardous waste or medical Dumpsters. It's wise to use your grabbing stick in case you encouter sharp objects.

Look through apartment Dumpsters and home garbage cans, and you may come across furniture, artwork, computers, lawn mowers, TVs, old CD players, vacuum cleaners, even bicycles. Find out from your city's sanitation department when "big trash" nights are scheduled for a neighborhood—it's a chance for homeowners to discard large pieces that don't fit into ordinary trash bins. Target Dumpsters of shops you're interested in, like toy stores, bookstores, or furniture stores. And lastly, don't get discouraged if you don't find something valuable the first day. Keep returning and eventually you'll see that people throw away the darndest things.

project: window shutter mail holder

A small window shutter, a ubiquitous Dumpster treasure, can easily be transformed into a letter holder.

Cut a piece of plywood to the same dimensions as the shutter. Using wood glue, attach the plywood to the back of the shutter. (This ensures that your letters won't fall out the other side.) Apply a fresh coat of paint in whatever color you choose. Hang your mail holder, slots angled up, near your mail slot, desk, or wherever else mail collects in your house.

profile: the life cycle of refuse

Freecycle is an internet-connected band of environmentally conscious folks who, rather than pile their castoffs into landfills, give them away to each other. How it works: You sign up to receive postings by email, and the first person to respond to an offer for a giveaway gets the item for free. It's a simple premise and one that works almost flawlessly. "It's free recycling on one hand, and feeds the free cycle of giving on the other," explains DERON BEAL, the founder and executive director of the organization.

In Tucson, Arizona, where Beal and his wife live, it's illegal to go Dumpster diving. It's even illegal to go through a trash bin that's sitting out on the curb. "Not only are we living in a hugely wasteful society, but the government is actually forcing people to throw things away," he says.

But Freecycle is doing more than its fair share to ameliorate this woeful situation. According to Beal, trading on the website has kept more than 200 tons of trash a day from being thrown into landfills, which is exactly what a midsize landfill takes in daily. So far, he's calculated that Freecycle has resulted in one less full landfill in the world.

"The coolest thing is not consuming at all."

With new countries signing on and more than 2 million members, the movement is "growing like bonkers!" he says. Of course, there are some items that can't be saved—like the four telephone poles Beal wanted to bring home. At that, his wife drew the line. "She didn't want them to be sitting around the perimeter of our house for five years until I figured out what to do with them," he says.

entering contests

WE'VE ALL WONDERED WHAT IT WOULD BE LIKE TO WIN A HUGE STASH OF CASH. What would we do with all that money? Buy gold-flecked toilet paper and a house and yacht for ourselves and every member of our extended family, pay off loans, quit our jobs, travel the world, and, most importantly, never worry about money again. Simply indulging the fantasy is motive enough to start entering contests. You know what they say: You can't win if you don't play!

what you'll need

- *Internet access or access to magazines that offer sweepstakes*
- *Stamps*
- *Pen*
- *Envelopes and index cards in the sizes specified by the sweepstakes instructions*

resources

How to Win Lotteries, Sweepstakes, and Contests in the 21st Century, 2nd ed., by Steve Ledoux (Santa Monica Press, 2004).

The Prize Winner of Defiance, Ohio: How My Mother Raised 10 Kids on 25 Words or Less, by Terry Ryan and Suze Orman (Simon & Schuster, 2002).

Contest Queen, by Carol Shaffer, et al. (Truman Publishing, 2002).

Best Publications
PO Box 421163
Plymouth, MN 55442
www.bestsweepstakes.com: A contests and sweepstakes newsletter published weekly by Best Publications.

www.contestalley.com: Enter to win everything from iPods to trips to Disneyland.

http://contests.about.com/library/blprize.htm: A list of online sweepstakes.

www.recipecontests.com: Cooking contests central.

overview

Companies sponsor contests as a way to promote their goods and services. Some sweepstakes require nothing more from entrants than sending in your name and address, while others solicit creative entries like recipes, poems, or slogans, or require you to write essays, answer trivia, or submit photos. For "sweepers" (those who enter sweepstakes as a hobby), the internet has opened up a whole new world of resources to mine, though many still use "snail-mail" (the U.S. Postal Service) as well. Without having to spend a dime, sweepers are enticed to participate in contests that sometimes offer unfathomably large sums of money or other expensive prizes. Some of the best-known ones are American Family Publishers Sweepstakes, Publishers Clearing House, and Reader's Digest Sweepstakes, all of which hawk magazine subscriptions on the same form as the sweepstakes entries. Fast-food companies, food retailers, travel agencies, radio stations, newspapers, magazines, and any other entity that has a chance of nabbing a customer by offering prizes also sponsor sweepstakes.

history

In Roman times, emperors commonly gave parting gifts to their guests as door-prize drawings, but Augustus Caesar was the first to conduct a public lottery as a means to raise money to make repairs to the public infrastructure in Rome. There's also mention of a lottery in the Bible—a way for Moses to award land west of the Jordan River to the tribes of Israel. In modern times, the Irish Hospitals' Sweepstakes in 1930 was the biggest of its kind; it was promoted internationally, reaching eager participants in the U.S. and Canada, which had abolished lotteries at the time. But by 1964, New Hampshire had created a state lottery, the first of its kind that was legal in the 20th century.

getting started

- *FIRST, DO SOME RESEARCH to figure out what types of sweepstakes you're interested in. Thousands of companies offer ways to win their goods or services, so it's up to you to narrow down the vast array of choices. If you've got a knack for creating recipes, taking photos, or writing poetry, look for contests soliciting those types of entries. (See resources for websites and newsletters that publish sweepstakes details.)*

- *WINNING SWEEPSTAKES TAKES PERSISTENCE, which requires time and energy. But there are shortcuts. If an automated form is available, for example, use it to save time. But if they ask for 3-by-5-inch index cards, be sure to stick to the rules—some companies immediately toss entries that don't arrive in the proper form. And remember, the more difficult the entry process, the better your chances are of winning. Even a simple thing like requiring that you print your name in all capital letters or that you use an odd-size envelope or card deters some potential contestants from entering, so don't be one of them.*

- *IT'S EASY TO GET BURNED OUT if you're entering too many contests at once. Pace yourself by entering a few every month throughout the year, rather than going through sweepstakes spurts. Don't wait till the last minute to send in your forms—it would be a shame to be disqualified because your entry was late. If there is no maximum number of entries, it's better to spread yours over the course of the sweepstakes timeline rather than send them in a huge group at the end. When there are a large number of entries and one is going to be picked from the heap, it's better to have your cards distributed throughout the whole pile rather than be clumped together in one spot.*

- *ONCE YOU'VE ENTERED, it's just a matter of waiting for the news. Obviously, the more contests you enter, the higher your chance of winning. The most popular contests will have far smaller odds of winning. In fact, the odds of winning a sweepstakes, contest, or legal lottery are 400 million to 1 against winning a grand prize of $500,000. Read the fine print carefully if you want to calculate your odds.*

project: homemade envelopes and index cards for contest entries

Using store-bought envelopes and index cards for entering contests can be expensive, especially since you aren't guaranteed a win. Instead of buying new ones, try making your own; sweepstakes companies don't care how your entries arrive, as long as they do.

Old calendar pages make great envelopes because of the weight and broad size of the pages. Before you start cutting them up, first undo a standard envelope to use as a template. Cut the pages to match the size and shape of the standard envelope, then fold and fix the edges together with a glue stick. Shopping bags, construction paper, or heavy-weight, glossy magazine pages make good envelopes, too.

When it comes to the index cards, the main thing is to make sure the dimensions are right. Instead of wasting new index cards for contest entries, reuse your resources: Write on the backs of old, blurry photos that you were going to toss anyway and send them in. You can also cut birthday and holiday cards you've received down to the right size.

falconry

TYPICALLY ASSOCIATED WITH THE TALES OF KING ARTHUR and other medieval legends, falconry, also known as the "sport of kings," is less a hobby than a lifestyle. Falconers tend to be obsessed with training their birds, and spend a great deal of time and effort to that end. Once the rigorous training is complete, however, the powerful connection lasts a lifetime.

what you'll need

- *Falcon*

- *Anklets (leather straps that go around bird's legs)*

- *Bells (to attach to the bird's tail or around its neck)*

- *Bewits (strips of leather used to attach bells to the bird's leg)*

- *Block perch (a perch for a falcon)*

- *Creance (cord attached to the bird for training purposes)*

- *Gauntlet (glove that protects the falconer from the bird's talons)*

- *Hood (leather head cover)*

- *I.D. tag (in case the bird wanders)*

- *Jesses (leather strips that keep birds on a leash)*

- *Leash (allows falconer to attach the bird to his glove)*

- *Lure (fake bait used for training)*

- *Scale (for weighing the bird before a hunt)*

overview

Falconry is the sport (or art) of training falcons to hunt for game. Training methods vary, but essentially, falcons are rewarded with food when they bring back their prey. During training, the bird wears bells and tethers on its legs and a hood over its head to keep it from being distracted by sights and sounds beyond the trainer. Motivated by edible rewards, the bird is trained to return to the falconer first from short distances, then from longer distances on outdoor perches, eventually free of tethers. The falcon then learns how to chase a lure, which is held by the falconer and swung around in wide circles. Once the bird is fully trained, it can start to hunt in open fields. The hood is removed, the tethers are undone, and the falcon flies off in search of prey, then leads the falconer to it or brings it back. Falconers gauge whether their bird will be willing to fly for prey by weighing them—the less they weigh, the hungrier they are, and thus the more eager to hunt for food. Falconers don't starve their birds, but during the week they work on building muscle by training them and rewarding them with meat. Toward the end of the week, to get ready for a weekend hunt, falconers cut back on the food so their bird is hungry enough to seek prey.

history

Falconry dates as far back as 2000 B.C.E., according to images and art found on tapestries in China. It was also an important hunting technique in the Arab world, where it is still commonly practiced. A drawing dated 1700 B.C.E. and found in the ruins of Khorsabad (now Iraq) shows a man bearing a hawk on his wrist. The Crusaders learned falconry from the Arabs and introduced the sport to Europeans. Falconry was favored by the noble classes in medieval Europe, as well as in feudal Japan, since only the wealthy could afford to raise these expensive birds of prey. Falconry went in and out of favor in England, and by the time guns became commonly used for hunting, its popularity had waned. The first falconry organization in the U.S., the Peregrine Club, was founded in 1934 (though it folded during World War II). The North American Falconers Association was founded in 1961. Today, falconry is used in some urban areas as a method of pest abatement to control animals like pigeons and jackrabbits.

getting started

- *FALCONRY IS MONITORED by government authorities because it is a form of hunting. Falconers must have state and federal licenses to practice. The falconer's license requires you to pass a written test, get your equipment examined, and complete a two-year apprenticeship with a licensed falconer. There are between 3,000 and 4,000 licensed falconers in the U.S., and you can find them by contacting a falconers' group near you. Call around until you find someone who's interested in sponsoring you.*

- *THERE ARE OTHER FACTORS to consider before diving in. A bird of prey is not a pet: You are training it to hunt. You'll need to have a proper facility to house the bird, called a mews—the dimensions of which are also mandated by law based on the size of the bird—as well as the means to provide your bird with food and medical care. Naturally, you should like the outdoors and have access to open fields where the falcons can go hunting. And you should set aside a good chunk of time to spend with the bird, whether it's for training, feeding, or heading out to a field.*

- *OBTAINING A FALCON is strictly regulated by the government. There are three classes of falconry license: apprentice, general, and master class. Licensed falconers with two years of experience can buy captive-bred birds from breeders (see resources). Apprentice falconers must capture their birds with their sponsors, and, in the U.S., they have two choices: red-tailed hawks or American kestrels that are at least three months old. If the birds are captured at a younger age, they will lose their ability to live in the wild and thus become permanently dependent on their owners.*

hobby hazard: Before plunging into this hobby, consider the pets already on your premises. Though most raptors can carry only up to half their own body weight (for a red-tailed hawk, for example, that's only 2.5 pounds [about 1 kg]), they can eat larger prey, like your pet rabbit. Cats and dogs, however, learn to keep their distance from the birds by observing how the birds react to them. Many falconers have hunting dogs, such as beagles and pointers, which form a relationship with the falcons and learn to work with them on hunts.

project: clean your falconry gloves

There's no way around it: Hunting animals invariably means dealing with blood and entrails. After each hunt, you'll need to clean your gloves in preparation for the next one. The best way to do this is to use a sharp knife or blade to scrape off the dried gunk, then soak the gloves in warm water. With a scouring sponge and soap, scrape off the remaining residue from the gloves, wring them, then place them in a warm and sunny spot to dry. To keep the leather supple, rub beeswax over your gloves.

resources

Falconry: Art and Practice, by Emma Ford (Sterling Publishing, 1998).

Falconry Basics: A Handbook for Beginners, by Tony Hall (Swan Hill Press, 2004).

www.americanfalconry.com: American Falconry Magazine, a quarterly publication dedicated to the sport.

www.themodernapprentice.com: Offers an overview of the sport and each of the pieces of equipment.

www.n-a-f-a.org: The North American Falconer's Association's site provides membership information, a photo gallery, and a members-only forum.

www.northwoodsfalconry.com: Falcons and hawks for sale, along with every type of falconry equipment.

fantasy sports leagues

FOR SPORTS FANS WHO SEEK THE THRILL OF HIGH-STAKES ACTION, joining a fantasy sports league is the way to experience it. The risks are based on sports players' real performances, so the excitement is quite real, even if the leagues are pure fiction. You control your own team members, come up with your own set of rules, and put together your own ideal team of starters. Follow your team's every triumph and defeat, agonize over every fumble and foul, as you live the life of a general manager. It's a wild ride, so get ready to rumble!

what you'll need

Depending on how and where you want to play, you'll need either a computer or some like-minded friends. To play with friends, you'll need access to sports statistics (that is, box scores). You'll need to play during the sport's actual season, so it's important to get set up with your opposing players before the season starts. You will also need a name for your league and your team.

resources

www.fantasysports.org: Fantasy Sports Magazine, a quarterly magazine for fantasy football and baseball fans.

http://football.fantasysports.yahoo.com: Yahoo's fantasy football leagues, free of charge.

games.espn.go.com/frontpage: ESPN's fantasy league website.

overview

Fantasy sports leagues are made up of league "owners" who assemble a "team" of professional athletes and compete against other fantasy teams by comparing the statistics established by the athletes during their real-life games. Statistics can be calculated manually, or by using computer software programs. What's more, fantasy sports leagues have evolved from a fun hobby to a lucrative internet industry with plenty of gambling involved.

history

The most popular and oldest fantasy sports game is the All-Star Baseball board game, manufactured by Cadaco-Ellis in 1941 and designed by baseball player Ethan Allen. APBA, a game company created in 1951 by Richard Seitz, offered a baseball simulation table game using cards to represent each major-league player and his stats from previous seasons. APBA eventually created games for football, golf, basketball, hockey, bowling, and saddle racing. The first recorded fantasy football league was dubbed the Greater Oakland Professional Pigskin Prognosticators League. It was created in Oakland, California, in 1962 in the basement of Wilfred Winkenbach, who was a limited partner of the Oakland Raiders.

Fantasy baseball swung into full gear in 1980 with the creation of Rotisserie League Baseball, organized by New York–based writer Daniel Okrent and his pals (they assembled at a restaurant called La Rotisserie Française to play). Each member acted as an owner of a team, drafted members from a list of active major-league baseball players, followed their stats during the season, and compiled their scores according to a special set of rules they devised *(see getting started)*. Today, each sport—football, baseball, hockey, basketball, even sumo wrestling and fishing—has its own fantasy league.

getting started

There are two ways to participate in a fantasy sports league: join an existing league or start one of your own.

- *TO START YOUR OWN, decide which sport you want to follow, find other members (an even number of players makes scheduling easier), and assign a "commissioner," the person who essentially runs the league. Setting up a league is a time-consuming endeavor, so start at least a month before the season starts, and be prepared for a lot of back-and-forth with potential players by email and phone. Now you can establish a set of rules and a scoring system for your league. For example, for football, if your favorite quarterback throws a touchdown, you score X number of points for your team. The rules are different for each game, so be sure to finalize your scoring method before the season starts and get sign-offs from other league members acknowledging that they understand the rules. Next, set up a roster of players with a starting set (those who actually accrue points during the week). Each week, the fantasy teams play against each other. You'll have to draft your team players just like in real life, so have your members pick a number out of a hat to see who goes first, then pick your teams. When the games start, each week the owners put together their lineup of starters and the teams compete.*

- *JOINING AN EXISTING LEAGUE is easy (though it may lack some of the excitement and creativity involved in starting your own league). Just follow the instructions provided online: Pick your team and watch the games, and the game organizers will keep score for you. Depending on which league you choose, there may be a fee to join.*

project: traveling trophy

If you've organized your own fantasy sports league, make your own traveling trophy to be passed around to the winners. You can pick up an old trophy at a thrift store and customize it with your own plaque, or order a new one online with engraving. Or for a football league, you can find an autographed helmet or other item with sentimental value once owned by a football luminary. It doesn't have to be perfect, just tangible evidence for the winning team to boast about—before they pass it to the next winners.

if you like this hobby, you might enjoy:

- Baseball card trading *(see page 26)*
- Beer brewing *(see page 38)*
- Car modding *(see page 56)*
- Coaching a sports team
- Games (Chess, D&D, Go, Pente, Tournament Scrabble)
- Historical reenactment *(see page 118)*
- Miniature wargaming *(see page 138)*
- Radio control vehicles *(see page 170)*
- Soapbox derby *(see page 188)*
- Ultimate Frisbee

faux finishing

FOR CREATIVE TYPES, white walls and ordinary furnishings are blank canvases begging to be customized. With a few magical tools and some paints, you can transform humdrum drywall into aged plaster, add rich wood grain to particle board furniture, or a lovely patina to your Home Depot fixtures. The possibilities are endless.

what you'll need

Supplies depend on the specific type of faux finish, but here are some basics to have on hand. Each project will call for a certain type of paint, but, generally speaking, latex paints are used for faux finishes on walls. Latex is also easiest for beginners to paint with.

● *Wall or wooden object to finish*

● *Paintbrushes and rollers*

● *Paint trays*

● *Latex gloves*

● *Drop cloths*

● *Rags for cleanup*

● *Painters' tape*

● *Steel wool*

● *Sea sponges*

● *Paint for base coat*

● *Glazes*

● *Crackle paint or other type of specialty paint*

● *Wood stains*

● *Varnish*

● *Wax*

overview

Faux finishes are a variety of techniques that decorative painters use to create the appearance of different finishes on walls and other surfaces (in French, *faux* means "fake"). Some examples are Venetian or aged plaster, gold leafing, decoupage *(see Decoupage)*, distressed paint, stenciling, wood grain, marble, limestone, and trompe l'oeil ("trick the eye" in French), which is a technique that uses painting to create the illusion of three-dimensional reality.

history

Faux finishing has been practiced since the time of the ancient Egyptians; it is said that pharaohs hired artists to emulate wood grain on stone walls as far back as the third dynasty, about 2600 B.C.E. The Greeks and Romans adopted and improved on the technique, and mural painting became commonly used in the homes of the wealthy citizens of Pompeii and Herculaneum. The rich loved to see portraits of themselves plastered (literally) all over their walls. During the Renaissance, Italians began experimenting with fresco techniques, covering the walls of churches and homes with religious or bucolic scenes. Artists also realized they could emulate natural materials with the stroke of a brush. They used faux marble and faux wood finishes, instead of the real thing, to decorate the interiors and exteriors of large buildings, as cost-saving measures. While the Italians developed a realistic but loose style, the French often incorporated elaborate but whimsical trompe l'oeil designs that bore an uncanny resemblance to the real thing. In recent years, faux finishing has become a byword in home décor, as well as a popular hobby for the DIY crowd.

getting started

First, decide what item or surface you'd like to add a faux finish to. There are many possibilities, but for the purposes of this book we'll focus on what you'll need to do to add a faux finish to your walls or furnishings.

- *YOU CAN EASILY add texture to bland sheetrock walls with just a few tools and materials. To apply a Venetian plaster finish, for example, apply a thin layer of plaster with a trowel, smoothing it onto the wall in an X pattern, then let it dry. Continue to smooth on layers with alternating sizes of trowel until the finish has a slight gloss. Other faux finishing ideas for walls: painting horizontal or vertical stripes using painting tape as your guides, sponging color onto the walls using a sea sponge, stenciling, trompe l'oeil, murals, and even metallic finishes. The choices are endless!*

- *IF YOU'RE LOOKING to add a bit of flair to your mass-market, flat-pack furnishings, you've got a few choices there, too. If it's been painted or has some other type of finish on it, you'll first need to strip the finish completely using a sander or chemical paint stripper. If you want to add a distressed look to your dresser, for example, first apply a basecoat color, let it dry, then add your topcoat and let it dry. Next, using a fine-grit sandpaper, start lightly sanding the corners and edges of the dresser, removing areas of the topcoat to make the piece look slightly weathered. Other faux finishing ideas for furnishings: crackle paint, adding wood or leather grain, stenciling, stamping, or painting borders.*

resources

Faux Finishing for the First Time, by Rhonda Rainey (Sterling Publishing, 2000).

The Paint Effects Bible: 100 Recipes for Faux Finishes, by Kerry Skinner (Firefly Books, 2003).

www.fauxfinishermagazine.com: *Faux Finisher Magazine,* a quarterly publication covering a variety of techniques.

www.fauxlikeapro.com: Shop for supplies, sign up for a class, or get an online tutorial.

project: antique your new brass

Faux finishes don't have to be limited to walls. You can dress up just about any surface. Suppose you've got shiny new brass fixtures that just scream, "Home Depot!" Try an elegant, aged finish for a look usually seen only on genuine antique pieces.

WHAT YOU'LL NEED:
New brass fixture, such as a light switch plate or doorknob
Sandpaper
Paintbrushes
Burnt umber oil paint
Artist's oil, a type of finishing oil found at art supply stores
Rags

1] First, sand the brassy areas of your fixture with a light, circular motion to add roughness and texture to the surface.

2] Dip a brush in the burnt umber paint, then in the artist's oil. Apply a coat of the mix to your surface, then wipe off any excess with a rag. The more indents, cracks, and textured parts there are, the more authentic the finish will look.

3] Let the paint dry overnight before mounting your faux antique fixture on the wall.

fish keeping

DOGS, CATS, HAMSTERS, AND BIRDS command a great deal of time and attention as pets. Fish, however, are mostly self-sufficient animals looking for a blissful domesticated existence. Keeping fish can be as simple as changing the water in a fishbowl every couple of days, or as complicated as setting up a full saltwater aquarium complete with live coral and exotic marine life. Sitting back and watching the fish glide around is better than TV any day.

what you'll need

- Aquarium
- Water-filtration system
- Fish
- Fish food
- Heater
- Thermometer
- Air pump
- Kits for testing ammonia and nitrate levels
- Gravel and aquarium decorations

resources

Manual of Fish Health, by Chris Andrews, et al (Firefly Books, 2003).

Setting up a Tropical Aquarium: Week by Week, by Stuart Thraves (Firefly Books, 2004).

www.aquahobby.com: Bilingual Brazilian site in English and Portuguese about fish keeping, including beautiful photos and links to the latest news.

www.aquatic-hobbyist.com: An active forum as well as a comprehensive species index for fish hobbyists.

www.tfhmagazine.com: The official website of the *Tropical Fish Hobbyist* magazine, with links to a variety of resources.

overview

Fish keeping involves housing, feeding, and caring for fish in an aquarium. Keeping freshwater fish, such as goldfish, guppies, and angelfish, is most popular, because they survive the longest with the least amount of maintenance. Most modern aquariums come equipped with the necessary filtration system to keep these fish alive for many years. They will grow in size as they age, depending on how often they're fed and how much room they have to grow in.

Creating a marine aquarium is more expensive and requires more know-how, but many fish keepers enjoy the challenge (and the beauty) of re-creating a miniature sea environment in their home. Brackish water aquariums involve combinations of freshwater and marine fish keeping, and maintaining a precise level of salt in the water.

history

Containing fish in a domesticated environment was first practiced in 3500 B.C.E. by ancient Sumerians, who caught wild fish in ponds and, before eating them, kept them alive in small tanks. The Chinese kept carp and developed decorative koi ponds more than 2,000 years ago. Goldfish first made their way into Europe in 1691 from China, and though people liked the idea of keeping fish indoors, they did not understand the necessity of filtering the water until 1805, when Robert Warrington discovered that cycling the water is crucial to keeping fish alive.

The British brought fish keeping to the mainstream in 1851 by displaying them in ornate, cast-iron-framed aquariums at the Great Exhibition in London. These days, exotic fish, from the Zambian Cichlid to the Cuban Hogfish, can be purchased from all over the world.

getting started

Start with a fishbowl or a small aquarium (a two- or three-gallon tank is a nice size for two or three fish). Clean the tank, gravel, and any aquarium decorations you've got thoroughly with a mild cleaner like dishwashing soap and rinse them all thoroughly. Find a good spot for your aquarium—one where you'll have easy access for viewing and maintainance, but out of direct sunlight and away from the heater or air conditioner. Follow the instructions for setting up the filtration system carefully. Once that's done, add your clean gravel, affix your plants and any other aquarium decorations to the gravel, then fill the tank to within an inch of the top with water. Filtered water is best for the fish, but you can check with your local fish store about whether your local tap water is satisfactory. Turn on the filter system, then add the heater and thermometer, setting it at the temperature your fish like best (this may require some research).

Now let the whole system run for a full day. While it's running, you can go buy your fish. Low-maintenance fish like goldfish, guppies, or betta fish are best for beginners. When the aquarium is ready, put in your fish, and watch them swim contentedly. You can submerge the fish-filled bag in the aquarium to allow the fish to adjust to the new water temperature, or just pour them right in.

project: make your own aquarium décor

You can immediately change the look and feel of an aquarium by posting a large photo of a seascape or other environment behind it. You can also add colorful rocks and coral to the bottom of the tank for the fish to swim by. Ceramic pieces are also great for glass tanks. You can paint anything you put inside with either latex or oil-based paint. Just keep in mind that organic additions may change the constitution of the water, so check for the right amount of salinity and acidity after you've added them.

profile: guppy love

"This may sound strange," says fish keeper GARY PHIPPS, "but I do believe that my fish have connected with me in their own little ways. Whenever I walk near the tank, they'll come to the glass and follow me. If I open the canopy, they immediately swim over to the top right corner where I always feed them."

So much for the theory that fish don't feel. The fishes' response is a testament to their owners' dedication to them. Having grown up with an aquarium in the house as a kid, Phipps carried on the tradition in his own home in Sidney, Ohio, as an adult. He bought his first saltwater aquarium a few years ago—a 35-gallon (132 L) hexagonal tank—but soon graduated to a 75-gallon (284 L) affair that he proudly displays on his website, www.ohioreef.com.

"I started out with just fish, but the desire to keep corals quickly took over," he says. After getting the tank settled in and stabilized, he began adding easy-to-keep corals, then slowly progressed to anemones and the more challenging corals, and finally a clam. "It was a long, sometimes frustrating two years, but I'm very happy with the way my tank has matured," he says. Along with the corals, Phipps also cares for several types of exotic fish, starfish, snails, and hermit crabs, and is proud of the fact that he's been able to keep the animals alive and thriving for so long.

"You just can't ignore the beautiful colors of a reef aquarium. My biggest enjoyment is just sitting back and observing my tank," he says. "It's very relaxing after a long day."

"First, be patient. Nothing but disaster comes quickly in this hobby. Secondly, do your research before you purchase any equipment or livestock. You need to be sure that you can meet the needs of any fish or plants you purchase."

fly tying

FLY TYING IS ALL ABOUT OUTWITTING THE FISH. You might wonder how difficult it could be to entice a marine creature to nibble on your line. But it's much more complicated than simply attaching some shiny baubles. Try tying a fly to see if you can nab yourself a fish.

what you'll need

- *Tools for working with small items, such as a vise, hackle pliers and hackle gauges, surgical scissors, toothpicks, and tweezers*

- *Bobbins (keeps tension on the thread while you tie the fly)*

Almost anything that successfully attracts a fish can be used as material for fly tying. Most typical flies include:

- *Thread*

- *Hooks (different sizes, shapes, and weights)*

- *Yarns and chenille*

- *Pieces of animal hair, like deer, rabbit, or elk*

- *Flosses*

- *Tinsel*

- *Paintbrush bristles*

- *Beads*

overview

Fly tying is the art of making the artificial lures (flies) that are used in fly fishing. Lures come in a variety of shapes and sizes, and are made to imitate insects and attract the attention of fish. Imitation flies trick fish into believing they're edible insects, while attractors are bright-colored lures that grab the fish's interest. Fly tiers, who must be well versed in what aquatic insects look like, attach fur, thread, and other objects to hooks to create authentic-looking replicas of live lures. The most common way of making ties is by wrapping thread tightly around the hook, then tying on the additional ornament. Sounds simple, but it's actually a detailed, painstaking process.

history

Fly fishing has been traced back to ancient Greece, when people typically caught fish on a hook dressed with a red yarn. There's also proof that fly tying and fly-fishing were practiced in the Middle Ages in Europe, as detailed in German texts depicting scenes of fishing trout and graylings using a feathered hook. Manuscripts from the 14th and 15th centuries also describe fly-fishing techniques. In 1496, Dame Juliana Berners wrote the first English book on the subject, called *Treatise of Fishing with an Angle*, describing how to tie flies. Some of these original designs are still tied today. In 1653, Izaak Walton codified these flies in his tome, *The Compleat Angler*. As the equipment grew more sophisticated, the art of fly tying became more widely practiced. Most of the modern techniques in use today were developed in Scotland and northern England in the 19th century.

if you like this hobby, you might enjoy:

- Eco-friendly travel
- Bonsai *(see page 46)*
- Fish keeping *(see page 98)*
- Meditation
- Species protection *(see page 192)*

getting started

- THE BEST WAY to learn the basics of fly tying is by following some simple patterns or watching an instructional video (see project and resources). The premise is pleasing in its simplicity: You'll tie different kinds of material to a hook (or to a string that you'll attach to a hook) in an effort to catch a fish—hook, line, and sinker.

- ONCE YOU'VE gathered your tools and materials and learned a little about the basics, practice tying some flies. Don't be afraid to toss aside the first few flies. In fact, it's best to buy a pack of 25 hooks to practice on. Your goal is to make as realistic or eye-catching a lure as possible, keeping in mind that a fish's vision is blissfully limited. Bright, shiny materials with lots of reflection are a good place to start. But don't get discouraged if your first efforts don't snag a fish for you. Fly tiers spend years creating flies and observing which ones attract particular fish. Even then, there's an element of chance when it comes to whether a fish will go for a lure. That lingering mystery is part of the draw of this hobby for dedicated practitioners.

project: learn the single-handed fly-cast grip

So, you've tied some flies, now it's time to get out there and test them. But first, it's important that you learn to grip a fly rod correctly. First, adjust your feet. If you're using your right arm as the casting arm, place your right foot slightly ahead of your left foot, but keep it underneath your casting arm. If you're using your right hand to cast over the left shoulder, the left foot should be slightly more forward than the right foot. Stand with your feet comfortably set hip-width apart, so you can transfer your weight easily. This is the traditional stance.

When it comes to holding the fly rod, it's important not to grip the rod too tightly. You won't be able to move smoothly and you'll tire your hand muscles quickly. The best way to grip a rod is to hold it with the thumb on top and somewhat to the left of the center of the rod, so you make a V with your thumb and forefinger, much like holding a tennis racket. Choose a rod that's narrow enough to enclose with your hand. Practice the grip so you can find the balance between a hard and a soft grip. For further fly-fishing techniques, it's best to take a class, where you can practice with the guidance of an expert.

fly-fishing basics:
The fly-fishing technique is used to catch a variety of fish, but is especially enticing to trout and salmon. Fly rods are long and light for easy casting, and fly line is heavier than regular fishing line to provide the heft needed to cast the nearly weightless fly. Since flies are meant to mimic the favorite food of the fish you're hoping to catch, you might choose a line that floats or one that sinks, depending on what's on the menu.

Rather than fishing from boats, fly fishermen stand thigh-deep in water in their pursuit of fish. Many (though definitely not all) fly fishermen opt for the catch-and-release method, skipping the fillet o'-fish and, instead, savoring the opportunity to commune with the great outdoors.

resources

Basic Fly Tying: All the Skills and Tools You Need to Get Started, by Wayne Luallen, et al (Stackpole Books, 2002).

Fly Tying Made Clear and Simple, by Skip Morris (Frank Amato Publications, 1992).

http://www.activeangler.com: Tips and tricks, articles, and photo galleries related to fly fishing.

www.flyfisherman.com: Fly Fisherman magazine, a bimonthly publication dedicated to the quiet sport.

www.flytyingworld.com: Fly-Tying World is an international fly-tiers' site, for info sharing and connecting tiers to each other.

www.tie1on.net/startth.htm: Step-by-step guide with illustration on how to tie flies.

www.umpqua.com: Online retailer of fly-tying material and hooks.

fossil hunting

FROZEN IN TIME, FOSSILS represent the types of creatures and plant life that inhabited the Earth for millions of years. They have been discovered in deserts, oceans, rainforests, riverbanks, mountains, parks, and anywhere else life has existed. Searching for and examining these rare treasures will give you a glimpse into basic evolutionary concepts and illuminate the earth's beauty and diversity.

what you'll need

- Hardhat (if you're hunting in quarries or caves)
- Safety goggles (for when you hammer rocks)
- Sturdy footwear
- Magnifying glass
- Geological hammer (or "rock pick" made of extra-hardened steel, with one square end and a chisel-shaped or pointed end)
- Chisel
- Wrapping materials
- Canvas bag or backpack for carrying specimens
- Mallet
- Trowel
- Brushes
- Field notebook and pencil or pen

overview

Simply put, a fossil is the remains or trace of an animal or plant that lived on earth, usually embedded in rock, or over time transformed into rock. Fossil collecting or hunting can be done anywhere rocks are found. Igneous rocks (those that come from volcanoes like granite, basalt, and so on.) and metamorphic rocks (like slates and marbles) most likely don't hold fossils because the very act of their formation erased all evidence of life. The best types for finding fossils are sedimentary rocks—limestones, sandstones, and shales—formed by the layering and compacting of finely ground bits of rocks and minerals; they're typically found along hillsides and mountain trails, near river or creek shores, or in quarries. In these types of rocks the shape of the organism is more likely to have been kept intact by being covered immediately in layers of sediment instead of decomposing in the usual way. Fossils are collected with a variety of specialty tools like chisels, which allow for careful separation of the portion of rock containing a fossil from the larger piece.

history

Leonardo Da Vinci was not only a supremely talented artist, he was also a great scientific thinker. One of the first to realize that fossils were remnants of ancient life forms, he regarded them as research tools that reveal the mysteries of the origin of life. Until that time, fossils were believed to be works of the devil, forces of nature, or remains of animals that died in Noah's flood or some other natural catastrophe, depending on who you asked. Da Vinci was the keen observer who actually connected marine fossils to the idea that the Earth used to be mostly covered in water. By the 1700s, the Age of Enlightenment, both scientists and laymen had started collecting and examining fossils more closely. In the mid-17th century, Danish scientist Nicolaus Steno developed the notion that the lowest layers of rock on Earth were the first to be created—the oldest strata. British scientist John Ray was a leader in spreading the idea that fossils could be millions of years old. In the early 1800s, scholars like Georges Cuvier and William Smith specified the varying layers of rock strata and began classifying fossils in detail.

getting started

First, do some research on where fossil hunters in your area have had luck finding fossils. Consult the staff at a nearby natural history museum and examine a geological map and guidebook at your local library. Join a rock and mineral club where you can meet people who'll share information about accessible fossil hunting sites.

When you're ready to start your hunt, choose a promising site, such as a quarry. Be sure to check with the property owner if it's privately owned. Note that national parks typically discourage people from hammering rocks or taking away any souvenirs. Now just look down. Any rock you see might be a veritable goldmine of information about your part of the Earth. If observing sedimentary rocks, note that fossils could be completely enclosed in the layers. How can you find a fossil in there? Look on the top, bottom, and sides—get out that hand lens, if necessary. If you see a hump, a squiggle, a crack, or anything else that looks potentially fossil-like, it's time to bust the rock open.

Depending on how and where the fossil is embedded, there are several different ways to remove the fossil from the rock. Whatever method you choose, you'll need to first brush off any dirt and soot, then you may need to soak the fossil in solvents—gasoline, kerosene, or alcohol. Some fossils must be placed in boiling water, then freezing water in order to loosen them for removal. You can also use tools like chisels and rock saws to remove fossils. More advanced fossil hunters will use ultrasonic devices, electric etchers and engravers, and different types of grinders to separate a fossil from the surrounding rock. It's painstaking work that must be done with great care so the fossil is not shattered or ruined.

amber is a fossil: What we wear as jewelry—luminous, honey-colored amber—has been in the making for millions of years. Amber is fossilized tree resin that actually hasn't been turned to stone like most fossils. Instead, over the course of 30 to 90 million years, it hardens through a different process. Insects, spiders, plant structures, and crustaceans have been found perfectly preserved within these fossils. Amber has long been prized for its decorative value. Amber objects have been found in Mycenaean tombs, in Neolithic remains in Denmark, and at sites from Britain's Bronze Age. Inside the Catherine Palace in Tsarskoye Selo outside St. Petersburg, Russia, an entire room is decorated with elaborately carved panels of amber.

project: make your own fossil

Learn a little more about how ancient fossils formed by making your own modern version of one. This project simulates a type of fossil that forms in mud that later turns into rock.

Select a leaf you would like to preserve. Mix some water with a handful of plaster of paris until you have a smooth, thick paste. Spread the plaster of paris onto a piece of cardboard so it's an inch thick and a bit larger than the leaf.

Cover the leaf with petroleum jelly, then position it on the plaster. Press down with a heavy weight on the leaf so it's firmly affixed to the plaster, then let it dry in a warm spot. Remove the leaf when the plaster is completely dry (imagining that ancient leaf gradually decomposing and flaking away, leaving only its impression in the mud), and you've got yourself a "fossil"!

resources

World Encyclopedia of Fossils and Fossil-Collecting, by Steve Parker (Lorenz Books, 2006).

Fossils: A Golden Guide from St. Martin's Press, by Frank H.T. Rhodes, et al (St. Martin's Press, 2001).

www.colossal-fossil-site.com: A vast, comprehensive, and entertaining site about everything fossil-related, including tips on how to find specific types of fossils.

www.fossilnews.com: A monthly magazine for amateur fossil enthusiasts.

www.fossils-facts-and-finds.com: Information and photos of all types of fossils.

framing

MAKING YOUR OWN FRAMES IS NOT ONLY A COST-EFFECTIVE HOBBY, it's also a creative one: Frames don't have to be made of wood. Almost any square (or rectangular, round, or diamond-shaped) object can be used to surround a piece of art—a CD case *(see project)*, strings tied together and nailed into the wall, even old glass-paned windows can frame prized images.

what you'll need

- Picture frame molding (softer wood is easier to deal with)
- Glass or acrylic cut to size
- Measuring tape and pencil
- Miter saw (or hand saw and miter box)
- Frame corner clamps
- Wood glue
- Frame corner brads called "V nails"
- Backing material (can be cardboard cut to fit) and mounting tape
- Small nails or a staple gun
- Hanging hardware (like a hook, frame bracket, or picture wire)

overview

Frames serve a variety of functions: They protect photos and pieces of art, they help focus the viewer's eye on the art, and, with more elaborate pieces, they complement and add an ornamental element to the piece. Framing a picture with wood pieces typically entails five steps: cutting a mat, cutting the frame, clamping the frame, joining the frame, then finishing the frame. Because having frames custom-made at frame shops can be expensive, some enterprising hobbyists have taken it upon themselves to build their own at home.

history

The very earliest "frames" date to the second century B.C.E.; they were the decorative borders drawn around Etruscan cave paintings. The Middle Ages marked the beginning of the use of carved wooden frames to display art. Many of the architectural motifs reflected in churches were also used in frames to signify the art's distinguished status. Gold leaf was first used to coat wooden frames in Italy and Spain, where dark churches benefited from frames that reflected light. Frames in northern European churches, which were better lit, reflected a greater variety of styles, patterns, colors, and materials.

At the time, artists usually constructed the frames in which their art was displayed, allowing for harmony between art and frame. But by the time the Renaissance had spread throughout Europe, artists tended to focus on their art. More and more, framing was left to furniture makers and woodcarvers, and frames were built separately from the pieces they held. By the 17th century, frames were frequently quite sculptural and elaborate, in keeping with the Baroque and Rococo paintings they displayed. It was not until the arrival of the Industrial Revolution that frames stopped being objects of opulent artistic expression and began to be mass produced.

getting started

- *TO BUILD A WOODEN FRAME, FIRST FIGURE OUT how much wood you need. Picture frame molding is the easiest material for beginners because it already has the L-shaped cutout, called a rabbet, that will hold the art and glass in place. Measure the dimensions of all sides of the art (measure the sides of the mat if you have one) and add them up to get the distance around all four sides of the art. Then measure the width of the frame wood you'll be using and multiply by eight, and add this number to the total of the four sides. This is the length of wood you will need to start making the frame.*

- *NEXT, MEASURE AND CUT the framing wood at 45-degree angles using a miter saw. Make sure the direction of the angled cuts is correct—first, each end will be cut in the opposite direction, and second, the rabbet will end up on the shorter side of each piece so it is on the inside of the frame after you make the angled cuts. Measure the length between the angled cuts by measuring along the outside edge of the rabbet where the glass and art will sit—not the inside or outside of the framing wood itself.*

- *NOW ARRANGE the pieces as a frame to make sure the cuts are correct. Attach the pieces with a small amount of wood glue, carefully aligning the corners and putting them in corner clamps while the glue dries. Tighten the corner clamps, then, to secure, hammer two V nails into each corner of the frame.*

- *AFTER THE GLUE IS DRY, take off the clamps and sand the frame, and then stain, paint, or finish it. Put the glass, art, and then the backing into the frame and secure it with small nails lightly pounded into the frame (so as not to break the glass) or staples from a staple gun. After adding a picture-hanging hook or picture wire, you are ready to display your work of art inside your newly created work of art.*

resources

The Encyclopedia of Picture-Framing Techniques: A Comprehensive Visual Guide to Traditional and Contemporary Techniques, by Robert Cunning (Sterling Publishing, 2002).

Mat, Mount, and Frame It Yourself, by David Logan (Watson-Guptill Publications, 2002).

www.clubframeco.com: Perfect for the beginning framer, this site's got everything from step-by-step tutorials to an online shop.

www.pictureframingmagazine.com: *Picture Framing* magazine, a monthly magazine featuring various framing techniques and new products.

project: make a cd case frame

We all have old CD cases lying around disused and empty. Instead of tossing them in the trash, use them as an inventive way to show off your favorite photos or small pieces of art. For CD jewelboxes that have two transparent sides (both front and back), you can display two photos.

1) First, cut two pieces of decorative paper (such as wrapping paper) into the exact size of the front and back of the CD jewelbox. You can use the existing CD cover as a guide. These papers will serve as the background or mats for your artwork.

2) Now cut a square (or rectangle or circle) out of the center of both pieces of paper. Glue a photo or piece of art to the back of each mat so it's centered inside the hole you've cut.

3) Dab some clear glue onto the corners of each paper square and stick one on each side of the CD case, art facing out.

4) Open the case slightly, and you've got yourself a handsome standing frame.

furniture restoration

TIME TAKES ITS TOLL ON EVERYTHING—including furniture. But that's no reason to pass up a good-looking chair with good bones at a thrift store or to turn away your grandmother's lovely Eames coffee table. With a bit of elbow grease and a few handy tools, you can bring life and function back to almost any piece.

what you'll need

- Drop cloth
- Rubber gloves
- Safety goggles, eye mask, and particle mask
- Cotton rags
- Natural-bristle paintbrush
- Steel wool and brass-bristle brush
- Paint or varnish stripper
- Sandpaper or sanding block
- Wood filler (for holes)
- Grain filler
- Oxalic acid (to remove stains in wood)
- Wood stain
- Glaze
- Sanding sealer

overview

Restoring furniture typically entails stripping the old varnish off the piece, then refinishing it, or mending a piece that is broken. Truly valuable antique pieces should be restored professionally in order to ensure the authenticity of old finishing practices and the integrity of the original structure. But for thrift-store finds, or even your own workaday furnishings that have been banged up over the years, restoring them yourself is fairly easy and gratifying. You can take on structural work, like recaning chairs, adding new straps to seating, and replacing table legs, or focus on finish work, like removing candle wax, hiding a scratch in the varnish, or refinishing an entire piece. The point is to bring the piece back to its original glory.

history

It's hard to pinpoint exactly when people started restoring furniture, because very few pieces from ancient civilizations like Egypt, Asia, Greece, and Rome have survived. Some furnishings, made of native woods like acacia, sycamore, cedar, and ebony, have been found in kings' tombs. Over the centuries, furnishings have been revered for their detail and craftsmanship, and restoring them has become a priority for those interested in preserving a bit of history. Panel-and-frame construction techniques had been perfected by the 16th century, elevating the craft and making for higher-quality furniture. In subsequent years, different types of furniture styles went in and out of fashion: King Louis(es), Queen Anne, Chippendale, Art Nouveau, Arts and Crafts, Art Deco, Bauhaus, and Shaker. Today, antiques dealers and collectors scour markets and estate sales in search of these treasures and attempt to restore them to their original glory. Antiques are pieces of furniture made 100 or more years ago, while vintage pieces are those made in the last 100 years. These days, mass-produced furniture is made with wood veneer or other types of less expensive wood substitutes like MDF (medium-density fiberboard) and comes packaged in flat boxes, ready to assemble. Thankfully, restoring these will be left to future generations.

getting started

Before undertaking serious restoration, reupholstery, and refinishing work, it's best to consult a book or website *(see resources)*. Please note: If the piece is too valuable to sacrifice to the hands of a beginner, hire a professional. Otherwise, if your midcentury bureau has a few scrapes and dings, you can handle the refinishing job yourself. When a piece of furniture is sporting finish that has nearly worn off or that has scrapes and dings that need to be covered up, it's time for a refinishing job.

1) *THE FIRST STEP is to strip the old finish, which can be done either by sanding or with a chemical paint stripper. For sanding, you can use a sanding block or an electric sander that you can run over the entire piece. For finer, more delicate woods, be careful when using the electric sander, because it tends to strip away layers quickly—you don't want to sand away the wood! If you use a chemical stripper, be sure to wear heavy rubber gloves and an eye mask, and work in a well-ventilated spot, preferably outside. Apply a coat of the stripper, then wait the allotted time, and with a putty knife, scrape off the finish. You might need to use steel wool or a brass-bristle brush for stubborn spots.*

2) *ONCE YOU HAVE CLEANED off the finish, sand the wood smooth until there are no bumps or lumps, wipe off all the dust, then choose the wood stain you're going to use.*

3) *APPLY THE STAIN according to the manufacturer's instructions. After the stain has dried, you can add a sanding sealer for extra protection, after which you sand again with 220-grit sandpaper. End with a polyurethane or oil-based finish to give your piece a polish.*

project: remove a blemish

If your favorite desk has a stain or scratch but doesn't need a complete overhaul, here's how to repair the flaw.

1) Clean the blemished area carefully with a rag that's been dipped in paint thinner to wipe off any clinging dust and dirt.

2) Pour furniture oil onto superfine steel wool. With a light hand, carefully rub the scratched or spotted part with the steel wool. Be sure you go with the grain, not against it. Keep rubbing until you can't see the scratch or spot anymore.

3) Apply stain over the treated area only, as necessary. To match the stain, look closely at the samples provided at the hardware store. You might want to test a few different stains on the back of the piece you're going to refinish before applying it to the damaged spot.

resources

The Complete Guide to Repairing and Restoring Furniture, by W.J. Cook (Lorenz Books, 2003).

Restoring Antique Furniture: A Complete Guide, by Richard Lyons (Dover Publications, 2000).

www.furnitureknowledge.com: How-tos, links to experts in your area, and woodworking tools for sale.

www.refinishfurniture.com: Answers commonly asked questions and provides an online source for supplies.

www.woodworking.com: Offers links to articles on restoration and a forum where you can ask the experts.

genealogy

WHY IS YOUR HAIR RED? Why does everyone in your family have perfect pitch? Do a little digging into your family history and you just might stumble onto the answers. Genealogy research opens the dusty doors of our history and helps us discover where we came from and define who we are.

what you'll need

- *Family names and other possible information leads*
- *Internet access*
- *Library card*

resources

How to Do Everything with Your Genealogy, by George G. Morgan (McGraw-Hill Osborne Media, 2004).

Genealogy 101: How to Trace Your Family's History, by Barbara Renick and the National Genealogical Society (Rutledge Hill Press, 2003).

www.archives.gov/genealogy: The U.S. National Archives in Washington, D.C., lists the U.S. Censuses and other resources for genealogists.

www.familychronicle.com: Magazine for genealogy hobbyists.

www.familysearch.org: The Church of Jesus Christ of Latter-day Saints portal into historical research.

www.genealogy.com: This website's "Learning Center" link is a goldmine of information about how to begin tracking your ancestry.

www.geneaologymagazine.com: *American Geneaology* magazine, features research tips and resources.

www.marthastewart.com: Type in "family tree" in the search box, and you'll get a decorative printable template to fill in.

www.worldgenweb.org: Free advice from a worldwide network of volunteer genealogists.

overview

Genealogy is the study and investigation of ancestry and family histories. It entails collecting information about relatives from generations past and plotting a family tree. A variety of tools will help with these investigations. In 1969, the Church of Jesus Christ of Latter-day Saints compiled an immense list (called the International Genealogical Index) of the records of hundreds of millions of people living in the U.S., Canada, and Europe between the years 1500 and 1900. The church did this as a way to perform temple ordinances, such as baptism and confirmation, on behalf of the deceased. Records such as birth, marriage, and death certificates, travel itineraries, and the U.S. Census all facilitate finding family histories. Many online companies now offer assistance—for a fee, of course—in tracking down missing links.

history

Keeping records of people's names and lineages goes back thousands of years. The Bible reveals that Hebrew men were required to document their descent from Aaron to be accepted into priesthood. During the Roman Empire, members of the patrician class needed documentation of their ancestry to maintain their status. The Greeks kept track of genealogy in an attempt to prove they were descendants of gods, and in ancient Egypt meticulous records were kept of pharaohs and their dynasties. The Inca civilization also kept genealogical records, though they had no alphabet. Native Americans kept track of their relatives on totem poles, and their petroglyphs clearly demonstrate their need to document their lineage. During the European Middle Ages, people were granted positions of nobility based on their proven pedigree, and the Catholic Church required parishioners to keep track of their heredity to prove their nobility. In Colonial America, churches were the first to keep such records, which were subsequently handed over to town managers, the equivalent of today's town registrars.

getting started

So, you want to know if you're a descendant of Benjamin Franklin? You've got many different leads to pursue. First thing on the long list is to gather as much information as you can from family members about names of ancestors and dates of birth, marriage, death, and other significant life events. Start with the present and work backward in time, keeping careful track of every piece of information. You can talk to your parents, grandparents, aunts, uncles, and anyone else who might know something about your family. For information about those who are no longer living, ask the person who was closest to them.

You'll find living histories in your family books, photo albums, cookbooks, any type of official documentation (including certificates, school records, wills, and trusts), jewelry, letters, newspaper clippings, resumes, scrapbooks, and yearbooks. For further research, go to community and genealogy libraries near where your family lived (or visit their websites), and look into the Family History Library of the Church of Jesus Christ of Latter-day Saints. When you feel you've exhausted your research or your own interest, begin charting your family tree.

> **"Information you gather from living family members will put you miles ahead of just jumping online."**

project: record a living history interview

No letter or state-issued certificate can replace the firsthand testimony of a relative's personal account of your family history. Bring an MP3 recorder, tape recorder, or video camera, but also bring pen and paper to jot down the spelling of names, notes, and questions. If your interviewee can't remember exact dates, you can come up with approximate ones by asking whether certain events happened before a couple was married or a baby was born. It's more important to get personal anecdotes and a sense of what life was like for your ancestors. Some topics to address with interviewees: incidents from their childhood, hobbies they were engaged in, family traditions, what schools were like, what subjects they learned, how they made major life decisions like whom to marry or where to move, what their parents did for work, whether they knew their grandparents, and impressions of the significant historical events of the time.

profile: connecting family ties

Last year, a woman doing genealogy research through Ancestry.com discovered a number of interesting facts about her relatives: where they were born, where they went to school, what jobs they held. She also discovered that in her family, two brothers fought against each other in the Civil War. Now she's on a quest to find out what events led to that surprising development.

"Everybody wants to find great information, a hero, someone amazing in their family tree that they can embrace and can be proud of, like George Washington or one of the Founding Fathers," says MARY KAY EVANS, a spokesperson for Ancestry.com, a comprehensive website with billions of genealogical records. "And most people do find amazing stories, even if their relatives might not necessarily be proclaimed heroes."

The company comprises four websites, each of which helps customers find family records; some services are free, while others require paid subscriptions. The fact that the websites receive millions of hits per day is a tribute to the internet's role in drastically changing the nature of this hobby. "If you wanted to know something about your family just ten years ago, you had to go to the library," Evans says. "But that's not the case anymore. Being able to access 6 billion records that are only available at [a facility in Washington, D.C.] while sitting at home in your pajamas is pretty amazing."

gilding

GOLD'S LUSTER has always symbolized the life of luxury. But you don't have to be Liberace or Ivana Trump to surround yourself with the shimmering stuff. Gilding elevates ordinary household accessories and furniture into works of art worthy of royalty, or even you.

what you'll need

The glue that makes the gold leaf stick to the intended surface is called "size." Water-based size dries quickly and tacks more easily, while oil-based size works best on hard, smooth surfaces, but takes longer to dry and reach tack state.

- *220-grit sandpaper*
- *Primer-sealer*
- *Bole color paint*
- *Adhesive size (water- or oil-based)*
- *Gold leaf*
- *Gilder's brush*

overview

Gilding is the art of putting a thin layer of gold on a surface to make it appear as if the entire piece is made of solid gold. The process of turning gold into thin sheets is called gold leafing and is done by pounding the metal into very thin sheets without breaking or tearing it. Hobbyists can buy readymade gold leaf, or if they're channeling Midas, they can make gold leaf themselves. Gold leaf can be used decoratively on walls, doors, and furniture, or on smaller objects, such as picture frames, mirrors, book covers *(see Bookbinding)*, buttons, toys, and on pottery, porcelain, and glass.

history

Gilding dates back thousands of years. Ancient Egyptians gilded wood and lesser metals like bronze by overlaying the surfaces with a thin layer of gold leaf, bound to the object with a paste called gesso. The technique is also mentioned several times in the Old Testament. The Romans gilded the ceilings of their temples and palaces, and used the technique to embellish private residences during the height of the empire. In the Middle Ages, gilding was also added to Bibles and prayer books that were handmade by master artisans.

The gilding method has changed very little since ancient Egyptian times. An illustration from about 2500 B.C.E. depicts gold being beaten with a rounded stone, a common modern practice, too, and some of the gold leaves found in Egyptian ruins are the same size as those used today, though a bit thicker. The durability of this ancient art form is demonstrated in King Tutankhamen's 3,000-year-old throne in Luxor—the burnished parts are still in immaculate condition.

getting started

For beginners embarking on a gilding project, it's best to use a gilding kit, which includes gold leaf, the size, sandpaper, brush, and cotton fabric. The kit will provide the right type of gold leaf for your gilding project, whether it's exterior, interior, on a metal or wood surface, or for walls. Kits offering different types of metal gilding material, such as aluminum, copper, silver, and bronze, are also available. Whichever surface you decide to gild, whether it's a tabletop or an entire piece of furniture, these are the basic steps you'll follow.

1) *FIRST, SAND THE SURFACE of the object you're going to gild with 220-grit sandpaper.*

2) *REMOVE THE SAND DUST, then apply a primer-sealer, followed by a base color, referred to as the "bole" color (originally, bole was a clay paste applied underneath the gilding), if necessary (the packaging information for your kit should clarify whether it is).*

3) *AFTER THE SEALER DRIES, it's time to apply adhesive size, which is the glue used to attach the leaf to the surface. Test the tackiness of the adhesive—you want it to be not quite wet, but not completely dry. When the size is ready, carefully fold back the protective paper and place one edge of the gold leaf on the prepared spot. Starting from one end and moving toward the other, begin carefully rolling the gold leaf onto the surface. You can then gently rub the gold leaf with a gilder's brush to be sure that it has affixed smoothly.*

project: gild a frame

Transform a dingy, thrift-store frame into a work of Renaissance-inspired art with these simple steps.

1) First, sand the wood frame with sandpaper, then paint a coat of primer. When that dries, paint the outside edge of the frame with black acrylic paint.

2) Mix together equal parts silver and gray satin-finish acrylic paint, and apply it to the interior of the frame. Let it dry. With a foam brush, apply a coat of sizing to the interior and wait for that ideal tacky quality, which takes about an hour.

3) Take some silver leaf fragments with your brush and press them randomly onto the frame. Dust a pinch of gold mica flakes over the silver leaf. The flakes should adhere to the surface. Dip a dry sponge into some silver mica powder, then brush it over the silver leaf and gold flakes.

4) With a clean foam brush, apply a thin coat of sizing to the black-painted area, and wait for it to get tacky. Dip another foam brush into gold mica powder, then brush it over the black-painted area. Let it set for 15 minutes, then brush off the excess powder with a softening brush.

5) After letting the frame dry for a couple of days, add a protective layer of acrylic.

resources

The Book of Gilding, by Liz Wagstaff (Southwater, 2003).

Annie Sloan Decorative Gilding: A Practical Guide, by Annie Sloan and Geoff Dann (Reader's Digest Association, 1996).

www.gildedplanet.com: Lists purveyors of gold-, silver-, and copper-leafing supplies, and handy gold-leafing tutorials.

www.goldleafcompany.com: Online supplier of gold-leafing kits, instructional books, and finished gilded pieces.

www.hgtv.com: Specific gold leafing instructions for common objects and many other gilding projects.

gourd crafting

FEW FOODS SERVE DUAL PURPOSES, BUT THE VERSATILE GOURD can be used as food *and* as a functional, readymade container. Ancient civilizations learned long ago to use these multipurpose provisions as receptacles out of necessity, but we get to make and use them simply for our own artistic purposes.

what you'll need

- Dried gourd

- Scouring pad (if needed)

- Pencil and chalk

- Cutting tools such as a jigsaw, keyhole saw, or coping saw

- Sandpaper

- Craft knives

- Woodburning tool (optional)

- Paints or enamels for embellishing

- Dust mask

- Spoons, chopsticks, coat hangers, old knives (for cleaning out the gourd)

- Finish for the exterior, such as linseed oil, paste wax or floor wax, or furniture oil

overview

Gourd crafting is the process of transforming gourds into pieces of art, useful home accessories, or musical instruments. Gourds are trailing or climbing plants related to the melon, pumpkin, and squash that bear fruits with a hard rind. In Africa, south Asia, and the Caribbean, gourds are made into string instruments and drums. In South American countries like Argentina, Brazil, and Paraguay, gourds are traditionally used as receptacles for yerba maté, a tea made from a relative of the holly. In the U.S., some use gourds to make birdhouses for purple martins, birds valued for their beauty and the belief that they might help control mosquitoes. The gourd's tough outer shell makes it easy to carve into sculptures, masks, and baskets. And if you want something brighter than the gourd's natural color (generally in the tawny range, once they're dried), you can paint or stain them. The art of gourding has become quite popular, as evidenced by the thousands of people who attend the North Carolina Gourd Festival in Raleigh every September.

history

The gourd's naturally bowl-like shape has made it a useful vessel in many different cultures for thousands of years. In tropical and temperate climates, where gourds grow best, they were used for hauling water, as cooking and eating utensils like ladles, for storing supplies, as bird feeders, baby bottles, infant bathtubs, cradles, and musical instruments. It's hard to specify exactly what date gourds came to be used, but in Gainesville, Florida, archaeologists found gourd seeds and fragments, suggesting they were used by humans, that date back to 11,000 B.C.E.

getting started

First, decide what you'll do with the gourd. Do you want to make a bowl, a musical instrument, a birdhouse? Once you've decided, you can look for the right gourd for your project. If you're making a vertical object that stands upright, choose a tall gourd with a flat bottom. If you're going to carve the piece, look for one with a smooth surface and a thick, dense shell. Gourds have a skin on top of their smooth shell (the shiny green, bright yellow, or orange skin you've noticed on fresh gourds). It gets pretty ratty during the drying process, and it's hard to know what the shell underneath will look like, so look for a gourd that's already been cleaned. You'll find suppliers of cleaned, dried gourds for craft projects on the internet, if you don't have a source nearby.

1) *TO PREPARE YOUR OWN GOURD, remove the outer skin, if necessary, by soaking it for about 15 minutes then scrubbing it with a scouring pad.*

2) *NEXT, OPEN THE GOURD and remove the seeds and dried pulp. Be sure to wear a paper dust mask because the dust from the pulp can be a respiratory irritant. Use a spoon and other utensils to scoop out the stuff; if you use a knife, wrap duct tape around the blade to protect the interior surface of the gourd from damage. Work your tool around until all the matter is loosened and ground into small enough pieces to remove.*

3) *SAND THE INTERIOR of the gourd until it's smooth and clean it with a damp cloth. If you haven't already, do the same with the exterior, too, using a scouring pad or sandpaper to make it smooth.*

4) *THEN IT'S TIME TO FINISH the exterior, which you can do however you wish—with any type of acrylic paint or paste wax, furniture wax, shoe polish, even spray paint, or decoupage (see Decoupage).*

project: make a lidded box

Gourds make ideal containers, and adding a lid makes it that much more convenient to keep out dust balls. Once you've followed the steps outlined in getting started, simply cut off the top portion of the gourd, which will serve as the lid. To make a snug lid, cut at an angle, rather than straight across, so you create a beveled edge. You can buy a hinge made of leather or fabric to connect the top to the body of your box.

if you like this hobby, you might enjoy:

- African violet cultivation *(see page 14)*
- Basketry *(see page 28)*
- Decoupage *(see page 70)*
- Drying flowers *(see page 86)*
- Pottery *(see page 164)*

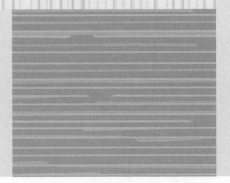

resources

Quick and Easy Gourd Crafts, by Mickey Baskett (Sterling Publishing, 2005).

The Complete Book of Gourd Craft, by Ginger Summit and Jim Widess (Sterling Publishing, 1998).

www.carvingmagazine.com: *Carving Magazine,* a quarterly publication dedicated to carving of all varieties.

www.fernsinkgourds.com: Online retailer of gourds, with instructions on what to do with them.

www.gourd-art.com: An informative site that details all you need to know about gourds, from growing them to drying them, and offers books for sale.

www.gourdgoods.com: Tasteful purveyor of gourd accessories.

gravestone rubbing

THE BEAUTY OF A GRAVESTONE is not only built into its architecture and design but found within the grains of the stone, the cracks and chips and erosion that occur naturally over time. The fact that it stands as the last physical remnant of a loved one adds that much more significance to these monuments. Gravestone rubbings allow us to bring home an image of these symbolic markers.

what you'll need

- *Large sheet of paper (butcher paper, newsprint, or vellum tissue)*
- *Lumber crayon, pencil, or rubbing wax*
- *Small slanted paintbrush*
- *Small natural-bristle brush for cleaning*
- *Masking tape*
- *Cardboard tube*

resources

Making Paper and Fabric Rubbings: Capturing Design from Brasses, Gravestones, Carved Doors, Coins and More, by Cecily Barth Firestein (Lark Books, 2001).

New York Is a Rubber's Paradise, by Roberta Halporn (Center for Thanatology Research & Education, 1998).

www.gravestoneartwear.com: Purveyor of gravestone rubbing kits.

www.gravestonestudies.org: The Association for Gravestone Studies is dedicated to preserving gravestones.

www.savinggraves.org: A site dedicated to restoring and maintaining graves around the country.

overview

A gravestone rubbing is made by using paper and coloring utensils to create an impression of the relief images on the gravestone. It's a way for people to take home a keepsake of gravestones of family members or famous people. It's also practiced by genealogists who want to preserve evidence of their family history *(see Genealogy).* Though gravestone rubbing is illegal in some states because rubbings can damage old gravestones, many cemeteries simply ask you to apply for a permit so they can control and monitor the number of rubbings produced.

history

The stone-rubbing technique has been dated back to 300 B.C.E. in China, where it was used as a method for making multiple copies of records. Laws, slogans, and messages from the emperors were carved in stone, then transferred to parchment by rubbing with colored wax. A few Asian countries still feature enormous temple rubbings.

project: 3-D foil rubbing

Most rubbings are done using wax or pencil. For a completely different look—and a decidedly more Las Vegas aesthetic—try this alternative method: foil rubbing. Simply place a sheet of aluminum foil on the gravestone (dull side facing you so you don't go blind) and, using a damp sponge, press gently, covering the entire face of the stone. Be careful not to tear the foil. When you're finished, you can take home your rubbing by carefully placing it in an art portfolio, where it can be laid flat and protected. Put it in the trunk of your car immediately and try not to make sudden turns or stops!

getting started

When negotiating the etiquette of this kind of hobby, it's important to abide by all rules, written and unwritten. First, call the cemetery you want to visit and ask permission to rub your preferred gravestone. If you don't know which one you're interested in yet and want to peruse the cemetery, make sure you get approval from the cemetery superintendent before you create any gravestone rubbings. You may discover that you're fascinated by a specific type of gravestone, maybe a certain motif or era.

1) *LOOK FOR GRAVESTONES that are in good condition, without any signs of fracture. The best kinds of stones are polished granite and solid slate. Warning: Stones that look like they have air pockets will likely crumble under the pressure of rubbing. Tap lightly on the stone, and if it sounds hollow, move on to another.*

2) *IF YOU NEED TO CLEAN the stone before you begin, use a soft brush and plain water, no harsh detergents, cleaning solutions, or vigorous scrubbing. Test the paper and color you'll be using to make sure it doesn't bleed through, and be sure to avoid using permanent color pens or markers.*

3) *NOW COVER the entire face of the gravestone with the paper and secure it on all sides with masking tape. Start rubbing gently over the entire paper, beginning in the center and using the broad, flat surface of a crayon or the side of the sharpened pencil lead. Try to keep the strokes even so the color stays consistent.*

4) *WHEN YOU'RE DONE, write the date and location in an unobtrusive place at the edge of the paper, roll it up, and place it in the cardboard tube. Carefully remove any masking tape from the stone.*

profile: art of stone

ROBERTA HALPORN *is a self-professed expert on death. As the director of the Center for Thanatology Research, Halporn has rubbed* more than her share of gravestones. In fact, she sells gravestone rubbing kits on her website (www.thanatology.org), along with scores of books and pamphlets she's written about gravestones from the Colonial period, Victorian garden cemeteries, and more. Through the observation of thousands of gravestones, she's discovered a few handy keys to interpreting symbols. For example, a candle represents a life's work extinguished; a gate, the entrance to heaven; grapes, the body of Christ; a moon is renewed life; a palm tree indicates martyrdom; and a yew tree stands for immortality.

"I've been kicked out of the best places," she says. Halporn has collected (or at least attempted to collect) rubbings from Prague, the Curaçao Islands, all across the eastern seaboard, New Orleans, and the Sea Islands off Charleston, South Carolina, sites of significant African American gravestones. Among her favorite treasures are rubbings of the gravestones of Frederick Douglass, Sojourner Truth, Leonard Bernstein, Benjamin Franklin, and F. Scott and Zelda Fitzgerald.

"Always ask permission before making gravestone rubbings, and your biggest concern should be to not hurt the stones."

Halporn can go on at length about different cultures' rituals relating to death and gravestones. But why the fascination with rubbings? "If you do it properly, you take home an exact copy of the original, and that includes its size [and texture]," she explains. That beats a photo any day.

ham radioing

WHEN ARMAGEDDON FINALLY ARRIVES, most of our newfangled forms of communication are going to cease working. The ham radio, however, will never fail. So forget your cell phone charger—rig up a ham radio before you're over and out.

what you'll need

- *Ham radio license*

- *Ham radio equipment, either home built or a commercial set such as: Handheld VHF or UHF two-way radio (VHF falls between 30 MHz and 300 MHz, while UHF falls between 300 MHz and 3 GHz)*

- *Shortwave or HF two-way radio transceiver*

- *Mobile VHF or UHF radio to be mounted in a car*

- *Low-power shortwave radios that come in DIY kits*

overview

Amateur radio operating uses two-way radio to communicate with other ham radio operators for fun or as a public service. More than 3 million people enjoy this hobby around the world. Operators must pass an exam and be licensed by the FCC, which reserves radio frequencies for use by hams at intervals from just above the AM broadcast frequencies to microwave frequencies. Ham operators can talk to their friends, family, and strangers on their radio frequencies. People also use the airwaves to broadcast public announcements. Though voice transmissions are the most common form of communication, corresponding via Morse code is still a popular pastime.

history

It's well known that, in 1895, the Italian Guglielmo Marconi was the first to send a radio signal. The first wireless signal flashed across the English Channel in 1899, and a couple of years later the first letter was telegraphed from England to Newfoundland, making it the first successful radiotelegraph message. In the ensuing years, inventors started experimenting with transporting communications via Morse code. By the time the U.S. Congress passed the Radio Act of 1912, which among many other things confined private use of wavelengths to about 650 feet (200 m), people had already perfected the "ham" or amateur radio signals.

During World War I, civilian radio activities were prohibited, but the restrictions ended in 1919. Advancements in vacuum-tube technology, which extended the range of radio waves, boosted the amateur radio industry, and by 1922 there were more than 500 radio stations. At an international radiotelegraph conference in 1927, radio band standards were set by treaty, and in 1961 the first satellite carrying amateur radio, called Oscar, was launched. Since then several new band stations have been established for amateur radio operators to use. Throughout the years, ham radio has also been used to unite the disenfranchised populace, as happened in 1958 when Radio Rebelde in Cuba urged workers to strike against Fidel Castro.

getting started

- *FOR THIS TYPE OF HOBBY, it's best to get started by joining an amateurs' club, because the members can give you important information about local operating practices, what equipment to buy, and other types of technical advice. To operate your own radio, you'll need to apply for a radio license certified by the FCC. There are three classes of licenses: technician, general, and amateur extra. The entry level, called Technician, is granted after you successfully pass a 35-question multiple-choice written test. Technicians may operate on bands above 50 MHz, or up to 80-meter amateur bands. General grades require passing the aforementioned test, plus a five-word-per-minute telegraphy test and a 35-question multiple-choice general exam. The highest license class is amateur extra, which requires you to pass the same tests as the general, plus a third multiple-choice exam with 50 questions.*

- *ONCE YOU HAVE A LICENSE, set up your radio equipment and check the frequencies, which will depend on atmospheric conditions on any given day. Be sure you're within your allotted frequency, as indicated on your license. Tune the band to find a frequency, then tune the transmitter into "dummy" mode. Fiddle with the frequency to make sure you're not interfering with another conversation, then start transmitting. First ask if the frequency is clear, then call CQ, which means you'll be talking to any open stations that might be listening. Look for a clear frequency by asking, "Is this frequency in use?" Wait a moment, then transmit the same message. If the frequency is clear, start your call by saying, "This is (say your call sign and your location) calling." Continue saying this until someone responds. When they do, speak in your natural voice, enunciate clearly, and make your responses short. If you allow some time between your answers, other parties might have a chance to join in the conversation. Remember to identify your station every 10 minutes as required by law. When you're ready to sign off, make it short and sweet, as in "Ten-four, good buddy!"*

project: radio contesting

Have some fun with your fellow ham operators by organizing a contest. An amateur radio station, which can be run by one person or an entire team, tries to contact as many other ham radio stations as possible in an allotted period of time to exchange information. Rules for each competition differ and are based on the radio bands that can be used, as well as the kind of information that has to be exchanged in each contact. Each contact adds up to a score, which determines the ranking of each station. It's a great way to test your message-handling skills and see if you could be the bearer of information during emergencies. Look for contests sponsored by amateur radio clubs and magazines. Also check the American Radio Relay League website, http://www.arrl.org/contests/.

resources

Ham Radio Operator's Guide, by Carl Bergquist (Prompt, 2001).

Now You're Talking! All You Need to Get Your First Ham Radio License, by Dean R. Straw, et al (American Radio Relay League, 2003).

www.aesham.com: Online purveyor of ham radio equipment.

www.arrl.org/qst: QST magazine, the official journal of the National Association for Amateur Radio.

www.cq-amateur-radio.com: CQ Amateur Radio magazine, with links to amateur radio—related events all over the country.

www.fcc.gov: The Federal Communications Commission's official site, from which you can download the question pool for the ham radio license.

www.hello-radio.org: Operated by the American Radio Relay League, the site offers links to local clubs, and how to study for the license exam.

historical reenactment

FOR THOSE WHO HAVE ALWAYS DREAMED OF FIGHTING HEROIC BATTLES that determine the fate of an entire nation and strategizing the best course of defense for an army of 20,000 warriors—or just love the idea of wearing armor—joining a historical reenactment group is your ticket to time travel.

what you'll need

- Costume, weapons, and other battle supplies, either handmade or store-bought (see resources)

- Historical character to play (see project)

- Coparticipants, who can be found at local living-history groups and societies

- Knowledge of the historical period you're interested in

resources

www.costumepage.org/tcpmake2.html: Instructions on how to make everything from braided laces and straps to waxed leather armor for period costumes.

www.panix.com/ffwlinden/enact.html: A comprehensive list of historical reenactment links, with updated events information.

www.sca.org: The Society for Creative Anachronism is a 30,000-member group that researches and reenacts pre-17th-century European historical events. Each reenactment organization has a rule book of its own; for SCA rules of play, see www.sca.org/docs/govdocs.pdf.

www.worldwartwohrs.org: World War II Historical Re-enactment Society's site includes information about upcoming events, message boards, photo galleries, and how to join the organization.

overview

The premise of this hobby is to re-create historic battles, either for an audience or for players' own enjoyment. They wear costumes that replicate the uniforms of their chosen era and use the same combat techniques and weapons that were used during that time. At least two types of battle techniques are practiced, both with realistic-looking but blunt weapons: rec fighting, in which participants work together to stage a fight with a predetermined outcome, and fratricidal combat, a competitive sport whereby armored players try to "eliminate" their opponents, sometimes in battles that last for several days. Specific safety rules are observed during fratricidal combat, which may involve one-on-one confrontations or multiple combatants.

Reenactment societies cover the entire arc of history—from battles fought in ancient Roman times to the Middle Ages to the French Revolution and World War I, all the way up to modern events such as the Korean and Vietnam wars. Hobbyists (both men and women) can choose the time period they're most interested in and find groups that reenact those specific eras. Medieval history buffs can become members of organizations like the Society for Creative Anachronism or Markland, both of which focus on that period in history, while Civil War–era enthusiasts would be more interested in the American Civil War Historical Reenactment Society.

history

People have been reenacting battles as long as battles have been fought. The Romans re-created their own epic victories in front of hordes of spectators in the Coliseum and took it quite seriously—they fought to the death! They even filled the Coliseum with water in order to reconstruct naval battles. In the United States, just a few years after the Civil War had ended, reenactments were staged on the original battlefields with veterans from both sides playing themselves. In the 1960s, the commemoration of the Civil War's 100th anniversary launched the modern version of historical reenactment as we know it today.

getting started

Generally speaking, living-history groups are a welcoming lot. It's just a matter of finding one that interests you. To that end, consider the eras of history you're most fascinated by—medieval times, World War I, perhaps as far back as the Trojan War? You'll also have to decide whether you're interested in performing for an audience, like at Renaissance Fairs, or if you'd prefer to enjoy the hobby with a small group.

To find an organization near you, search for activities in your local paper or on the internet during the spring and summer, when most of these events take place. Some groups allow a grace period for prospective members to observe before asking them to commit to membership fees. Searching for appropriate gear or making it yourself is part of the fun and teaches you a great deal about the time.

"We can educate the public about history and challenge ourselves, but there's also the social aspect of it. We're a tight-knit group, and many of us keep in close contact. We're really like a family."

project: create a historical persona

In the world of historical reenactment, the persona you take on will impact how you experience the game. Once you've decided which period in history to tackle, try this exercise to help you home in on what type of character you want to play.

1] What's your character's name and how old are you? Refer to resources to find a historically accurate moniker and pinpoint what type of character you'll play, such as a wet-behind-the-ears soldier or a seasoned general. This is your chance to role-play any type of personality you're fascinated by.

2] Where were you born and what's your nationality? This will decide what side of the battle you land on.

3] When not on the battlefield, what do you do? Are you, for example, a merchant, an artisan, or a member of the royalty? How educated are you? Typically, the higher the education level, the higher the military post.

4] Apart from the war you're engaging in, what world events are happening at this time? Do you have any family fighting in the war? If so, on what side?

profile: time traveler

During the week, MARY BETH KOLBER is a 27-year-old high school English teacher from Point Pleasant, New Jersey. On the weekends, she transforms into Cerdwen Einara, a medieval Celtic housewife whose hobbies include drop-spinning thread and fratricidal combat. For the uninitiated, the latter means fighting against other medieval characters.

It sounds more violent than it is—the worst injuries she's witnessed during her eight years on the battlefield are bloody noses. And they're typically due to the improper use of the padded armor that participants are required to wear or tripping over a shoelace. Warriors must stick to a set of strict fighting guidelines specified by Markland, the 500-member organization Kolber belongs to.

But skirmishes are not the only recreational activities associated with historical reenactment. Kolber also demonstrates the drop-spin technique, sews costumes, kicks up her heels doing period dancing and singing, participates in period paper making and period fencing, practices archery, and joins her husband in his obsession with medieval cookery. It's no wonder the organization voted her Aeldorman, Celtic for head honcho of the group.

ice sculpture

AT BIRTHDAYS, WEDDINGS, GRADUATIONS, or any special occasion, ice sculptures always draw crowds. Perhaps it's the mastery suggested by the ability to carve delightful objects out of such fickle material, or maybe it's the inevitability of its disappearance that makes us enjoy ice sculptures all the more while they last. Part of the fun for carvers is the temporal nature of a dazzling sculpture that literally transforms into a puddle of water. Though pros use chainsaws to build large-scale sculptures, hobbyists can just as easily use chisels and picks to create smaller wonders.

what you'll need

Ice sculpting can be done the easy way or the hard way. Those who are not inclined to break out the chainsaw can buy a mold from an online retailer (see resources), pour the water in, let it freeze, and—voilà!—unmold a sculpture. If you're not afraid of power tools, here are some of the things you'll need:

- Gasoline-powered or electric chainsaw for cutting and shaping ice
- Heat gun
- Die grinder for detail work
- Gloves
- Acrylic eye mask (safety goggles)
- Ice pick
- Chisels and a dremel tool
- Template paper or a template
- Heavy-duty tongs
- Multiprong chipper

overview

Ice sculpting involves using carving tools to shape blocks of ice into functional or decorative structures. To achieve the best results, the ice should be made from clean, filtered water. Commercial companies that make ice sculptures for special occasions like weddings or corporate events make their own ice and molds; hobbyists can purchase molds and either make their own ice or buy it online. Depending on the size of the sculpture and the complexity of the shape, the whole process takes between five and seven hours: three to four hours to freeze the block of ice (if it's around the size of an 8-quart container) and a couple of hours to carve out the pattern. Beginners can clear out their freezers to make blocks, but if you get hooked, you might want to invest in a dedicated freezer for your hobby. You can also buy blocks of carving ice; the average size is a 300-pound block that is 40 inches high by 20 inches wide by 10 inches thick.

Functional sculptures, like ice bowls and ice bars that hold bottles of liquor and food, for example, are made from molds. Decorative sculptures, such as animal figures, angels, brides and grooms, hearts, snowmen—you name it—are done freehand or with templates or patterns as guides. Depending on the temperature of the space they're displayed in, ice sculptures can last about six hours indoors and four hours outside. Dry ice is typically used in storage to keep the sculpture from melting.

To celebrate this unique art form, ice-sculpting festivals are held throughout the world. In cold-weather cities like Harbin in northeastern China, where the winter temperature hovers around 40°F below zero (-40°C), residents celebrate their surroundings with an annual ice and snow sculpture festival featuring building-sized works that depict bears, mythological characters, and abstract art. Every year, the Ice Sculpture World Championship is held in Fairbanks, Alaska, where the public can watch expert sculptors create elaborate montages like dancing seahorses and nude women descending a staircase.

history

For hundreds of years, carved ice has been used for utilitarian purposes from food preservation to housing. Some historians claim hunters and gatherers in northern countries used ice to store and preserve food and, of course, build igloos. Alexander the Great is said to have sent his slaves to the mountains to gather ice to keep his drinks cool. It was stored in underground trenches, where temperatures were lower. In France, as long as 200 years ago, chefs used ice to keep food cold. Ice has also been appreciated for its decorative, luminous qualities: As early as the 16th century, ice sculptures were used as centerpieces at banquets in wealthy homes, palaces, chateaux, and even monasteries throughout Europe, the Middle East, and China.

getting started

It goes without saying (one can hope) that you won't pick up a chainsaw without learning how to use it safely. If you're not already familiar with this powerful power tool, arrange to get some lessons from somebody who is or stick to hand-operated tools like chisels and die grinders. Once you're ready, here, in broad strokes, are the steps you'll need to follow to create a sculpture.

1) *YOUR FIRST STEP is to get yourself a block of ice, and the easiest way to do that is to buy one (see resources). Commercial vendors' ice blocks are made of purified water that has been frozen slowly over several days, then trimmed and boxed.*

2) *MAKE A ROUGH DRAWING of the shape you want to carve out on ice carving template paper (see resources). Keep your design simple for your first project, such as a basic geometric shape, letters, or numbers.*

3) *THEN PUT ON your gloves and carve the mold into the general outline of your chosen design, at first using a chainsaw, then, for detailed portions, using die grinders, picks, and chippers. Obviously, it's important to keep the temperature of your work area as cool as possible—your basement or garage would be best.*

4) *APPLY YOUR DRAWING or template to the block, then carve your design into the ice using the die grinder and chisels. You can use the heat gun to smooth out any mistakes, as well as to round and gloss the ice.*

project: make an ice castle

You don't necessarily need chainsaws and specialized tools to make an ice sculpture. For a simple home project—and to wow the kids—try your hand at an ice castle.

1) Take square ice cubes from your freezer (you can add food coloring before freezing the water for even more drama) and stack them on top of each other to create a little castle.

2) To make the cubes stick together, trickle a few drops of water where the cubes join, then put the whole structure back in the freezer.

3) Using a butter knife or nail file, smooth out some of the rough edges after the sculpture has frozen.

4) Your ice castle is ready to take center stage on your dining table or sideboard. To develop your theme, you can add embellishments to your castle, such as plastic figurines, animals, or faux flowers.

resources

Ice Carving Made Easy, by Joseph Amendola (John Wiley, 1994).

www.icecarvers.com: Source for blocks of ice and ice sculptures.

ikebana

THE QUIET ELEGANCE AND TRANQUILITY of a Japanese garden can be achieved within a vase with the placement of a few carefully chosen flowers. As your eyes follow the arc of one long-stemmed beauty to the sudden burst of color of a juxtaposed flower, you'll appreciate the gracefulness of this ancient art.

what you'll need

- Container, such as a vase or a bamboo or wire basket

- Marbles or pebbles

- Different types of stem holders

- Variety of flowers: those typically used include bamboo, narcissus, camellia, rohdea (a type of lily), the delicate leaves of nandina, chrysanthemum, Japanese iris, Calla lily, freesia, bird of paradise, weeping willow, and plum, quince, or apricot tree branches

overview

Ikebana is the Japanese art of arranging flowers, which takes into consideration the natural flow, harmony, and balance of the blossoms in relation to the vessel that contains them. Compared to the Western aesthetic of flower arrangement, which tends to focus on achieving symmetry, an abundance of flowers, and bright color, ikebana arrangements are typically asymmetrical and incorporate into the design everything from the shape of flowers to the leaves, branches, and even the empty space surrounding the vase. The three main Japanese philosophical principles taken into consideration when creating these arrangements are mankind, earth, and heaven; each flower and plant material represents one of these three elements, and, as practiced in Japan, ikebana is meant to evoke a connection with nature.

history

Ikebana's roots can be traced to the introduction of Buddhism to Japan. The discipline developed with the practice of Buddhism and the offering of flowers; monks created these arrangements to decorate the altars of temples. Over the more than 600 years that ikebana has been practiced in Japan, specific styles have developed. For example, *rikka*, the most formal style of ikebana, uses wiring to arrange plant materials according to strict rules and consists of nine main stems, each one of a specific length, angle, and character. The modern practice was established around 1930, when women became educated in this art as part of their preparation for marriage.

resources

Ikebana: Japanese Flower Arranging for Today's Interiors, by Michelle Cornell and Diane Norman (Rizzoli, 2002).

Ikebana: Step By Step Japanese Flower Arrangement, by Reiko Takenaka (Japan Publications, USA, 1995).

www.ichiyoart.com: Online purveyor of ikebana supplies.

www.ikebana.org: Incredible photo gallery showing examples of all the different schools of ikebana.

www.ikebanahq.org: Comprehensive website detailing the basics of ikebana.

getting started

Because of the subjectivity of this highly adaptable art form, it's best to carefully study a variety of ikebana arrangements in order to get a sense of what kinds of materials and plants organically harmonize. Ikebana arrangements have three basic components: the area under the water, the space between the top of the water and the top of the vessel, and all the space beyond the top of the container.

The very first thing to consider in ikebana is the container and how it will figure into the overall design. Decide whether it's going to be the star player of the arrangement, or whether it will act as an understated vessel for the flowers. Then begin choosing your flowers carefully. (See *what you'll need* for a list of those typically used.) The flowers you choose should complement both each other and the container in texture and color. With every placement of branch and flower, step back and observe the arrangement from a distance to be sure everything is in balance. Ikebana is a subtle undertaking, but with observation and lots of practice, it's absolutely achievable.

if you like this hobby, you might enjoy:

- African violet cultivation *(see page 14)*
- Aromatherapy
- Basketry *(see page 28)*
- Bonsai *(see page 46)*
- Calligraphy *(see page 50)*
- Drying flowers *(see page 86)*
- Orchid cultivation
- Reiki
- Spiritual retreats
- Gourd crafting *(see page 112)*
- Topiary *(see page 204)*

project: make a nageire arrangement

Nageire, developed in the 16th century, is a type of ikebana arrangement that literally means "throw in." The unfussy arrangement is typically used as a centerpiece at tea ceremonies. To achieve the desired wispy look, use a long vase with a narrow neck. Place a long stem of folded New Zealand flax leaf (available at plant nurseries) inside the vase, then take another flax leaf, tie a knot at the top of the long stem, and place it inside the vase. Add two or three pieces of brightly colored flowers like red anthurium in varying heights, slide in a couple of blooming birds of paradise, and your ikebana arrangement is complete.

journaling & blogging

DOGS ARE SAID TO BE MAN'S BEST FRIEND, but a journal is arguably more useful. It can serve as your most steadfast, trustworthy confidante—no judgments, no criticism, and, best of all, no exorbitant hourly fees! Blogging can also serve as a cathartic outlet, but with millions of prying eyes (whether or not they've been invited) scouring your public chronicles, beware of the juicy bits you decide to share.

what you'll need

JOURNALING BY HAND:

- Blank book or notebook
- Writing utensil
- Photos or other mementos (optional)

JOURNALING ON THE COMPUTER OR BLOGGING:

- Computer
- Internet connection (for blogging)

resources

Journaling from the Heart, by Eldanna Bouton (Whole Heart Publications, 2000).

Visual Journaling: Going Deeper than Words, by Barbara Ganim (Quest Books, 1999).

www.flaxart.com: Fancy pens and journals galore.

www.thelibraryshop.org/journals.html: Purveyor of a wide selection of journals.

Blog sites ready for uploads: www.myspace.com; www.xanga.com; www.blogspot.com; www.livejournal.com; www.opendiary.com.

overview

Journaling entails writing down the details of one's life in the form of a diary. You can write in a journal on a daily, weekly, or monthly basis—the idea is to keep a log of activities, feelings, and impressions of your life as it happens. Journals can also be less text-based, like scrapbooks or sketchbooks. People keep them as an outlet for self-expression, to maintain a record of events, or to serve as a private confessional.

Blogs are essentially online journals, but rather than being stashed away in a private place, they're broadcast for the public to read and respond to. Bloggers write about all sorts of subjects—from the minutiae of their daily lives to their political opinions to their favorite shopping finds. They can add photos of themselves and anything else to their blogs, making for a more entertaining viewing experience for the audience. Blogs can be elaborate, customized websites or live on massive servers like Myspace.com and Friendster.com, which allow millions of people to upload their own names, profiles, and photos and invite others to comment.

history

One of the first published diaries, as we define it in modern times, is that of Samuel Pepys, a British member of Parliament. Pepys recorded in detail his personal account of important events for nearly the entire decade of the 1660s, including the Great Plague of London. British author Virginia Woolf was another well-known diarist who detailed her fraught life in journals that were published in five volumes. Another famous example of this genre is Anne Frank's Diary of a Young Girl, a first-person account of her life in Amsterdam during the Nazi invasion.

Blogging, which comes from the word weblog, began almost as soon as access to the internet became available. One of the first bloggers is Justin Hall, who wrote about his daily life and his observations about the internet and pop culture in 1994 when he was a student at Swarthmore College.

getting started

For many people, the innermost thoughts and events of their private lives are just that—private. For others, airing their daily experiences on the internet is a form of catharsis and a simple way to let friends and family know what they're up to.

If you prefer a private venue for your thoughts, go with a handwritten journal. Find a beautiful blank one that will inspire you to open it up and write in it every day. You can organize your journal by date, by subject, or any other category that makes sense to you. To get your creative expression flowing, set aside a specific time every day to sit down and write out your thoughts for 30 minutes or more. You can write in a stream-of-consciousness style or follow traditional grammatical guidelines—whichever way encourages you to continue writing. But don't fret over grammar and spelling; this exercise is for your eyes only, unless you decide to share it with others.

If you're more interested in blogging, you can download blogging software from a variety of resources (see resources), or just sign up for your own page on one of the widely used blogging sites like Myspace.com. A note of warning here, though it may seem obvious: Anyone with access to the internet can read about your ventures, so keep that in mind when you detail the accounts of last night's binge!

project: write an email to your future self

It's always a kick to see old photos of yourself, but try reading about what you were thinking about 10 years ago. Futureme.org, a website created by Matt Sly and Jay Patrikios, allows people to send themselves an email one year, five years, or up to thirty years from now. What you write in your email to yourself is up to you. You can list some of your goals and see if you've hit them by the time the email arrives in your inbox: "I hope that within five years I'm the owner of my own business," you might say, or "I better be married and have a couple of kids by the time I'm 35."

profile: the blogging life

In San Francisco, if you're single and under 30, you've got no cred without a blog. REBECCA GHOLDSTON is a perfect example of this phenomenon. She and her roommate (who also happens to be named Rebecca) keep a joint blog "full of all the mundane details of our lives in San Francisco," which happens to draw plenty of attention from her own crew.

"It's turned into the easiest way to keep in touch with friends and family all over the world," Gholdston says. "It's a great way to share all the photos, entertaining stories, and random thoughts." Maintaining her own blog was an easy transition for Gholdston, who started out on Madlib-style, fill-in-the-blank blogs like Friendster and Myspace. "It seemed like the next step up from all these 'look at me, look at me' online profile sites," she says.

Though anyone can log on and see what Gholdston is up to on a daily (almost hourly) basis—from which train she took to the sushi bar, to which friends crashed on her couch, to what she cooked for a party celebrating the season finale of Lost—she says it's mostly her friends who read her blog and post comments. "We end up having a daily dialogue in the comments section of each post," she says.

Though there may be a bit of exhibitionism in this lighthearted blog, Gholdston keeps her private thoughts in a separate journal. "I usually keep one of those embarrassing private journals that only gets seriously written in during times of heartbreak," she says.

kite flying

LAUNCHING A KITE INTO THE SKY happens to be one of life's few unadulterated joys that transcends age. What better way to while away a breezy day than to send one of these simple marvels of aerial engineering aloft?

what you'll need

- *Kite, complete with string*
- *Windy day*
- *Wide-open space*

resources

The Kite Making Handbook, by Rosella Guerra and Giuseppe Ferlegna (David & Charles Publishers, 2004).

25 Kites that Fly, by Leslie Hunt (Dover Publications, 1971).

www.aka.kite.org: The American Kitefliers Association offers a forum, an event calendar, and information about national kite month (April).

www.kitebuilder.com: Offers information, plans, and active forums where kite builders swap information.

www.kites.org/zoo: The Virtual Kite Zoo details different types of kites, what to do with them, and how to fix them when they have a run-in with a fence or tree.

overview

Flying a kite entails causing a small sail-like object to catch a wind current and take flight. Kites fly the way airplanes do: The flow of air generates low pressure above the kite and high pressure under the kite, propelling it in the direction of the low pressure. In essence, the kite is able to fly by pushing down on the wind. Kites come in many different forms and shapes. They're typically made with taut fabrics such as nylon and spars made of lightweight malleable woods like bamboo to stretch the fabric in place. They can be simple flat designs, or can feature bright fabrics and geometric shapes, or be elaborate affairs, such as boxes, cylinders, biplanes, butterflies, and so on. The fancier versions, called stunt kites, allow kite flyers to very closely control the direction the kite is flying and make it do acrobatic tricks. Some hobbyists take their competitive spirits to the skies by entering kite-flying competitions.

history

It's widely believed that kites originated in China about 3,000 years ago, where perfect natural materials for kite-flying—bamboo and silk—were readily available. Legend has it that the first kite was accidentally made when a windblown Chinese farmer affixed some thread to his hat to keep it attached to himself. Around 200 B.C.E., the Chinese military commander Han Hsin was said to have flown a kite to his enemy's borders to measure (via the length of the kite string) how far his troops would have to travel. In Japan, kites were flown to repel malevolent spirits and bring good luck. The European military brought kites back to their countries from Asian destinations, and in the U.S., Benjamin Franklin's famous kite-flying adventure during a thunderstorm led to the development of his electricity theory. In modern history, kites were used to help in the creation of the airplane.

getting started

Start with a simple, lightweight, single-line kite. You can choose different kites depending on where you plan to fly them and the speed of the wind. Diamond kites and deltas (triangular kites) work better in light winds, which range from 8 to 15 miles per hour (13 to 24 kph), while the bigger varieties like box kites and parafoils soar with the rush of 25-mile-per-hour (40 kph) winds.

On a windy day, find an open area where you can fly your kite without obstructions. Stand with your back to the wind and, holding the kite up by its bridle (the place where the kite string attaches), gradually let the line feed out from the reel. Let the wind carry the kite away from you, and when you notice its nose—the top point—pointing upward, pull on the line a little; the kite will ascend farther. Keep up the pulls and tugs until the kite finds a rhythm and can maintain its altitude. If the wind is too weak for the kite to take off by itself, place it against a post or another vertical object, unroll the line, and pull the kite up.

project: make a diamond kite

WHAT YOU'LL NEED

*2 sticks of bamboo, one 40 inches (1 m) long
    and the other about 35 inches (89 cm) long*
Sturdy paper or sail fabric about 40 inches (1 m) square
A tail, or anything else you'd like to decorate
Garden twine
Scotch tape and epoxy
Whittling knife
Pencil
Scissors

1] Orient the bamboo sticks (or "spars") perpendicularly, with the short one going across horizontally. Position the horizontal spar about 1 foot (30.5 cm) from the top of the vertical spar. Using twine, fasten the pieces of wood to each other where they cross, and add some epoxy to secure them. Carve out a small indentation at each tip of the spars, which the twine will be wrapped around.

2] Measure around the edge of the diamond defined by the spars, then cut your twine to that measurement. Make a loop about an inch (2.5 cm) in diameter for the top of the kite and secure it to the frame by wrapping the twine tightly around the top notch several times. Then pull the twine to a notch on the horizontal spar, stretching it tight, and wrap it. Continue on to the bottom notch, where you will again make a loop and wrap the twine. Stretch the twine to the remaining side notch, wrap it, pull it back up to the top of the frame, and tie it securely. Before you cut off the excess twine, be sure it's as tight as it can be without bending the spars.

3] Lay out your fabric or paper on a large, flat surface and place the frame on top of it. Using a pencil, trace the diamond shape defined by the twine onto the fabric. Add about an inch margin to these lines and cut along the outer lines. Apply epoxy to the spars and set the frame into place on the fabric. Spread more epoxy along the outer edges of the fabric and fold it over the twine to secure the edges, tugging gently to make the fabric as taut as possible.

4] Now cut a piece of twine about 4 feet (22 cm) long, and tie each end to the top and bottom loops on your kite. Pinch the loose twine and tie another loop in it at about the place where the two spars cross—this is where you'll tie your flying line. You can also tie a tail to the end of the kite for embellishment. Attach a flying line to that last loop you made in the twine. Find a nice, steady, mild wind, start running with the kite in your hand, let out the string, and watch it take off.

knitting

KNIT ONE, PURL TWO. These days, you can hear this mantra coming as frequently from downtown coffee shops as senior rec centers. Decades after our grandmothers picked up their knitting needles for the first time, the hobby has wound its way into the lives of women (and men) of every age. In fact, knitting is turning out to be the national obsession that bridge was for our parents.

what you'll need

- *Pattern*
- *Knitting needles*
- *Yarn*
- *Scissors*
- *Tape measure*
- *Stitch holder*
- *Stitch marker*

resources

Knitting Rules! The Yarn Harlot's Bag of Knitting Tricks, by Stephanie Pearl-McPhee (Storey Publishing, 2006).

The Knitting Answer Book: Solutions to Every Problem You'll ever Face; Answers to Every Question You'll ever Ask, by Margaret Radcliffe (Storey Publishing, 2005).

Knit Wit: 30 Easy and Hip Projects, by Amy R. Singer (HarperCollins, 2004).

Stitch 'n Bitch: The Knitter's Handbook, by Debbie Stoller (Workman Publishing, 2004).

www.woolworks.org: Patterns, discussions, photo galleries, and links to online stores.

www.yarn.com: Retailer of every type of knitting tool, yarn, and accessory.

overview

Knitting is the craft of turning yarn into larger pieces of fabric or garments by looping it around itself using two needles. Machines can be used for knitting, but for hobbyists, knitting by hand is typically the more rewarding pastime. Different techniques are used to knit different types of projects; each type of project requires a specific size of needle, which may be either metal, plastic, or wood and either straight or circular.

Most hand knitting begins by attaching a series of yarn loops to a needle that's pointed at one end and has a knob at the other to prevent the loops from slipping off. A second needle is then used to create another row of loops, which are then slipped through a loop from the first needle. As more and more rows build up, they form a stretchy piece of fabric. Learn even the most basic stitches and you can knit yourself a scarf, sweater, or blanket.

history

The first example of knitting dates back to the Nazca culture in Peru, around 100 B.C.E., when shapes of animals and humans were knitted along the edges of cloth using colorful yarns. Other remnants of ancient knitting are rudimentary sandals, originating in Saudi Arabia around 300 C.E., and other similarly knitted footwear found in Egyptian graves. The craft was brought to Europe from Arabian countries around 400 C.E., and by the late Middle Ages several guilds had been established. Knitting became popular in England and Scotland, where woolen caps and other cold-weather accessories were necessities. A variety of machines were developed during the Industrial Revolution, making it easy to shape the knitted fabrics for garments and make knitting a commercial industry. By the 1800s, most knitting was done by machine rather than by hand, but the hobby continued to be popular. During World War I and World War II, droves of volunteer knitters banded together to knit warm clothing for soldiers (as well as ordinary citizens). Today, handmade clothing and accessories are regarded in high esteem, thus the resurgence in the popularity of knitting.

getting started

First, decide what kind of knitting project you're interested in taking on; *see resources* for books and websites offering all sorts of options for beginners, from legwarmers to scarves to ice cream pint cozies. The pattern will specify what type of knitting needle (size 10 and larger is best for beginners, as are circular needles) and yarn you will use. Remember: The simpler the project, the easier it is to finish.

Beginners should ask knitting shop clerks for help in choosing the right type of yarn. Approach knitting as you would approach a recipe in a cookbook. First, if it hasn't been done for you, unwind your skeins of yarn, rolling each one into a loose ball so it doesn't tangle when you start pulling. Now you're ready to "cast on" (create your first row of loops) according to the instructions in your pattern. As you knit, you may find it helpful to use row counters to help you keep track of when you stop and start at the end of a knitting session. Once you're finished with a piece, you'll cast off the live stitches and finish it as the pattern describes.

profile: kitschy knitter

For a process-oriented craftster like DEBBIE BRISSON, knitting is not the means to an end, it is the end. She often realizes that she's knit far beyond her row count and ends up unraveling some of her work. "I love the act of knitting. It's like meditation to me," she says. "After a tough day, it's all I want to do."

Brisson's knitting adventures have not only yielded plenty of warm scarves and sweaters, they've also launched her on the unexpected path of publishing. She is the author of Museum of Kitschy Stitches *(Quirk Books, 2006), a collection of hilarious, yet quite earnest, images of knitwear from the 1970s. There, in glorious Technicolor, is a photo of a suave chap sporting an ascot and a cocky sneer, enveloped in a taupe-colored, hip-length, double-breasted knit jacket. Another shows an impossibly perky blonde wearing an impossibly short, knit micro-mini dress, leg kicked up coyly behind her.*

"There's something about an outdated fashion sense that everyone can relate to," she says. "My own wardrobe from the '80s could fill an entire [kitsch] gallery." Check out Brisson's first book, and her blog, written by her alter ego, Stitchy McYarnpants, www.stitchymcyarnpants.com, to see for yourself.

project: felted scarf

When a knitted sweater has served out its lifespan in its original form, give it a new reason for living by felting it and stitching up a patchwork scarf. Felting is done by washing and agitating a knitted piece of apparel in hot water so that the fibers mesh together and form a nice, tight weave. Use a sweater that's 100 percent wool for best results.

1) Bring a large pot of water to a boil, then add the sweater and let it boil for about half an hour. If the sweater is old and has been washed, it shouldn't bleed.

2) Take the sweater out, and, when it cools off, wring out as much water as you can. Put it in a warm dryer until it is completely dry. Cut the fabric into 4-inch (10 cm) squares, sew them together in a long strip, and you've got yourself a brand-new woolen scarf. You may need to use two sweaters, depending on the size of your garment.

3) If you want more color, boil two sweaters and alternate the squares.

knotting

WE MAKE KNOTS EVERY DAY FOR A NUMBER OF ORDINARY TASKS: tying a necktie, our shoelaces, or a ribbon around a gift. But knotting can be a far more complex art—a puzzler for the brain and a challenge for your fine motor skills. Fidgety hands were never better occupied!

what you'll need

- *Rope or string*

- *Knot-tying instructions (see resources)*

resources

The Ashley Book of Knots, by Cliffod Ashley (Doubleday, 1944).

The Morrow Guide to Knots, by Mario Bignon and Guido Regazonni (Collins, 1982).

The Klutz Book of Knots, by John Cassidy (Klutz, 1985).

www.geocities.com/roo_two/knotindex. html: Step-by-step, illustrated instructions for all types of knots.

www.realknots.com: Comprehensive collection of knotting links.

overview

Knotting is the act of interlocking rope or string. The skill is essential to a variety of sports, such as fly fishing, rock climbing, and calf-roping, as well as decorative arts like jewelry making and macramé. Knots are also useful for everyday purposes like tying bowties and neckties, keeping shoes tightly laced and bathrobes from coming open, hanging clothes lines and porch swings, and many other mundane projects. Knotting is also an essential part of sailing; most notably it is used in tying ropes that control the sail's functions.

There are hundreds of different knots, and each one has its own (often-descriptive) name and purpose. There's the noose, the breast plate, the timber hitch, the figure eight, and the carrick-bend to list just a handful.

history

Functional knots, for hunting, fishing, sailing, and everyday fastening and wrapping, have been used for thousands of years. In China, for example, knotting dates back to about 700 B.C.E., and was later developed into a recognized art form during the Tang and Song dynasties. In South America, knots were used by the Incas to keep records and as a method of communication, as well as for decorative uses.

The most famous story in the history of knots is the legend of the Gordian Knot. In the 9th century B.C.E., the city of Phrygia, temporarily bereft of a king, decided that the next man to arrive to their city in an ox-carried cart would be named king. A young man named Midas turned out to be the first to drive into town with his father, Gordias, and as such was anointed king. The legendary ox cart was then tied to a post with a complex knot. And as they were apt to do, the people of that time predicted that the person who would untie that knot would become the king of all of Asia. Alexander the Great arrived in 333 B.C.E. and tried his hand at untying the knot. Legend has it that, in his frustration, he ended up using his sword to cut the knot. And of course, ultimately he conquered most of Asia.

Sailors have played a big role in knot tying throughout history. While spending month after month aboard ship, many sailors whiled away the time learning how to tie knots into both decorative and functional pieces, such as handles for baskets and chests, life preservers, handcuffs for prisoners, and belts. Many of these techniques were taught to the next generation of sailors. The use of the word *knot* in calculating the speed of a boat also derives from old maritime knotting techniques. Sailors would throw a float attached to a knotted rope overboard, marking the distance between the knots. They were able to count the number of knots that went through their hands in a given amount of time, which became the measure for sailing speed.

getting started

For each knot, there's a purpose, and to that end, you must first decide what you'd like your knot to accomplish. If it's a knot for rock climbing, you'll need a tutorial that will give you step-by-step instructions on how to tie sturdy knots that will keep you safe, even when you're poised high on a rock wall. Fly-tying instructions will show you how to tie your fly so the lure stays on your line, even in a fast-rushing river *(see Fly Tying)*. An anchor hitch on a sailboat will attach a line to an object, such as an anchor. If you're tying knots just for the fun of it, the best way to learn is to sit down with some rope and an instruction book and knot away. This hobby takes patience, but any knot you tangle you can untangle and begin again.

project: how to tie a bow

Do you find yourself tying your shoelaces more than once a day? The truth is, if done correctly, the bow should stay put throughout the day, no matter how far you walk, and should come undone with a quick pull.

You may have thought you mastered this technique when you were four years old, but read on to see if you really know how to tie the perfect bow:

1] First, start with a simple overhand knot—that is, cross one side of the lace over, then under, the other and pull it tight.

2] Make one end of the lace into a loop, then wrap the other lace around the loop right where your thumb is holding it in place (wrap the lace around your thumb, too). Now, a lot of you were probably taught just to wrap once at this point—but you're going to wrap twice instead.

3] Finish the bow by pushing the middle of the lace you were wrapping with through that double-wrapped part to form a second loop. Pull on the loops to tighten the knot. Now, run along!

lego building

FOR AS LONG AS MOST OF US HAVE BEEN ALIVE, Legos have symbolized constructive creativity and innovative play. Throw a few Lego bricks in front of a kid and watch her invent an imaginary world of castles and trucks and streets and schools and villages. The fun doesn't have to end with childhood. Adults have appropriated these iconic plastic playthings and are carrying on the mini-architectural tradition.

what you'll need

- *Legos*
- *Building plan* (see resources)

resources

The Unofficial LegoBuilder's Guide, by Allan Bedford (No Starch Press, 2005).

Ultimate Lego Book, by DK Publishing (DK Children, 1999).

The Brick Testament, by Brendan Powell Smith (Quirk Books, 2003).

http://afol.meetup.com: Type in your zip code to find Lego builders in your vicinity.

www.lego.com: The official site for all your Lego needs.

www.legofan.org: Forums, FAQs, and links to all sorts of Lego fan sites.

overview

Legos are small, colorful plastic bricks that snap together to make larger structures. They come in a variety of sizes and shapes, as well as themes that can be made into all manner of diminutive or life-sized objects: ships, buildings, airplanes, robots, villages, farms, people, and just about anything else. Serious hobbyists use them to build elaborate sculptures. Some examples include a replica of the Chrysler Building, a life-sized harpsichord, an iPod, Han Solo frozen in Carbonite, a full-size car, a pinhole camera, a Loch Ness monster, medieval castles, and London's Trafalgar Square. For almost any imaginable scenario, there's probably a Lego depiction of it somewhere in the world. The company sells hundreds of different types of kits to satisfy the full range of building expertise.

history

Legos' illustrious history begins in the small village of Billund, Denmark, inside the shop of Ole Kirk Christiansen, a furniture maker. In 1932, Christiansen began making petite renditions of his pieces to show prospective customers his designs, which then inspired him to make small wooden toys, like cars and trucks. A couple of years later, he came up with the name *Lego,* from *leg godt,* which means to "play well" in Danish. As his toy business grew, Christiansen and his son, Godtfred, started buying samples of small plastic bricks that connected to each other, made by a company called Kiddicraft and designed by a Brit named Hilary Harry Fisher Page. Lego designed similar pieces and improved upon the design, adding the small round studs on top of each brick to serve as solid-locking pieces that attach the bricks together but can be easily taken apart. When Godtfred took over the business in 1958, the Lego brick as we know it was developed. Lego first became popular in Europe, then, as it was exported to other countries, morphed into a household name all over the world. The first Legoland theme park opened in Billund, Denmark, in 1968, and another opened in Carlsband, California, in 1999. In 1993, a group called Adult Fans of Legos was formed to connect like-minded Lego enthusiasts.

getting started

The experience of real Lego fanatics suggests that it's easy to get hooked—in a big way—on this hobby. Be aware that if you get serious about it, you'll be investing a lot of time, energy, and money in Legos. You can get a taste of the hobby without too much expense, though. Start with a small Lego kit, available at most toy stores, and try your hand at putting it together to get the feel for—or remind yourself of—what these little plastic bricks can do. When you're sure Legos aren't just a passing fancy, join a Lego club, like Adult Fans of Legos (see resources). You can browse online discussion groups, following threads of messages about all kinds of large-scale Lego projects, and ask about joining a group that's involved in building something that piques your interest. Or you can start your own project—whatever inspires you. It helps to learn the Lego lingo, all of which is also detailed on hobby sites. For example, minifigs are little Lego people who feature prominently in staged scenes; LTC stands for Lego Train Group; MOC is an acronym for "my own creations." Look on eBay and other auction sites for vintage Lego kits.

project: computer-assisted lego construction

There's no end to the sculptures and scenes you can make using Legos. Want a model of your house? A miniature sculpture of your kid? A three-dimensional interpretation of your favorite painting? You can build almost anything using Lego's Digital Designer, a software program that allows you to design your project brick by brick, customizing everything, including color, much as an architect would use a computer-assisted design program. After you download the program from http://factory.lego.com, you select the appropriate types of digital bricks and click them in place. Once your electronic design is complete, you can print out a list of all the bricks you need and either order them online or buy them at a store, depending on how eager you are to build your Lego masterpiece.

profile: a testament to obsession

Like most kids, BRENDAN POWELL SMITH grew up playing with Legos and then moved on to other things. By the time he turned 13, the bricks were boxed away in the basement. Thirteen years later, Legos came to mind again as he and his girlfriend were browsing through eBay auctions. The collections started, and the sculptures followed soon after. First he made an 8-foot-tall skyscraper, then a Lego Colosseum. "These were fun, but I was looking for an even more interesting challenge," Smith recalls.

As a philosophy and religion major in college, Smith had always been interested in the stories of the Bible, so his first idea was to create a few famous Biblical dioramas, like the Garden of Eden, the Last Supper, or Moses holding the Ten Commandments. "But as I started constructing the Garden of Eden, it occurred to me that this could be something larger, that it could be a way to retell these stories in a way that was novel and compelling," he says.

Thus was born the Brick Testament, a series of photographs of Lego-built scenes and characters from the Bible. Though he's not a religious person, Smith went into this project well aware of the prickliness of the subject. "I knew that illustrating Bible stories in Lego would turn a few heads, but I wanted there to be more to it than just the novelty factor," he says. "I wanted people to be drawn into the stories—to be visually engaged by the quality of the constructions, the photography, and the dramatics of the little plastic people." It started with six stories on the website www.bricktestament.com, then blossomed into a series of books by the same name (see resources). So far, Powell has created 222 illustrated Bible stories in his Mountain View, California, home, each of which took about a week to build.

magic

YOU'VE WONDERED LONG ENOUGH about how magicians can make objects disappear, or levitate, or pull off complicated card tricks. It's time to take matters into your own hands and see what materializes.

what you'll need

- Book of magic tricks
- Magic kit or set containing illusions and gags
- Deck of cards
- Coins
- Rope
- Pieces of fabric
- Shot glass
- Rubber finger tip
- Cups and balls
- Top hat
- Cape

overview

Magic is the art of staging optical illusions to entertain audiences, making them believe that what they are seeing is really happening. Magicians can play for large audiences or a few up-close observers. In their sleight-of-hand tricks, magicians pull rabbits and birds out of hats, long scarves out of gloves, flowers out of their palms, coins from behind children's ears, and perform other such entertaining marvels. In night clubs or magic clubs, however, it's a different story. Famous magicians like David Copperfield, Siegfried & Roy, and Penn & Teller wow huge audiences by "chopping" people in half, levitating them, and other such astonishing feats.

history

An Egyptian papyrus from 1700 B.C.E. shows a magician named Dedi enthralling his audience with various tricks, among them making pigeons and chickens evaporate and displacing a ball under cups. These old favorites have been around for centuries and are part of the repertoire of many modern magicians. In the Middle Ages, magicians performed at fairs and circuses, although that was a hazardous time to be even remotely associated with the idea of "magic."

By the 18th century, magic shows began to crop up in Britain, Europe, and Australia. In the mid-1800s, the Frenchman Jean-Eugène Robert-Houdin, a former watchmaker, established his reputation as the father of modern magic. He is the first conjuror known to use electricity, and was actually sent by his government to its colony in Algeria in 1856 on a mission to use his magic act to intimidate the Algerians, who were beginning to get restless under French rule. Some years later, in the United States, a young man named Erich Weisz took the name Harry Houdini to honor Robert-Houdin and went on to become an iconic escape artist. The vaudeville years were good ones for magicians, but things got a bit quiet after that, until showman Doug Henning came to the public's attention. He appeared on Broadway in *The Magic Show* in 1974 and ushered in a whole new era for conjurors. David Blaine is another magician of note, famous for being buried inside a glass coffin in an office building with only water as sustenance, for standing on a 90-foot pillar for 34 hours without any apparent props, and for hanging 30 feet in the air from a Plexiglas box in front of London's City Hall for 44 days.

getting started

- *LEAPING INTO the world of magic can be as straightforward as buying a kit and following instructions that will introduce you to the basics of sleight-of-hand, but it isn't easy to do well. The real trick is to distract your audience without being obvious. Practicing is a big part of this hobby. You not only have to get the motions down right, you have to master the key to magic: diversion. While performing a trick with one hand, you distract your audience by snapping the fingers of your other hand or by waving it around—anything to avert their eyes from what's going on in the hand you're tricking them with. This is one of the most important and subtle aspects of magic, and it requires both manual dexterity and good acting skills. Other techniques for distraction include chatting with your audience, asking them questions, answering their questions, and telling stories. You should memorize your lines, so you can focus on the trick at hand.*

- *JOIN A MAGICIANS' organization, such as the Society of American Magicians, meet some of the experts, and ask them to work with you in perfecting your techniques. Go to a magic club, or a magic store, and ask about local magicians. They are a friendly bunch, especially if you compliment their skills.*

- *READING MAGIC BOOKS is a good way to start your research, and investing in an instructional DVD can provide demonstrations that the books can't convey as well. You can also buy tricks at magic shops that come with instructions.*

resources

Self-Working Table Magic: Ninety-Seven Foolproof Tricks with Everyday Objects, by Karl Fulves (Dover, 1981).

Mark Wilson's Complete Course in Magic, by Mark Wilson (Running Press Book Publishers, 2003).

www.magicsam.com: The Society of American Magicians site offers a gateway to magicians everywhere.

www.penguinmagic.com: Levitation effects, card tricks, and "mentalism" for sale.

www.tannenmagic.com: Pick up all your tricks here.

project: make a coin disappear

Amaze your friends, and make small children squeal with glee, with this classic trick.

1) Place a coin on a table with your left hand.

2) Bring your right hand over to the left hand, then with the three middle fingers of your left hand, slip the coin toward you and off the table. Make sure it lands on your lap so it doesn't make a conspicuous sound, and say something as you do it, like "Isn't this cool?"

3) Immediately after the coin hits your lap, pretend you're picking it up from the table where it should be. Keep your fingers enclosed as if you're holding it. Look at your hand as if the coin is there as you keep moving it away from your body.

4) Now, rub your fingers together, make a fist, and suddenly open up your palm. Enhance the drama with your favored magical expression—perhaps "abracadabra!" or "voilà!"

making preserves

NO GOOD BREAKFAST IS COMPLETE WITHOUT a juicy dollop of fruit preserves on a piece of toast or croissant. There's a flavor to please every palate—from Concord grape and strawberry to red currant or whiskey-spiked orange marmalade. Even bananas can be made into a delicious jam. Sure, store-bought preserves may be easier, but nothing can substitute for these homemade treats.

what you'll need

- Fruit
- Canning jars, rings, and lids
- Large, open-topped pot or "water bath," for sterilizing jars
- Jar lifter or tongs
- Large pot for cooking the fruit
- Food grinder, blender, or food processor
- Liquid fruit pectin (if needed—depends on the fruit)
- Sugar
- Ladle
- Wide-mouth funnel
- Timer

overview

Preserving fruit involves cooking a mixture—primarily fruit and sugar—then vacuum-packing it in sterile jars. The process allows the fruit to keep for long periods of time without spoiling. Small differences in the cooking technique will result in different products: Jams are cooked until thick and contain unstrained fruits; jellies are clear, thickened spreads made with strained fruit juice; preserves, made by just barely cooking the fruits through, are usually quite liquid with large pieces of fruit; and marmalades are citrus-based preserves that contain bits of the rind as well as the flesh of the fruit.

history

The first fruit preserves weren't made to create delicious condiments. In those days, long before refrigeration, the main concern was finding a way to get foods to keep so you wouldn't starve come winter. By the 1st century C.E., the ancient Romans had documented several methods for storing fruits—drying them, pickling them in brine or vinegar or wine, or covering them with honey. A few centuries later, after sugarcane had made its way from New Guinea to the Middle East, the Arabs created some concoctions that resemble modern-day fruit preserves. Crusaders apparently brought these back home to Europe, and by the Middle Ages preserves were being enjoyed on the Continent, at least among the wealthy, who could afford the sugar.

hobby hazard: Simply cleaning your canning jars with the hot water from your faucet, or even in your dishwasher, will not guarantee sterilization. The jars have to be immersed in boiling water for at least 10 minutes to be considered sterilized. If they're not sterilized, you might be subjecting yourself (and those you feed) to botulism food poisoning or another type of undesirable bacteria. So be sure to boil those pretty little jars.

getting started

You'll want to follow a recipe, at least until you become familiar with the steps. But here's an overview of the basic preserve-making process. First, you'll sterilize your canning jars and all the rings and lids that come with them by submerging them in boiling water for 10 minutes. While the jars are sterilizing, wash and dry the fruit you want to preserve, peel and seed it if necessary, remove stems or caps, and cut away any bad parts. Process the food in a grinder or blender until it's pureed, but chunky. Pour the puree into a large pot and stir in the sugar. Now bring the whole concoction to a rolling boil, all the while stirring. Add the fruit pectin, then return the mixture to a boil for a full minute; keep stirring to keep the mixture from burning or sticking to the pan. Take the pot off the stove and skim away any foam that may have accumulated on the top. Using the jar lifter, remove your jars from the boiling water, then wipe them dry with paper towels.

The best way to get the fruit into the jars is to ladle it through a wide-mouth funnel. Fill the jars to within about $1/8$ inch (3 mm) of the top, then position the lids and screw on the rings as tight as you can. Turn the jars upside down for about 10 minutes, then right side up. After a while, the lids will pop, indicating that they've been sealed. Now stock your larder shelves or generously present jars of jam to friends and family.

resources

Blue Ribbon Preserves: Secrets to Award-Winning Jams, Jellies, Marmalades and More, by Linda J. Amendt (HP Trade, 2001).

Perfect Pickles, Chutneys and Relishes: An Essential Practical Guide to Making Delicious Preserves at Home, with More Than 70 Step-by-Step Recipes and 300 Superb Photographs, by Catherine Atkinson (Southwater Publishing, 2005).

The Complete Book of Year-Round Small-Batch Preserving: Over 300 Delicious Recipes, by Ellie Topp (Firefly Books, 2001).

www.canningpantry.com: Online retailer for every type of canning equipment.

www.jelly.org: Recipes for all sorts of dishes using fruit preserves.

www.uga.edu/nchfp: The National Center for Home Food Preservation answers questions about safe and efficient methods of making jams and jellies.

project: make brandied cherries

These adults-only preserves are as delicious atop a bowl of ice cream as they are on a slice of toast. Makes 6 pints (2.8 L).

1) Wash, stem, and pit 6 pounds (4.1 kg) dark cherries. In a large stockpot, mix together 1 cup (200 g) sugar, 1 cup (240 ml) water, and $1/4$ cup (60 ml) freshly squeezed lemon juice.

2) Bring the mixture to a boil, then reduce the heat to a simmer. Now, add the cherries and cook over low heat until the mixture is piping hot, 10 to 15 minutes.

3) Remove the pot from the stove, add $1^{1}/4$ cup (300 ml) brandy, and mix thoroughly. The brandied cherries will keep, refrigerated, 9 to 12 months. If you want to keep them for longer than that or give jars of the cherries as gifts, sterilize 1-pint (473 ml) jars in a water bath according to the instructions specified in a good cookbook or preserving website *(see resources)* and ladle the mixture into the jars through a wide-mouth funnel, leaving about $1/8$ inch (13 mm) at the top. Seal as instructed in the recipe.

miniature wargaming

WHAT'S MORE APPEALING THAN CONTROLLING your own little civilization? We did it as kids, with our dollhouses and our G.I. Joe action figures. The same kind of enjoyment comes from orchestrating battle reenactments using figurines, but there's a higher level of detail and complexity. Wargamers go to great lengths to re-create scenes that accurately reflect the time and place of the battle they're attempting to reconstruct. For these hobbyists, miniature wargaming is serious fun.

what you'll need

- Toy soldiers

- Model paint (if painting your own)

- Miniature vehicles and weapons (optional)

- A rule book

- A place to play, preferably a dedicated tabletop

- A diorama or other created environment where the soldiers do battle (see project)

resources

www.frontline-figures.com: A manufacturer of model soldiers from Napoleonic to contemporary times.

www.kingandcountry.co.uk: The world's largest dealer of all-metal toy soldiers.

www.michtoy.com: Supplier of historical toy soldiers from a variety of manufacturers.

http://theminiaturespage.com: A web magazine for miniature wargamers.

www.miniwargames.com: *Miniature Wargames* magazine, a source for starter packs, rule books, and accessories.

www.toy-soldier.com: *Toy Soldier & Model Figure* magazine, with features about famous hobbyists, a forum for subscribers, and sources for accoutrements.

overview

Miniature battle reenactments require a few items: toy soldiers, their accompanying fighting gear (vehicles and weapons), and a setting (trees, mountains, roads), all of which can be painted to accurately resemble the time and place of the simulated war. The various figurines come in different sizes and scales, depending on the manufacturer, and correspond to the types of battles being fought. They are available for every imaginable era: Roman, Napoleonic, pirates, Civil War, World War I, World War II, and so on.

Before any action starts, all parties must agree to a set of rules, which can get quite complicated. This is a big part of the enjoyment for most hobbyists. The rules of engagement for miniature wargaming vary according to the time period, and can be found in a variety of books and websites *(see resources)*. Players can make up their own set of mutually agreed-upon rules, or they can buy a prepackaged miniature wargame set.

history

Some believe battle reenactments derive from of the ancient game of chess, an abstract version of military simulation, which scholars say was invented as long ago as 3000 B.C.E. The first written references to chess are from 7th-century Persia. Tacticians and war leaders have long used games to study warfare strategy and to plan battles before engaging in war. Legend has it that just before launching into the Franco-Prussian war of 1870–71, Prussian soldiers trained with a war game called the *Kriegsspiel*, a tactic that may have helped them outwit the French.

In 1913, H. G. Wells, known as the "father of miniature wargaming," wrote a book called *Little Wars*, in which he detailed rules for fighting battles with toy soldiers. And, of course, in 1974, Gary Gygax's company, Tactical Studies Rules, released the game Dungeons and Dragons, a perennially popular game that features fictional characters who wage battles against fantastical enemies and hunt for treasure.

getting started

The basic premise of miniature wargaming is that you are a military commander designating troops to fight against another commander on the battlefield. As the leader, it's up to you to prepare a strategy and act on it. Before that can happen, though, you need to find an opponent and ready your troops for battle (which usually means a fresh coat of paint). If none of your friends are up to the challenge, refer to sources like Miniature Wargames magazine to find other players in your area who might be willing to play. These magazines can also help you find complete starter kits for battle, including two matched armies with the right kind of troops and instructions for painting. Starter kits also contain rule booklets, which may be simpler for beginners than the compendious rule books that more advanced players use. Some kits include extras like terrain features and transport vessels.

"Start simple. A modern officer begins with a platoon of 30 men and has to be nursemaided by a sergeant. Pick an army with relatively few troop types and use simple tactics until you gain experience. And pick an army you can love—even when it loses!"

project: build your own diorama

Rather than investing in expensive battle sets, you can create a realistic war environment with everyday household items. First, decide on the scale of your soldiers and plan the diorama accordingly. Find a clean box and paint it with the setting of your choice—a beach, an open space, a jungle, and so on. Start with the back of the box, then add more elements as you move forward. Crumple up paper to simulate mountains. Use small wooden blocks as blank canvases on which to paint scenes or objects. For nighttime expeditions, cut a hole in the top of the box and shine a flashlight through for optimum effect.

profile: little wars, big ideas

Even after more than 65 years of experience under his command belt, PHILIP C. BARKER *still gets excited at the prospect of sitting down for a long, challenging session with his friends.* "Sitting at a table, watching small metal figures as if they were real soldiers who get tired, hungry, short of sleep, frightened, overconfident, victimized by the weather, and deserving of better generals," *he says.* "That's what I love about it."

Barker, who makes his home in London, still marvels at the fact that he gets to do "the one thing the world has decided I'm good at" *and loves that wargaming gives him the perfect excuse to buy and read expensive books. In fact, Barker has literally written the book on his favorite subject. The founder of the seminal organization Wargames Research Group, Barker and his cohorts published rules of ancient battles for miniature wargamers to use.*

How accurate to the time period are the rules? "Completely, and, in fact, much deeper research is required of a rule writer than, say, an academic historian," *Barker says.* "They can brush inconvenient bits under the carpet or erect great palaces of conjecture on a flimsy foundation of fact. We have to provide a system that is consistent with all the known facts or our customers will eat us alive!"

It all started for Barker when he read H. G. Wells's Little Wars *at the tender age of eight.* "I tried his rules out, but couldn't persuade any opponent to stay interested," *he says.* "I invented a lot of solo games." *He joined the Birmingham Wargames Club in 1962—he was its third member. Through the group, he met the wargamers with whom he ended up writing rule books. Though now officially retired from the Wargames Research Group, Barker still does consulting work for England's Ministry of Defense.*

mobile making

BABIES AREN'T THE ONLY ONES WHO APPRECIATE the free-floating elegance of mobiles. Nearly everyone likes the way they hover in the air and sometimes take a brief spin, as if to assert their disdain for gravity. The whimsical 20th-century artist Alexander Calder elevated floating sculptures to a new form of high art. Why not do the same?

what you'll need

- String
- Needle
- Wire
- Sticks, dowels, or a coat hanger
- Objects to hang, such as photos, figurines, fabric, plastic
- Clamps, clips, or glue to fasten objects to the wire

resources

Mobiles & Other Paper Windcatchers, by Noel Fiarotta and Phyllis Fiarotta (Sterling Publishing, 1996).

Alexander Calder and His Magical Mobiles, by Jean Lipman (Hudson Hills Press, 1981).

How to Make Mobiles, by Polly Pinder (Search Press, 1997).

www.calder.org: Everything you wanted to know about Alexander Calder.

www.mobilesculpture.com: Learn how to make winning mobiles and take inspiration from other hobbyists.

overview

A mobile is a hanging sculpture carefully balanced with weighted objects attached to rods so that the various parts of the whole structure move and spin in the breeze. Mobiles are typically hung from ceilings as delightful, ever-changing pieces of art or above a baby's crib as a focal point and distraction for the sleep-resistant child. Crafters can use almost any type of object to hang on the mobile, as long as the weight is carefully distributed. Glass ornaments, cardboard cut-outs, paper umbrellas, photos, toys, collectibles, and wooden figurines can all be hung on mobiles—it's up to the artist's imagination.

history

Alexander Calder is the artist who brought mobiles into the public vernacular in the 1930s. (Incidentally, it was French artist Marcel Duchamp who coined the word to describe Calder's work, which perhaps accounts for the reason we pronounce it "mo-beel.") As a kid, Calder started out making these kinetic sculptures for his sister by attaching toys to wires. He didn't originally intend to be an artist—perhaps the fact that his father was a sculptor and his mother was a painter made the career seem like less of a rebellion that it would have been for other people. He graduated from college with a degree in mechanical engineering in 1919, and worked at some engineering jobs. But he ended up going to art school in New York, then moved to Paris, where he met the famous artists of the day. In Paris, Calder created a marvelous miniature circus, complete with clowns, jugglers, and other circus characters, and a menagerie of animals—all made out of wire, cork, cloth, and other materials. Gradually, he turned to abstract forms and began creating mobiles, as well as stationary sculptures that came to be called stabiles in comparison. Over time, the mobile was appropriated by baby accessory manufacturers because of its ability to soothe infants.

getting started

First, decide what items you want to hang from your mobile. You can start with something relatively easy, like lightweight cardboard cutouts. Make them two-sided if your mobile is designed to spin. Arrange your cutouts on a table in the general outline of the mobile you want to make, keeping in mind the weight of the cutouts and their effect on the equilibrium of the mobile. Next, using a needle, thread a knotted string through the middle of the top of the cutout, then tie the other end of the string to the left end of a stick. Do the same with another cutout and tie it to the right end of the stick. Then tie one end of another piece of thread to the middle of that stick and the other end of the string to the left end of a second stick. Now attach your cutout to the right end of the second stick. Then connect those two pieces to a third stick by tying one end of a piece of thread toward the left end of the second stick to the third stick. Now attach a cutout to the left end of the third stick. You can keep going or, if you feel it's complete, tie one end of a piece of thread to the balancing point of the third stick, which should be around the middle-to-right side of the stick, and hang it with pride. You can experiment with balancing objects from the mobile.

project: make a mobile frame from a wire coat hanger

The medium for your mobile can be found in a very obvious spot: your own closet. To make the wire frame, follow these instructions, provided by www.enchantedlearning.com.

1) Using a wire clipper, cut two 1-foot (30.5 cm) lengths from two wire clothes hangers.

2) Using pliers, create a loop at the end of each piece.

3) Take one of the pieces of wire and bend it to form a loop in the middle. Pass the second wire piece through that center loop, and twist the second wire to make another loop that locks the two pieces together.

4) Now you can hang any objects you choose from the four loops at the ends of the wire pieces. Try a mobile made of toy cars, photographs, or hanging ornaments.

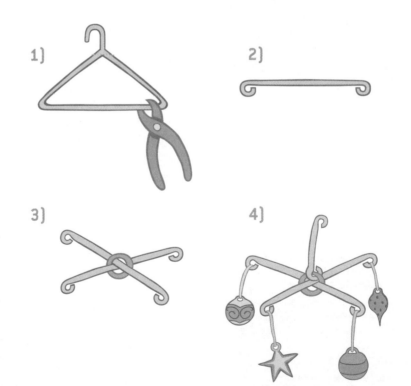

model aircraft

THE NEXT BEST THING TO FLYING A PLANE is flying a model plane—and it doesn't require going to pilot school and logging thousands of hours of practice. Sophisticated models offer would-be pilots control over precise turns, spins, and aerobatics that even real planes couldn't pull off. Come to think of it, model airplane flying might be even better than the real thing. Well, at least it's safer.

what you'll need

- *Model airplane kit*
- *Open space to fly*

resources

Model Aircraft Tips and Techniques: An Illustrated Guide, by Mike Ashey (Kalmbach Publishing Company, 1997).

Model Aircraft Aerodynamics, by Martin Simons (Nexus Special Interests, 1999).

www.greatplanes.com: These airplanes do all kinds of aeronautic tricks.

www.modelaircraft.org: The Academy of Model Aeronautics site offers a link to hobby shops by zip code.

www.modelairplanenews.com: *Model Airplane News* magazine's website links to many explanatory photos and hobbyist sites.

www.revell.com: One of the better-known brands in the model world.

overview

Model airplanes are miniature versions of life-size flying machines. For model airplane hobbyists the process of putting the planes together from scratch is a big part of the fun. In addition to the wide range of airplane designs, there is a huge variety in what the models can do and what they're made of. There are static planes (which are not meant to fly) for lovers of the pure form of a particular craft, and there are flying models. They can be made of balsa wood, foam, fiberglass, or plastic. They can be simple gliders or accurately detailed scale models.

With static models, hobbyists can buy model aircraft that can be built from scratch, including painting and customizing parts, readymade models, or those that snap together easily. Military planes and helicopters are very popular among model airplane hobbyists.

The standard scales used in plastic model kits are 1/32, 1/48, 1/72, and 1/144. Each scale has its own advantage. For example, 1/72 (or about 1 inch to 6 lifesize feet) is one of the most popular scales, making it easy to find parts and accessories at low cost. Fans of this scale appreciate that it has a compact size while being able to display a lot of detail. Models at 1/48 scale, however, allow for more detail as well as more accuracy than the 1/72 models. And some believe that the 1/32 models are the most representative of their lifesize counterparts because of the astounding level of detail.

With flying models, hobbyists can choose from three types: radio-controlled aircraft (*see Radio Control Vehicles*), which are flown with a remote control by a pilot on the ground; control-line aircraft, which are flown with the use of cables controlled by the pilot; and free-flight models, which are built to fly with no ground control.

history

Sir George Cayley, who was obsessed with flight from the time he was a child, first put together the fundamental structure of an airplane back in 1799. He was the first to fly a model glider in 1804, and nearly 50 years later he finally managed to send a man up into the air in a life-size glider. In the 1870s, Frenchman Alphonse Pénaud invented a rubber-band-powered flying machine featuring propellers and sold hand-built models of it to enthusiasts. In the 1930s, probably as a result of Charles Lindbergh's transatlantic flight in 1927, model airplane building became a popular hobby in the U.S. Over the years, the aircraft have grown increasingly sophisticated, with the use of motors, remote-control systems, and batteries.

getting started

The best way to get started with this hobby is to buy a kit. And it's probably a good idea to start with a simple model without a motor before moving on to the more complex varieties. If you want your airplane to fly, try a glider. Radio controlled models let you practice your piloting skills before moving on to more expensive, complicated, and heavier motor-powered planes. If you like old-fashioned wood, there are many beautiful balsa, maple, and plywood planes that are suitable for beginners. Find a good model store with knowledgeable staff and let them help you pick your kit. Then start assembling.

project: make a cardboard rocket

Fancy model aircraft are beautiful to behold, but this cardboard rocket is an easy way to get a model moving.

1) Start with a rectangular piece of light cardboard, keeping in mind the length of your sink or your bathtub—about 6 inches (15 cm) usually works nicely. Using scissors, cut a triangular point at one end. On the opposite end, sketch a long keyhole shape on the cardboard (a tight rectangle with a circle at the end; place the circle at about the middle of the cardboard rectangle) and cut that shape out.

2) Float your rocket in a freshly scrubbed sink filled with water.

3) Next, dribble a few drops of dishwashing liquid right into the circular part of the keyhole, and watch the rocket fly along the water.

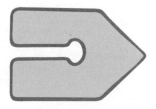

model railroading

THE ROMANCE OF TRAINS SPANS CULTURES AND GENERATIONS. Though putting together a model railroad is clearly an adult endeavor, watching that train chug over the tracks is a delight for hobbyists of all ages.

what you'll need

- *Train kit*
- *At least 16 square feet (4.9 sq m) of surface area (floor or long tables)*

project: make signs from old magazine ads

Part of the fun of this hobby is creating a realistic environment for your trains to traverse. Hark back to the slower, quieter days of the railroad by making small billboards using ads from vintage magazines. You'll find old magazines in vintage bookstores, flea markets, and garage sales. Just cut out that Coca-Cola or Pepsi ad you love, spread a thin layer of glue on the back, and either attach it to one of the buildings you've bought for the backdrop or onto a piece of cardboard the same size as the ad, for which you've built a small stand. To make it look more authentic, you can weather the sign by lightly applying white chalk.

overview

Model railroading involves assembling and powering trains on railroads. The amount of paraphernalia that accompanies this particular activity can be immense. You'll need locomotives, tracks, signals, and scenery such as roads, buildings, people, mountains, valleys, rivers, and anything else that evokes the great outdoors. Some hobbyists are more interested in constructing and expanding the miniature landscapes than others. Some people prefer to concentrate on the trains. Models come in different scales, or ratios, based on their real-life counterparts. Some hobbyists even build models big enough to ride on.

history

The first model railroad was probably built by Josef Ritter von Baader, a German engineer who assembled a model to impress the king of Bavaria and get him to agree to build a life-size railroad project. In 1838, a live model steam engine was built in Dresden. A few decades later, the British started selling steam-powered models commercially. In the U.S., Lionel and American Flyer were the first companies to produce electric-powered toy trains in around 1900. The 1920s were known as the golden age of toy trains, a time when exquisitely detailed models were being produced. By the 1950s, model trains had become the favorite hobby of many youngsters.

resources

How to Build and Detail Model Railroad Scenes, by Lous Sassi (Kalmback Publishing, 2004).

101 Projects for Your Model Railroad, by Robert Schleicher (Motorbooks International, 2002).

www.the-gauge.com: A forum for all levels of hobbyist.

www.nmra.org: The National Model Railroad Association's "Beginner's" link details everything you need to know to get started.

http://tmrc.mit.edu: The Tech Model Railway Club at the Massachusetts Institute of Technology is one of the oldest and most famous model-railroading clubs.

getting started

You can choose to make this hobby as simple or as complicated as you like, but remember two things: You'll need to invest money to buy the pieces, and you'll need lots of surface area. First, you must decide what scale of model you want. This information is typically noted by code letters like N, HO, S, and O, which correspond to various ratios of the miniature to the real thing. The most popular scale is HO, which means the ratio is 1:87—one foot (30.5 cm) on the model corresponds to 87 feet (26.5 m) of real train. Another popular one is N scale, which is 1:160. The best way to figure out which you'd prefer to spend hours of your time with is by visiting a hobby shop and handling the different model trains. Deciding on a scale also depends on how much room you have; the smaller ones, like N, pack in more details, occupy a smaller surface area, and focus more on the scenery.

When it's time to choose which train set to buy, invest in a high-quality one, especially when it comes to the locomotive. For tracks, go for nickel silver rails, which are more conductive and make the trains run better. Be sure to pick up some track pieces with turnabouts and curves, so you can vary the route.

profile: romancing the rails

Like many people his age (62), JIM SENESE received his first Lionel electric train when he was a boy. Every Christmas, his father would add to his train set, and soon enough, it became a year-round fixture in the basement of his house, where he would while away the evenings with his father after supper. "The train represented travel, power, and magic," he says. "It was my world in miniature." Senese passed along his love of trains to his son, who also began working on models as a youngster.

But long after his son left home, Senese continued to work on his model railroad, a prototypical set that features parts of a real railroad and uses locomotives and cars that real railroads did. Senese models a 4.5-mile (7.2-km) section of the Kansas City Terminal Railway, which takes up 660 square feet (201 m) of floor space. "I call it medium size, but my wife Bonnie calls it large," he says. The grain elevators, terminals, and other structures are modeled to look exactly like they do in real life, and are placed along the railroad where they actually appear along the tracks. He has chosen to model the scene as it was on October 25, 1980, at 3 P.M.

He even includes model cars, signs, and billboards from that date.

Senese's love of railroads led to his purchase of a real-life caboose. "The Missouri Pacific caboose followed me home one day," he explains. It had been purchased by the owner of a body shop in Tulsa who intended to use it as a playhouse for his grandchildren, but after giving up on the idea, he decided to dismantle it and sell the scrap metal. "Rather than let him torch this 52,000-pound (23.6 t) car, I made a

"I would suggest that new model railroaders think of the hobby as a 3-D art form. My opinion is that the real enjoyment comes from building the railroad, laying the track, constructing miniature buildings, making scenery, and then running trains like the real railroads do."

humanitarian offer, which he accepted," Senese explains. As expected, the shipping cost turned out to be higher than the purchase price. Now, it sits on Senese's acreage in the Oklahoma plains, on 39 feet (12 m) of regulation rail—safe from the welder's torch. "Someday it might become a cabana house if we put in a pool," he says. "Maybe it could be a playhouse for the grandkids."

model ships

FOR THOSE WITH A PREDILECTION FOR ALL THINGS NAUTICAL, model ship building (like most other model building hobbies) provides a fascinating, firsthand look into how these vessels are constructed—from the hull to the sails to the planks. Whether you're working on a 17th-century British frigate or a modern American battleship, the pieces you assemble will connect you to your seafaring id.

what you'll need

- Model ship kit
- Hobby knives, razor or jeweler's saws, and blades
- Needle files
- Clamps
- Carving tool set, such as gouges and chisels
- Drills with varying sizes of bits
- Tack hammer
- Tweezers
- Wire cutters
- Vise

overview

Model ships are miniature versions of life-size vessels, either of modern or historic design. Though traditionally constructed of wood, the kits sold today at hobby stores are mostly plastic, and a few are made of sheet metal. These kits can require extremely detailed workmanship. And, of course, you can research, design, and build your own from scratch, if you're inspired to.

As with other types of models, model ship kits come in a variety of sizes and designs: single-masted sails, two-masted sails, and three-masted sails for sailing ships. Hobbyists can choose from battle ships, merchant ships, navigation ships, and many other classic boat styles, as well as canoes. Most of these are meant to be displayed, but there are also remote-controlled models that can be raced. The ship's hull (or body) can be either made with one single piece of solid wood or glued together with two or more pieces of wood. Some come with preformed wood hulls for easy construction.

history

The ancient Egyptians built highly detailed wooden models of ships to sail the spirits of the dead to the next life. Some of these (showing the duties of the crew, their attire, and the mechanics of the ship) have been immaculately preserved in tombs and have given historians an accurate account of seafaring during that time. Other types of model ships dating back to 1100 C.E. have been found in early Christian churches in Europe, where they were said to be blessed by the clergy before their real-life eqivalents embarked upon long voyages. By the 18th century in Europe, model ship building was a craft that had been handed down from father to son for generations. Model ships from that period were constructed to show what the life-size vessels would look like and how they would operate. Another group of model ship builders were seamen who were stuck at sea for years and passed the time making small ships out of wood scraps and bone.

getting started

First, decide what type of model ship you're interested in. Historic wooden models, sailboats, submarines, and warships from various countries are just a few of your choices. Consider whether you want a radio-controlled model that you can launch on the water, and, if so, where you'll run it. Take into account how patient you are at working with small objects, then determine how involved you're willing to get in the ship building construction. When considering size, think about where you'll store the vessel and how you'll transport it to the water.

Ask the hobby store clerk for recommendations to match your interest and skill level. Start simple, then work your way up so you understand the terminology. And lastly, joining a modelers club is a great way to get help and guidance.

project: build a ship in a bottle

If you've always wondered how they do that—squeeze a ship into a bottle—there's no better way to learn than to build one yourself. There are a variety of kits on the market that take you through the process step by step and include every piece you need, though some additional tools may be necessary. You can choose what kind of ship you want: a *USS Constitution*, a pirate ship, the *Mayflower*, or the *Bounty*. The tiniest ones include wood toothpicks that serve as the masts and booms, a balsa strip for the rowboat, black tubing for the cannons, and white cotton for the sails. You can also customize the boat by painting it. One of the most economical brands available can be found at www.a2zhobbies.com.

resources

The Ship Model Builder's Assistant, by Charles G. Davis (Dover, 1988).

Ship Modeling from Stem to Stern, by Milton Roth (McGraw-Hill Professional, 1988).

www.historicships.com: Specializes in historic wooden model ship kits.

www.model-ships.com: Purveyor of both radio-controlled boats and display ships and ship-building tools.

www.shipmodeling.net: The Ship Modeling Forum offers a venue for hobbyists to ask questions, argue about best practices, and get tips.

moviemaking (with a video camera)

IT'S NOT JUST BLOCKBUSTER HOLLYWOOD MOVIES and highly paid method actors that get good reviews. Many an entertaining film has been made with the use of a low-budget video camera, a few friends, and access to credit cards. So if you've always had a brilliant idea for a movie—*Kramer vs. Kramer* meets *Shakespeare in Love*, say—get out there and film your vision.

what you'll need

- Digital video recorder
- Computer with lots of memory
- Editing software like iMovie or Final Cut Pro
- Screenplay
- Actors
- Script

resources

$30 Film School, 2nd ed., by Michael W. Dean (Course Technology PTR, 2006).

How to Shoot a Feature Film for Under $10,000 (And Not Go to Jail), by Bret Stern (Collins, 2002).

Setting Up Your Shots: Great Camera Moves Every Filmmaker Should Know, by Jeremy Vineyard (Michael Wiese Productions, 2000).

www.consumerreports.org: Consumer Reports offers paid subscribers objective reviews of all kinds of equipment, including camcorders.

www.digitalfilms.com: Make your own movies for free on this user-friendly website.

overview

This hobby involves planning, shooting, and editing your own film using a video recorder and the appropriate editing software. Making movies—whether with an expensive Hollywood crew and cast or at home with a simple video recorder—typically involves the same general steps: writing a script, finding actors to perform the lines from the script, and filming the movie using a video camera. The movie is then edited, each scene is spliced together sequentially, and finally the film is shown in its entirely.

For this exercise, you'll come up with a story line, write a script, scout locations, ask friends and family to play the roles, and, when it's time to shoot, follow the script. This won't be just another home movie that gets tossed into a box and stowed in the attic. This'll be the beginning of your *oeuvre*.

history

The first moving pictures were shown to audiences in the late 1800s, and it wasn't long before people began trying to sell movie cameras to the masses. Surely, they thought, since home photography was so popular, home filmmaking would be, too. The problem was that the equipment used at that time was cumbersome, complicated, and expensive. An early effort by Birt Acres and Robert W. Paul appeared in 1895 in England, and Acres used it to make several amateur films of his own. In 1898, another Acres-invented camera, the Birtac, and a cheaper rival device, the Biokam, were released. In 1923, in the United States, Bell & Howell, a company that established itself making cameras for Hollywood, released the Filmo, a 16-millimeter camera for amateur directors. Home moviemaking became much more affordable after the invention of the video cassette and, soon after, the handheld video camera, in the 1980s.

getting started

It's one thing to shoot home videos of your kids, your friends, and birthday parties, but it's quite another to put together an entire movie. Start with a short film; once you get the hang of it, you can experiment with longer features. You can still enlist the help of your friends and family, but delegate them to behind-the-scenes ranks, such as casting director (finding actors) or location scout.

1) FIRST, figure out your story. The most important thing to remember in film is the story arc—you need a beginning, a middle, and an end to your plot. Then it's time to develop a screenplay. You can do this loosely, summarizing for your actors what they're trying to convey in each scene (that's what Robert Altman does), or you can write a line-by-line script.

2) NEXT, figure out where you're going to shoot your movie. Public venues are free for small ventures, but so is your own home or your office. It's best to stick to what you know so you don't have to deal with unforeseen incidents.

3) WHEN IT'S TIME to shoot, follow a few tips from expert directors. Compose each shot (what you see in the camera) before you begin shooting and try to make it interesting: Rather than placing the characters smack in the middle of the camera, use the environment around them to add texture to the story. Avoid using the zoom button too much—that'll give your audience a headache—and keep the camera in focus. The best way to do this is to use a tripod, as handheld cameras invariably jostle around as you move or even breathe.

4) START FILMING early in the day to get the most natural light, which always produces the best results. Try shooting the same scene from different angles to experiment with which one turns out best, and don't forget to let the camera run a few seconds before and after you say "action!" and "cut!" This will make editing a lot easier later in the process.

5) EDITING is the production part of the process; it involves shaping all those yards (or megabytes) of footage into an actual story, and requires lots of time in front of the computer. Luckily, there are plenty of editing software programs to choose from that will walk you through the entire process. As you work, try to vary the kinds of shots and the length of takes you use. It will make for a more textured film. Too many abrupt cuts are jarring, while shots that go on too long may bore your audience. Experiment to see what works best for your film: fade-in and fade-out, sudden blackouts, and so on. And don't forget continuity—keep clothing, accessories, and the position of props consistent from shot to shot.

6) WHEN YOUR MOVIE is complete, roll out the metaphorical (or literal) red carpet and stage a viewing for friends and family. After all your hard work, you deserve to bask in the limelight.

project: make a storyboard

Every movie starts with a story, and it really helps to outline it in a storyboard, which is a series of illustrations detailing where actors will stand and what will be captured in each shot. Do you want a close-up on the character or a wide shot to show context? Sketching each scene—even if it's as rudimentary as stick figures—will give you an idea of how the movie will look and help keep your shooting organized.

mushroom hunting

EMBEDDED IN A PIZZA, tossed with a salad, or mixed with chicken and veggies in a stir-fry, mushrooms—morels, chanterelles, oyster mushrooms, hen of the woods, to name only some common ones—add earthy flavor and depth to all sorts of dishes. And, of course, their value does not stop in the kitchen: Healers have been prescribing mushroom cures for thousands of years to treat everything from asthma to high blood pressure. Then there's the "magic" variety, always tempting to those seeking a transcendent experience.

what you'll need

- Pocket knife
- Paper bags for mushroom collecting
- Field guide to mushrooms (see resources)

resources

The Mushroom Lover's Mushroom Cookbook and Primer, by Amy Farges (Workman, 2000).

Basically Morels: Mushroom Hunting, Cooking, Lore & Advice, by Larry Lonik (RKT Publishing, 2000).

A Field Guide to Mushrooms: North America, by Kent H. McKnight and Vera B. McKnight (Peterson Field Guides, Houghton Mifflin, 1998).

The Mushroom Hunter's Field Guide, by Alexander H. Smith and Nancy Smith Weber (University of Michigan Press, 1980).

www.fungi-zette.com: A newsletter/blog kept by a mushroom hunter with tips, anecdotes, and recipes.

www.morelmushroomhunting.com: Everything you wanted to know about morel mushrooms and more.

www.mushroomexpert.com: Facts, details, and other helpful information about mushrooms and mushroom hunting.

overview

Mushrooms are fungi, many of which are not only edible but delicious, and hunting for them involves foraging in the wild, usually at the roots of trees along wilderness trails. Some hobbyists think of mushroon hunting as a sport and organize contests to see who can pick the most. Pickers must take care to familiarize themselves with the identifying characteristics of mushrooms to avoid. (New mushroom hunters should see *resources* for field guides and organizations they can join, as well as the hobby hazards box.) There are about 1.5 million different species of mushroom, but some of the most common edible types found in North America are chanterelles and morels. Certain types of mushrooms can be expected to grow in specific areas, so do your research before setting out.

history

Images of mushrooms found in cave drawings in the Sahara have been traced back to the pre-Neolithic era, approximately 7,000 to 9,000 years ago. In ancient Egypt, mushrooms were considered so precious and flavorful that the pharaohs dictated that they could only be consumed by sovereigns and royals. In Japan and China, mushrooms have been used for centuries for their medicinal properties, specifically to benefit the liver and lungs, and as a cleanser of toxins. In Central and South America, ancient sculptures show that mushrooms were ingested during religious ceremonies. In fact, the Aztecs apparently described hallucinogenic mushrooms as the "flesh of the gods" and used them to commune with the gods and spirits. In the U.S., mushroom cultivation began in the late 19th century with spores brought over from the U.K. Today, a wide variety of wild and cultivated mushrooms are available to consumers, not only in gourmet produce shops but through garden-variety supermarkets.

hobby hazard:

Some mushrooms are poisonous and can lead to anything from minor stomach upset to the unmentionable. So at all costs, practice safety. The most important bylaw in mushroom hunting is "if in doubt, throw it out!" If you can't positively identify the mushroom, tasting it is not worth the risk. Even if you're confident that a mushroom is not poisonous, you should start with just a small taste to see if you experience an allergic reaction.

project: mushroom soup

Once you've filled your bag with morel mushrooms, it's time to show off your mushroom-hunting prowess and make a creamy morel soup. First, clean the mushrooms and cook them in butter and olive oil, along with shallots and parsley. Cream the mixture in a blender, then pour into a saucepan. Add just enough chicken broth to yield a dense but fluid soup. Add a hint of nutmeg, then let simmer for about 15 minutes. For a richer soup, add a cup of cream to each quart.

getting started

With this hobby, you shouldn't strike out on your own right away. First, you must research the types of mushrooms in your general vicinity so you know what to look for. Confirm your findings with an authority on the matter. The best way to do this is to go on outings with experienced mushroom hunters. Check with a mycological society near you to sign up for an organized field trip.

When you're ready to forage on your own, head out to a wilderness area with a field guide, keeping a close eye on the ground as you walk. If you think you've found an edible mushroom and can spot it in your field guide, pick a few of them. Be sure to pick up the entire base and some of the surrounding plants, which will help you identify your pickings. Take note of the size, smell, color, shape, and whether it's got gills or tubes. For those mushrooms you don't recognize or can't identify with absolute certainty, you can gather a few specimens to take home and conduct field tests on; just be sure to keep them separate from the mushrooms you recognize and know are safe.

The best time to hunt is right after a good spell of rain in the spring or the fall, but you can find mushrooms any time of year.

profile: mushroom maestro

"Almost everyone will eventually find a mushroom that doesn't agree with their system," points out mushroom hunter HERMAN BROWN, "but that's just one of the perils of trying anything new." Though he's been picking mushrooms for years, Brown says he has never had a bad reaction. It did, however, take him several years of foraging before he felt comfortable enough to eat a wild mushroom—and that was a chanterelle, which is fairly easy to identify.

In the mountains behind Santa Barbara, California, where Brown and his wife lived for many years before moving farther north to Greenville, they were surrounded by mushrooms, so his interest was naturally piqued. He loves foraging for them in the forest, bringing them home, and eating them—but only if he's identified them as edible. If they're not, he logs them in his growing list of mushrooms.

So far, he's found and recorded exotic varieties like the fuzzy truffle (Geopora cooperi), various stinkhorns, and a Ganoderma oregonense, an annual that can grow up to 15 inches (38 cm) wide. Not exactly slim pickins.

"First, never eat a wild mushroom unless you have it identified by someone who is either an expert or regularly consumes that species. Even that is no guarantee that you might not have a negative reaction. The popular advice is, when you try a new mushroom, start with a small amount and wait for a reaction."

needlework

GONE ARE THE DAYS WHEN NEEDLEWORK was relegated to grandmothers and great aunts. With all the modern and customizable designs for creating threaded art, people of all ages (though, yes, still mostly women) are putting needle to canvas and creating exquisitely detailed designs.

what you'll need

- Fabric or canvas
- Plan for a design (or choose fabric or canvas with a preprinted design)
- Thread or yarn
- Needle appropriate to the type of needlework you're doing

project: photo-to-cross-stitch conversion

Customize your embroidery by cross-stitching a photo of a loved one, or a landscape shot from your favorite vacation. For beginners, it's best to start with a simple photo of an object or one with few (or no) details in the background. Download the image to a software program available at either www.hobbyware.com or www.pcstitch.com. The program creates shadows and background colors, but you can customize this to your liking. For example, rather than stitching a black background for an object, you can use a black canvas that can easily serve as the backdrop. Then you're ready to start stitching.

overview

Needlework in general is the craft of using a needle to make decorative designs and textiles. Embroidery is a general term that describes decorating fabric with thread or yarn using stitches. Crewel is a type of embroidery that uses loosely twisted worsted yarn. Cross-stitch is an embroidery technique that uses only a double stitch forming an X. Needlepoint, also known as canvas work or tapestry work, is done with thread on a canvas mesh. The canvas can be a picture, an abstract design, or a repeated geometric pattern called bargello.

history

Embroidery goes back at least as far as 3000 B.C.E. Evidence shows that Egyptians, Babylonians, Moors, Phoenicians, and Hebrews used it for decorating their robes. The technique later spread through Spain and Sicily. During the Middle Ages, embroidery was used in church clothing and worn by rich traders and merchants.

In the 1500s, people began regularly using canvas as the background for needlepoint; they also used steel needles, which yielded more intricate work than the older needles made of such materials as bone, horn, or thorns. As with most such hobbies, needlepoint was practiced by the leisure class.

Needlework was used to create lavishly decorated fabrics all across the world. The Chinese used jewel-toned silk threads; in India, gold and silver metallic threads were used along with brightly colored ones. Italians crafted lace embroidery. Central and South Americans used floral designs in their patterns, while Russians employed bright, primary-color cross-stitch designs.

resources

The Needlepoint Book: A Complete Update of the Classic Guide, by Joe Ippolito Christensen (Simon & Schuster/Fireside, 1999).

Subversive Cross Stitch: 33 Designs for Your Surly Side, by Julie Jackson (Chronicle Books, 2006).

www.needlepoint.org: American Needlepoint Guild, with a membership program that offers books, seminars, and other benefits.

www.tnna.org: The National NeedleArts Association's comprehensive site, featuring a retail directory, local events, and educational resources.

getting started

Spend some time in a good specialty craft store. There's nothing like the gorgeous colors of the wools and threads to get you inspired. The store may also have a selection of books about various styles of needlework. Browse through them and see what most appeals to you. You may be able to get a readymade kit for your first project, with the pattern printed on fabric or canvas and the required threads or yarns already included.

Here are some tips to help you with whatever project you choose:

- *CHOOSE THE RIGHT size needle. For example, for needlepoint, you need one that will fall through the hole of the canvas and not catch at the eye of the needle. If you have to push the needle through the canvas, the holes will be stretched and the weave disturbed, causing uneven stitches and warping the canvas.*

- *GENERALLY, thread length should be about 18 inches (46 cm), or roughly from the tip of your middle finger to the bend of your elbow. If the thread is too long, it will wear thin from passing through the canvas or cloth too many times.*

- *WHEN IT'S TIME to thread, don't pull more than about 2 inches (5 cm) of the fiber through the eye of the needle. Start by stitching the smaller parts of the designs, then work your way to the larger areas.*

- *STITCH THE PALE WOOLS first so the darker fibers don't cling to the lighter ones and muddy up the color.*

profile: witty stitches

Just when you thought cross-stitch patterns were about to grow mold, along comes an injection of wit into the world of craft. JULIE JACKSON's sassy cross-stitch designs have given a new generation of clever crafters something new to stitch. With designs that spell out "Bite Me" and "Beeyatch" with a little bee buzzing along the border, Jackson has struck a nerve with young crafters who want to redefine the traditional meaning of these small forms of self-expression.

Growing up, Jackson marveled at her grandmother's handmade gems and dabbled in all kinds of crafts herself. So when, as an adult, she began resenting her work atmosphere, she naturally turned to cross-stitching to express her aggravation. "I was so frustrated from being stuck with an idiot boss, I guess I was looking for some kind of art therapy," she says. But browsing through craft shops in her home, Dallas, Texas, she was surrounded by frilly designs that just couldn't capture her mood.

"I decided to change the sentiments by changing the words. It was a way to express my frustration with the mendacity of a conservative office by adapting their favorite art form to suit my frame of mind," she said.

Coworkers started feeding her clever quips, and she posted them online—"just for kicks." Soon enough, the public pounced on these never-before-seen patterns: The union of something old (the medium) and something new (the message) was an immediate hit. Her website was picked up by a few blogs, and as often happens in the design world, it "spread across the web like wildfire." Soon she was selling her cross-stitch kits online and to major retailers like Target and Urban Outfitters.

As we observe crafting making a comeback in pop culture, Jackson says these hobbies fulfill a need that transcends generation gaps.

"Go to a craft store and look for some mainstream cutesy cross-stitch pattern that you can subvert for your own purposes!"

olive oil infusions

THE REVERED GREEK POET HOMER called olive oil "liquid gold," and for good reason. Not only is it one of the healthiest oils we consume, it makes just about everything taste better. Enhance your olive oil with a few herbs and spices, and you've created an enticing concoction that'll add amazing flavor to everything, from vinaigrettes to pasta. It's such an easy and satisfying undertaking, you'll find yourself filling up your cabinet with bottles of this golden oil.

what you'll need

- *Extra-virgin olive oil (the fragrant, fruity oil from the first pressing of the olive)*
- *Bottle with cork or airtight lid*
- *Funnel*
- *Fresh herbs, spices, or other flavoring ingredients*
- *Wooden skewer (for some ingredients)*
- *Mortar and pestle*

if you like this hobby, you might enjoy:

- Beer brewing *(see page 38)*
- Coffee roasting *(see page 60)*
- Community gardening
- Ice sculpture *(see page 120)*
- Making preserves *(see page 136)*
- Wine tasting

overview

Infusing olive oil with fruits, herbs, peppers, spices, and other flavorful ingredients adds wonderful new flavors and even texture to your oil. The process is remarkably easy: Chop the flavoring ingredients, add them to the oil, and let the mixture sit for a couple of weeks. The new concoction can then be used to dress salads; marinate meats, fish, and vegetables; or as a dip for bread. You'll take great satisfaction in seeing store-bought versions of your home-infused oils marketed at gourmet food shops for a pretty penny.

history

Olive trees were first cultivated around 5,000 years ago in Greece and spread to nearby countries. They are slow-growing but long-lived, with a maximum life span of more than a thousand years. Greek athletes rubbed olive oil on their bodies, perhaps believing in its healing or strengthening powers—sometimes the oil was given as a prize to the winner of a contest. Olive oil was also used to anoint kings and other royalty. Ancient Hebrews, such as King Solomon and King David, hired guards to protect their groves.

People have been adding flavors to olive oil for almost as long as they've been growing olive trees. Ancient Egyptians, Romans, and Greeks infused the oil with flowers and grasses to make medicine and ointments. Mycenaeans added ingredients like fennel, watercress, mint, sage, sesame, and rose. Consider taking a cue from these ancients and experimenting with some of these flavor additions yourself.

Olive oil has become extremely popular in the U.S. in the past decade, as Americans have become more interested in Mediterranean food and the healthful qualities of the oil. In the U.S. today, Americans devour more than 450 million pounds (204 million kg) of olive oil, more than twice the amount they consumed 10 years ago.

getting started

- *DECIDE what flavors you want to infuse your olive oil with. Herbs that work well with the oil include tarragon, basil, thyme, rosemary, cilantro, oregano, chives, mint, dill, bay leaf, and parsley. Spices that work well are cinnamon, cloves, cumin, coriander seeds, and nutmeg. Garlic cloves, hot peppers, and citrus zest add a pleasant zing. When adding citrus zest, peel it off the fruit in a long strip, run it through with a skewer, and push the skewer down into the bottle before filling it with olive oil. To infuse with herbs, first wash and dry them well, then bruise them slightly to free their aroma and flavor (or pound them with a mortar and pestle), drop them into a bottle, and top it off with oil. Seal the bottle tightly and let it sit in a cool, dry place for a couple of weeks for the flavors to fully take effect. When the oil is ready, drizzle it onto any of your favorite recipes or salads.*

- *THE OIL will keep for about six months to a year if you've only added thoroughly dry ingredients. If you used fresh herbs, garlic, or peppers, you'll need to use it within a few weeks. Store the oil in a cool, dark place, or refrigerate it (but be aware that it will turn temporarily cloudy at cold temperatures). Remember that, just like wine, olive oils come from different regions and already have their own distinct flavors, so you may need to experiment with infusions before you find your favorite combination of oil and ingredients.*

project: speedy herb-infused olive oil

If you're planning a big dinner party and can't wait two weeks for your special blend of herb-infused olive oil to steep, you can cut the time down to half a day with this method. Combine your favorite herbs and spices (a couple of cloves of garlic, a few pinches of fresh rosemary, a few flakes of red pepper, for example) in a bowl with half a cup of olive oil, add some lemon peel, and microwave the mixture for about a minute. Put it in the refrigerator for 12 hours, then let it sit out until it reaches room temperature. It's ready to serve.

resources

Flavored Oils: 50 Recipes for Cooking with Infused Oils, by Michael Chiarello, et. al. (Chronicle Books, 1995).

Olive Oil: Fresh Recipes from Leading Chefs by Sian Irvine, (ed.) (Periplus Editions, 2000).

www.oliveoilsource.com: Purveyor of all things related to olive oil, including recipes and accessories.

hobby hazard: Though infusing oil sounds fairly foolproof, there is a slight risk of botulism associated with this hobby. To avoid any potential risks, be sure to wash all the herbs thoroughly, leaving no specks of dirt encrusted in the mix. You can also add lemon juice or vinegar—an acidic agent—to the oil, at about one tablespoon per cup of oil. If you see any gas bubbles rising or any cloudiness in the bottle, or if the infused oil smells anything but sweet and flavorful, throw it out!

origami

ORIGAMI IS LIKE MAGIC. With a series of folds, a two-dimensional piece of paper is transformed into an elaborate, three-dimensional sculpture, evoking the grace and beauty of animals in flight, blooming botanicals, even food. But unlike magic, these patterns are by no means secret—creating these delicate sculptures simply takes practice and a skillful hand.

what you'll need

- *Origami paper*
- *Instructions* (see resources)

resources

Bugagami: An Origami Infestation of Insects and Other Creepy Crawlies at Your Fingertips, by Jeff Rutzky (Barnes & Noble, 2006).

Complete Origami: An A–Z of Facts and Folds, with Step-by-Step Instructions for over 100 Projects, by Eric Kenneway (St. Martin's Griffin, 1987).

Zoogami: An Origami Menagerie at Your Fingertips, by Gay Merrill Gross (Barnes & Noble, 2006).

www.artcity.com: Online source for origami paper and supplies.

www.origami-usa.org: Information about annual conventions, beautifully illustrated instructions, and children's projects.

www.paperfolding.com: Learn how to make origami dinosaurs and flowers, and read about the history of origami.

overview

Origami is the art of folding paper into geometric designs that resemble specific animals or objects. Typically, it begins with a square piece of colorful paper that is folded in a variety of different sequences without cutting the paper. Renditions of almost anything can be made with the origami technique, from flowers and fruits to fantastical creatures. Origami paper is sold at craft stores and comes in many patterns, colors, and weights.

history

Contrary to its name and our preconceptions, origami originated in the 1st century in China, not Japan. The art came into being along with the invention of paper. Origami was brought to Japan around 500 c.e. by Buddhist monks and was quickly elaborated upon and integrated into Japanese life. Members of the royal family would use butterfly-shaped papers to wrap wedding presents like sake and wine. For hundreds of years, the origami tradition was passed down by word of mouth from generation to generation. But in 1797, with the publication in Japan of the book *How to Fold 100 Cranes*, origami became accessible to everyone.

Modern-day origami has been greatly influenced by master Yoshizawa Akira, who wrote books illustrating new types of origami techniques in the 1950s. With help from Sam Randlett, Akira created a standardized set of origami diagram symbols, which became the universal way of communicating the techniques. Akira exhibited his works across the world and introduced the art form to the U.S. and other countries. New Yorker Lillian Oppenheimer, who is said to have become captivated by a figure of an origami bird when she first saw it in the 1940s, mastered the techniques and began teaching origami. She founded the Origami Center of America (now known as OrigamiUSA) in 1980.

getting started

To master this precise and detailed art, it's best to begin by practicing a technique devised by British origami expert John Smith, called Pureland origami. This restricts the folder to certain basic folds. For example, a mountain fold entails folding the paper in half and setting it up like a tent. A valley fold is the same maneuver but facing upward, like a V. An accordion fold, also known as a pleat fold, is one that requires making four or five horizontal folds to divide the paper into a series of equal-sized mountain and valley folds. And a blintz fold is done by laying out the square piece of paper and folding each corner over into the middle.

project: make a dollar-bill shirt

This classic model, courtesy of origami artist Jeff Rutzky, is often folded from currency and left as a server's tip.

1) For a green shirt, start with the back side up. Pinch the midpoint of each short edge, and unfold, then turn the bill over.

2) Using the pinch marks as a guide, valley-fold the long edges to the center, unfold, then turn the bill over.

3) Valley-fold over about 1/4 inch (6 mm) of the right side, then turn the bill over.

4) Valley-fold over about an inch (2.5 cm) of the left side, then turn over top to bottom.

5) Valley-fold the top and bottom edges back to the center on the existing creases. Crease firmly.

6) Mountain-fold the right edge behind. Crease firmly.

7) Valley-fold the left side's long edges about 1/16 inch (1.5 mm) to make the sleeve's cuffs. It doesn't have to be perfectly matched toward the middle, since it will be hidden.

8) Valley-fold the left side's top layers outward on the angle shown. Valley-fold the right side's top and bottom points inward to the center on the angle shown.

9) Softly valley-fold the left side, tucking the edge underneath the collar as far as it will go, then crease firmly. Rotate 90 degrees left.

10) You've got a finished shirt. Keep a few freshly "pressed" bills in your wallet or purse to leave for your favorite server as a tip!

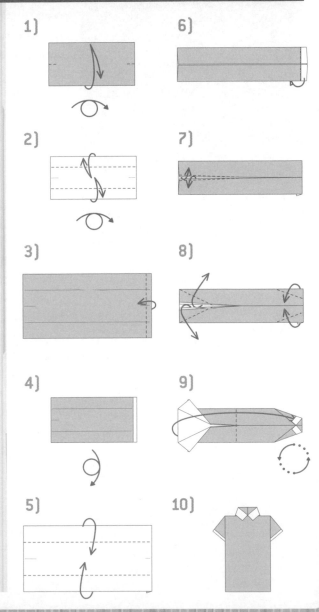

paint by numbers

THERE'S SOMETHING UNIVERSALLY SATISFYING about creating your own piece of art. So what if all you did was fill in some numbered areas with the corresponding paints? It was your hand that held the brush and so nimbly daubed those colors onto the canvas. Go ahead, you have permission to hang your newly minted painting in a prime spot.

what you'll need

- *Paint-by-numbers kit (see resources)*

- *Water for cleanup*

- *Picture frame or mini easel to display your finished work*

resources

Paint by Number: The How-to Craze That Swept the Nation, by William Bird (Princeton Architectural Press, 2001).

Paint-by-Number Kit: Everything You Need to Re-create 8 Vintage Masterpieces, by Dan Robbins (Chronicle, 2005). A fancy paint-by-numbers kit with eight postcard-size canvases with preprinted scenes and with eight little easels to display them on.

Whatever Happened to Paint-By-Numbers? A Humorous Personal Account of What It Took to Make Anyone an "Artist," by Dan Robbins (Possum Hill Press, 1998).

www.dickblick.com/categories/paintbynumber: Not your grandmother's paint-it-yourself kits, from a longtime art supply retailer.

www.tate.org.uk/shop/piy.htm: Paint-it-yourself projects for the truly artsy set.

overview

Completing a paint-by-numbers kit entails filling in numbered areas on the prepared canvas with correspondingly numbered paint colors. For example, the painter will paint number-3 yellow on the parts of the canvas that are marked 3, and so on, until the entire canvas is painted. Though the picture looks abstract in its early stages, by the end, you see how all those numbered shapes fit together to make a convincing picture, with highlights and shadows and all. Some regard paint by numbers as their entry into the world of painting—a way to become familiarized with colors, canvases, and brushes, as well as the way two-dimensional spots of color can be combined to create a 3-D effect. Others savor the kitschy aspects of this decidedly retro hobby.

history

In 1949, a 24-year-old children's coloring book illustrator and designer named Dan Robbins, who worked at the Palmer Paint Company in Detroit, produced the first paint-by-numbers kit. Called the Craft Master, it launched an enormously popular hobby in the 1950s. Each kit came with two brushes, as many as 90 numbered paints, and a numbered canvas. The themes available included animals, landscapes, flowers, clowns, and barns.

Though the popularity of the hobby waned in the ensuing years—it became a symbol for midcentury conformity and a lack of imagination—it's picking up steam again with the crafting set. You can find paint-by-number sets at hobby stores, art stores, drug stores, and online vendors, featuring every type of imagery and landscape, from traditional still lifes to nature scenes.

getting started

Buy a kit at your local craft store or from one of the websites listed in the resources. The kits are available with either acrylic or water-soluble oil paints, so the only cleaning solution you need is water, unless otherwise indicated on the kit. As with any painting project, it's best to cover up the floor, table, or whatever surface you'll be using with some type of tarp or covering before opening up the paints. Though older kits came with premixed colors, newer ones typically require mixing. Once you've mixed your paint, it's best to start from the center of the painting and work your way out so your hands and fingers don't smudge the areas you've already painted. It's also a good idea to paint all portions of the painting that require the color you've got on your brush before moving onto the next color. And remember to wait for each portion to dry before filling in other parts of the canvas. Like any work of art, your paint-by-numbers original deserves to be signed.

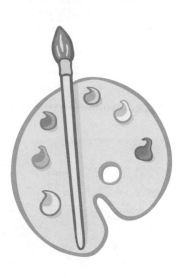

project: make your own paint-by-numbers canvas

If you're not so taken by the poodles and roses that seem to pervade the paint-by-numbers line, make your own canvas using a software program, such as the free one available at www.photodoodle.com. Just download the photo (or any image) you want to paint, and the program instantly transforms it into a paint-by-numbers-style canvas, complete with numbers and a corresponding color palette. Print it out on thick cardstock (you can also ask a printing company to print it on heavy paper or canvas), buy the matching paints at a craft store, and settle down for your next painting project. An appropriately themed canvas from Photodoodle, plus paints and brushes, would also make a fun gift for artistically inclined (but technically challenged) friends.

other painting kits: Canvases aren't the only media for DIY painting kits. A visit to the craft store will open up a whole world of painting project possibilities. You'll find wooden blocks, lamps, piggy banks, glass plates, model animals, and any number of other surfaces on which to paint. Ceramic studios have also cropped up all over the country, offering white dishware as canvases for burgeoning artists. You purchase and paint it, they fire it up and glaze it for you.

photography

PRESERVING THE IMAGE OF A FLEETING MOMENT is a miraculous invention that we take for granted. Without photographs, we would have no evidence of our grandparents' wedding, our eighth-grade winter ball, or just how tiny our children were when they were born. Photography is not only a respected art form, but a medium in which to capture spontaneous occurrences that might have gone otherwise unnoted.

what you'll need

- Camera (digital or film)
- Film (for film cameras)

resources

Shoot Like a Pro! Digital Photography Techniques, by Julie Adair King (McGraw-Hill Osborne Media, 2003).

Teach Yourself Photography, by Lee Frost (McGraw-Hill Osborne Media, 2004).

www.kodak.com: Online retailer of film and cameras, as well as links to helpful tips.

www.lomography.com: Lightweight, offbeat cameras that encourage experimentation, with a heavy emphasis on fun.

www.photographymuseum.com: Sometimes the best way to learn is by studying the masters. There are plenty of great photographs on the web, and the *American Museum of Photography* is a good place to start.

www.popphoto.com: The website for *Popular Photography*, a beautiful publication for pros and hobbyists.

overview

Photography is the process of making images using a camera. Clicking the shutter of a camera freezes the image by recording the light reflected from the object being photographed onto a light-sensitive medium. If a traditional camera is used, the image is captured on film then transferred to paper by a chemical process. Images taken with a digital camera are captured on a memory chip and can either be transferred to a computer disc or printed on paper.

history

The idea of "drawing with light" (the literal meaning of the word *photography*) dates back to ancient times and a device called the camera obscura, a darkened room or box with a small hole at one end. Because of the way the light reflects off objects outside the box, the scene in front of the hole is projected upside down onto the wall inside the box. During the Renaissance, scholars used the camera obscura to observe solar eclipses, which were too bright to look at straight-on. It wasn't till the 1820s that a Frenchman, Joseph-Nicéphore Niépce, figured out how to use one to capture a permanent image; he called the process heliography, and it took eight hours. By 1835, Louis-Jacques-Mandé Daguerre had found a way to decrease that time to about 30 minutes. Four years later, Thomas Wedgwood and William Henry Fox Talbot invented the process of using negative and positive images that formed the basis for modern photography. In 1900, Kodak made photography widely available to the general public by offering its $1 Brownie camera, a shoe-box-style cardboard camera that took 2¼-inch square photos and became an immediate hit. The first multilayered color film became available in the 1930s, and in 1963 the first instant color film was developed by Polaroid, followed by the Instamatic by Kodak. Today, though many people still use film in photography, digital cameras have become the more popular medium.

getting started

First, decide what kind of camera you're going to use. Though digital models have come a long way in their ability to capture details, some professional photographers will never leave their film cameras behind because of the warmth of a film-based photograph. Either way, you'll need to consult the instructions of whatever camera you buy to learn how to operate it best. Here are a few tips to help you take your best shots.

- *GIVE SOME THOUGHT to composing your shot, which means combining all the different elements in each shot so they work well together and achieve a kind of balance.*

- *TRY NOT TO always center the subject of your photo. You'll get a much more interesting image if you move it slightly to either side of the frame and combine it with a linear object that leads up to the subject.*

- *TRY FRAMING each shot both vertically and horizontally to see what works best.*

- *FOR PORTRAITS, the closer you are to your subject, the better the shot. Try either having them look directly at you or in another direction (or both—and choose which you like better later). Photograph children from their eye level rather than from above so they can look directly at the camera without craning their necks or squinting.*

- *IF YOU'RE SHOOTING outdoors, try to get your subjects to face the sun. Yes, they may have to struggle not to squint, but with bright sunlight behind them you'll be shooting silhouettes. (It may help to turn on the flash when you photograph people with their backs to the sun.) Actually, that's one of the reasons overcast skies make for the best kind of light.*

- *MAKE SURE your picture is in focus.*

project: photo trickery

You can practice serious photography all day, but if you're in the mood to try something more lighthearted, experiment with some of these whimsical techniques.

- Cover your flash with your finger, then shoot your subject in a dark room. Your photo will have a sexy, red glow.

- Invert a shot glass and place it up against the lens of your camera for a nifty fisheye effect.

- Cut out a small hole in the center of a piece of black paper, then position the hole in front of the lens before you snap your shot.

- Cover your lens with sheer pantyhose to achieve that Doris Day haze.

- Use translucent, colored sheets or your sunglasses to color the lens and, ultimately, the photo.

polaroid transfer

GAUZY AND IMPERFECT, Polaroids are the antithesis to crisp, digital photos. Still, the appeal of being instantly rewarded with a tangible picture makes this antiquated process a perennial favorite. With the Polaroid transfer process, candid photos are transformed into new works of art.

what you'll need

- Polaroid film (669, SX-70, 559, 59, or 809)
- Polaroid camera or Daylab Copy System Pro, to transfer images to film
- Ink roller
- Paper, fabric, or other mildly rough surface to transfer the image to
- Shallow tray large enough to hold the receptor sheet
- Scissors
- UV spray (optional)

resources

Photographer's Guide to Polaroid Transfer: Step-by-Step, by Christopher Grey (Amherst Media, 2001).

Polaroid Transfers: A Complete Visual Guide to Creating Image and Emulsion Transfers, by Kathleen Thormod Carr (Amphoto Books, 1997).

www.alternativephotography.com: Alternative ways to process photos.

www.betterphoto.com: Online photography courses, including a class on Polaroid transfers.

www.daylab.com: Retailer for Daylab Copy System Pro.

www.polaroid.com: Online retailer of Polaroid film, as well as tutorials on transfers and emulsion lifts.

overview

A Polaroid transfer involves peeling apart undeveloped Polaroid film, positioning it chemical side down on a wet sheet of paper or any other receptive material, then placing it under heat to create a print. The process requires specific types of Polaroid film, such as 669, SX-70, 559, 59, or 809. The image can be transferred onto any porous surface, including paper, fabric, wood, or unglazed ceramic. The surfaces are then sealed to protect the image. The resulting prints have a unique visual style that ranges from gauzy to a little ghostly.

history

The Polaroid camera was invented by Edwin Land, an American scientist inspired by his impatient three-year-old daughter who asked to see film developed into pictures right away. The first version of the camera was offered to the public in 1948, an improved version followed in 1963, and by 1972, the SX-70 superseded the peel-apart film by introducing dry Polaroid prints that developed in light. The first Polaroid transfer is said to have been created accidentally in the 1960s from peel-apart film. The story goes that a researcher inadvertently left the negative side of the film facing a countertop, and after lifting it up, saw that the inverted image was printed on the surface.

project: painted polaroids

The best part about Polaroid transfers is the endless variety of surfaces you can print on. But even if you decide to stick to paper, you can add sheen and shimmer to the transferred image—and another layer of interest and texture to your art—by painting the paper prior to printing. Before you submerge the paper in water, spray it with a coat of gold or silver paint. Let it dry, then follow the above steps to complete your Polaroid transfer. You'll notice that parts of the paper literally glisten in the light. Another option: After the whole piece has dried, you can scrape away or paint in parts of the image to achieve the effect you want.

getting started

First, decide if you're going to reproduce an image using a device like the Daylab Copy System Pro, which converts any 4-by-6-inch (10 by 15 cm) image into a Polaroid print, or if you're going to work with a Polaroid photo from the start. The Daylab system is an investment and requires some counter-top space, so beginners should consider creating prints exclusively from Polaroids at first. Next, organize three separate workspaces: one for exposing, another for treating the receptor sheet, and a flat surface where the negative will be transferred.

1) CUT SHEETS of paper to your chosen size. Wet your paper by submerging it in warm water, then use a paper towel to wipe away excess water. The instructions are the same for fabric.

2) CREATE YOUR photo using the Polaroid camera or the copier. Wait a few seconds (count to 8), then pry apart the film. Cut away the chemical pad from the film and place the film, chemical side down, on the damp paper or fabric.

3) USING THE INK ROLLER, gently roll back and forth in one direction a few times. The goal is to make sure every part of the image surface makes contact with the receptor surface. Pressing too hard may ruin the image.

4) IN THE TRAY in which you soaked the receptor sheet, either soak both the film and the receptor in warm water for about 20 seconds or just let it sit for 1 minute before slowly unpeeling the film. Voilà! You have your Polaroid transfer.

5) LET THE IMAGE DRY completely. Afterward, you can seal the surface with a coat of UV spray to prevent it from fading.

profile: dreamy results from polaroid transfer

For creative people like KATHLEEN CARR, straight photography definitely has its merits, but manipulating photographs takes the art form to a whole new level of customization and control. Carr, who's based in Kona, Hawaii, says her "fingers started to itch" after she experimented with hand-coloring black-and-white photos. After attending a workshop on Polaroid transfers, "I realized that Polaroid transfers were going to be my next step," she says. That next step launched her on an artistic path she would follow for the next 15 years.

Looking at her work, it's easy to see what she fell in love with. The ethereal renderings of horses in motion, a field of Monet-like mustard plants filling a landscape, and a graphic bamboo grove look less like photographs than watercolor paintings. In fact, Carr makes a point of printing her transfers onto watercolor paper to give her work "a certain softness and grittiness."

"I like the more dreamlike metaphoric, less literal, more subjective rendering," she says. "I realize the literal, straight photographic print is as beautiful as it can be. But the transfers let me achieve a totally different color palette, and the texture of the paper is completely different."

Carr uses a variety of media for her transfers—handmade papers, fabrics, almost anything porous. With transfers, it's not so much about subject matter as it is about lighting, contrast, and composition. For example, a landscape with a lot of details in the distance won't work as well with transfers because those details will get lost. She has mastered these kinds of subtleties after years of experimenting with this process, and has written two books on the subject to share her knowledge.

"If you notice that some parts of your transfer are darker than other parts, next time peel off the negative very slowly then rinse it underwater in a vinegar bath."

pottery

WHETHER USED FOR POTTING PLANTS, for plating meals, or simply for their decorative good looks, handmade ceramics are prized by those who own them. Making your own pottery will encourage you to appreciate its sculptural beauty all the more. Don't worry about getting your hands dirty—the clay will easily wash away, leaving you with an exquisite piece of art to call your own.

what you'll need

- *Pottery wheel and accessories (depending on method)*
- *Clay*
- *Mold*
- *Kiln*
- *Glaze*

resources

The Complete Potter's Companion, by Tony Birks (Bulfinch, 1998).

Hand-Building Techniques, by Joaquim Chavarria (Watson-Guptill Publications, 1999).

www.howtomakepottery.com: A step-by-step tutorial on how to make pottery, including wheel throwing, glazing, and firing.

www.claytimes.com: The website for Clay Times magazine, devoted to enthusiasts, hobbyists, and artists of pottery.

overview

There are three ways of making pottery: slipcasting, on a wheel, or by hand. Wet, malleable clay is shaped into forms using any of those methods, then left to dry. When it's dry, the piece is then "bisque fired" in a kiln at an extremely high temperature—from just under 1000°F (538°C) to more than 2000°F (1093°C), depending on the type of pottery. When the pottery is cool, it can then be painted with one or more glazes, which come in many different types, or left unglazed for an earthier look. The glazed pots must then be fired again, at even higher temperatures (these vary depending upon the glazes used). Some glazes give the object a glossy surface, while others are satiny or crystalline. The same methods are used for creating functional vessels, like vases, platters, cups, and planters, as for making purely decorative pieces of sculpture.

history

One of the oldest pieces of pottery discovered was found in Japan and dates back to the Jomon period, which began in 10,500 B.C.E. The potter's wheel is said to have been invented in Mesopotamia around 6000 B.C.E., though it's difficult to confirm precisely. By 5500 B.C.E., people were able to mass produce pottery and earthenware and make it available to the general public. Potters in ancient China developed their own techniques. It is believed that porcelain was first made by Chinese potters toward the end of the Han period (206 B.C.E.–C.E. 220), when pottery became more refined in body, form, and decoration. The Chinese made early vitreous wares (protoporcelain) before they developed the white vitreous ware (true porcelain) that was later so admired by Europeans. Glazing, which is applying a coating to the pottery that adds a glossy finish and makes it waterproof, is believed to have first been accomplished in the 9th century B.C.E. in Mesopotamia. Over the next few centuries, the technique was further refined in Rome and China.

In North America 2,000 years ago, the nomadic Native American people settled down to cultivate agriculture, and along with that came pottery, which was used to carry water, store foods, and protect seeds for planting. They also developed pots for cooking that were designed to be positioned over fire. In the New World, baked-clay pottery was made in the form of bricks and tiles in the early 1600s by Dutch immigrants in Virginia and Pennsylvania. In 1735, the first stoneware factory opened in New York. Other pottery plants began opening along the East Coast soon thereafter. In modern times, pottery took on the form of current artistic movements: Art Nouveau, Arts and Crafts, and Art Deco. In the 1950s, designers like Eva Zeisel, Russel Wright, and Edith Heath created pottery that typified midcentury American style.

getting started

For this type of hobby—one involving complicated techniques and a lot of expensive equipment—it's probably best for beginners to take a class. The teacher will provide much of the equipment and demonstrate the different techniques. You'll learn how to make pottery by hand, which involves shaping clay, then smoothing it with slurry, a thin mixture of clay and water. If the teacher instructs the class on how to use a potter's wheel (called "turning" or "throwing"), you'll attach a lump of clay to the center of the wheel, then cause the wheel to spin by using a pedal, kick wheel, treadle, or electric motor. As the wheel turns, the potter squeezes and pulls the clay into shape. It is then typically trimmed, allowed to dry to a hardened state, then put back on the wheel to be made even smoother. Thrown pots are usually symmetrical, because they are created by pulling the clay into shape while it spins on a vertical axis.

Another method you might learn in a class is slipcasting, which involves pouring a thin layer of liquid clay "slip" into a plaster mold that sucks the water from the slip and leaves a layer of clay the same shape as the mold. The process is repeated with more layers of slip until the mold is full. Then the potter removes the piece from the mold and the piece is allowed to dry completely.

All these pieces must then be fired at extremely high temperatures in a kiln. They are then smoothed with sandpaper and glazed with a finish, then fired again. The glaze can be applied by either dipping, pouring, spraying, or brushing on the glossy finish, and can be a combination of colors and textures.

project: fix a chip or crack in a pot

Not ready to throw your own pot yet? Familiarize yourself with the medium first by fixing the chips and cracks on the pieces you've got. Here are two perfectly simple solutions for repairing ceramics.

1) For chips, apply a coat of clear polyvinyl acetate adhesive (called PVA at the hardware store—or possibly just plain white glue) to the inside of the piece that fell off. Put it back into place and hold it down for a full minute. You can use a scraper or a sharp blade to scrape off the remaining adhesive after it's completely dried. Let the piece dry for a full day before using it again.

2) If you've got a crack, first spread PVA over it with a small brush and push the two sides of the cracked piece together for a minute. Scrape away the residue, and let it dry for a full day. If the piece is completely broken, you can apply constant pressure overnight by placing it in a larger vessel and filling the larger vessel with beans, which will hold the pieces together.

NOTE: PVA is not waterproof, so this method is only good for pottery that will not come in contact with liquids.

puppetry

MARIA VON TRAPP AND HER FLOCK OF stepchildren put on an unforgettable puppet show in *The Sound of Music*. Just watching the lonely goatherd yodeling up that mountain and the men blowing beer foam off their faces makes you want to join in the wicked fun. Don't be shy—you can learn how to control your own set of diminutive village people! You may even discover that you have a knack for ventriloquism.

what you'll need

- *Puppets*
- *Stage and sets*
- *Script*

resources

101 Hand Puppets: A Beginner's Guide to Puppeteering, by Richard Cummings (Dover Publications, 2002).

The Complete Book of Puppetry, by George Latshaw (Dover Publications, 2000).

www.creativeupuppets.com: Readymade puppets and make-your-own puppet kits are sold through this online store.

www.sagecraft.com/puppetry: All of your most urgent puppetry questions are ably addressed on this informative site.

overview

Puppetry involves putting on a puppet show on a stage. There are many different types of puppets, among them :

- Marionettes (controlled by strings)
- Hand puppets (a glovelike puppet controlled by the hand, which moves the arms, head, mouth, and sometimes even the eyes)
- Rod puppets (controlled by rods connected to the arms and possibly the legs)
- Ticklebugs (created by drawing the puppet's facial features directly on the middle finger and using the other fingers as arms and legs)
- Shadow puppets (two-dimensional puppets manipulated behind a screen and lit so that their shadows are projected onto the screen)

Some puppeteers use black lighting to hide themselves while showing off their puppets, while others wear black clothing to blend into the background. Ventriloquists typically have a puppet (or "dummy") with a movable mouth. They prop it on their knees and carry on a conversation without moving their own mouths. And every child is familiar with finger puppets—they fit over the fingers like the digits of a glove. In the hands of a skilled puppeteer, all sorts of items can be brought to life, from stuffed animals to cardboard boxes.

history

Puppetry originated in ancient China with the introduction of shadow puppets, which were also mentioned in Greek philosophical texts. By the Middle Ages, puppets were being used in church to tell stories from the Bible. (That's where the word *marionette* came from: It means "little Mary" in French.) Because many puppeteers incorporated humor and satire into their routines, they were kicked out of churches and ended up going from village to village to perform in fairs. In the 1700s, puppetry was considered a form of high art and entertainment for the wealthy classes, but has since become more of an entertaining forum for kids—think *Mister Rogers' Neighborhood*, *Sesame Street*, the Muppets, and Punch and Judy. But there are quite a few groups dedicated to puppet art for adults.

getting started

Putting on a puppet show is much like putting on a stage play from the production standpoint, except you'll be using puppets instead of actors. So first, conduct some research by going to see puppet performances to help you decide what kind of show you'd like to put on. You could also research puppet theater groups near you and ask to audition and join in. If you want to be a puppetmaster, you'll need to choose what type of storyline you'd be interested in performing: a fairytale for kids, a published play, comedy, satire, drama? Will your characters speak?

Go to a puppet shop and look at all the different varieties, testing them out to see what you're most comfortable using: a marionette, a hand puppet, a shadow puppet, or something else altogether.

The type (and number) of puppets will dictate what sort of stage you'll need. You can create a stage simply by tying a rope between two chairs and tossing a blanket over it. Even the back of a couch can serve as a puppet stage. Remember, all the world's a stage when it comes to your production. Whether you're going it alone or you've got a cohort, set up your music and start the show.

project: make a sock puppet

An oldie, but a goodie—sock puppets can be surprisingly expressive. Witness the following.

1) Start by putting a sock on your hand, with your fingers in the toe and the heel near the back of your wrist.

2) Next, make the puppet's mouth: Using a pair of scissors, cut a slit in the sock in the space between your fingers and your thumb, where your toes used to go. Then get the second sock from the pair and cut an oval piece measuring about 4 inches (10 cm) across and about 5 inches (12.5 cm) long. Cut out a piece of cardboard with the exact same measurements and attach the oval piece of sock to the cardboard with glue. Once the glue is dry, fold the oval in half.

3) Fit the folded oval into the slit you cut for the mouth and sew the raw edges of the sock all around the edges of the oval. Now your puppet is ready to talk.

4) You can stop right there, if you like. You have a functioning puppet. But if you want it to have a little more personality, add eyes, ears, hair, eyebrows, glasses, and more. The minimalist's way would just be to draw all that on with a Sharpie, but you could get fancy. Use yarn or cotton balls for hair, sew on buttons for eyes, shape pipe cleaners into eyeglasses—you know what to do.

quilting

A QUILT OFTEN SERVES AS A PSYCHOLOGICAL PORTRAIT of its maker. The eclectic, free-spirited quilter patches together fabrics in every color of the rainbow, the spare modernist uses carefully spaced geometric patterns, while the environmentalist reuses vintage fabrics. The common bond among them is their craft—it has endured over the centuries and continues to thrive.

what you'll need

- Fabric
- Scraps of fabric (if making a patchwork quilt)
- Batting
- Spool of quilting thread
- Thimble
- Ruler or straightedge
- Quilter's needle
- Fabric scissors
- Fabric pencil
- Sewing basket

resources

Your First Quilt Book (Or It Should Be!), by Carol Doak (That Patchwork Place, 1997).

Quirky Quilting: 20 Easy and Fun Projects, by Tomme J. Fente (HarperResource, 2004).

Quilter's Complete Guide, by Marianne Fons, et al. (Oxmoor House, 2001).

www.dsquilts.com: Denyse Schmidt's modern, elegantly designed quilts.

www.quiltinaday.com: Purveyor of instructional courses, books, and quilting accessories.

www.quiltuniversity.com: Online quilting courses.

overview

Quilting is the technique of sewing together two layers of fabric with a layer of batting (a fluffy sheet of cotton, wool, or synthetic fiber) in between. The top layer of the quilt is typically either one piece of fabric with elaborate stitching or a patchwork of fabric pieces—called blocks—that have been sewn together. Some quilts are made of embroidered blocks or appliqués, a patchwork of blocks onto which other pieces of fabric have been sewn. Some quilts also have a border that rims the entire piece. Quilts can be functional—used everyday as bedding, for example—or hung on a wall as decoration.

history

There's evidence of ancient quilted items from every continent. The first known prototype of a quilted article of clothing was found on an ivory carving of an Egyptian pharaoh dating back to 3400 B.C.E. In India, a banner made of silk pieces sewn together and hung in the caves of the Thousand Buddhas was constructed in the sixth century, and another fabric quilt thought to be from Mongolia dates back to approximately 200 C.E.

During the Roman Empire, quilted bedding—what they referred to as a "stuffed sack"—was used as a mattress. In medieval England, the invention was appropriated and referred to as the "cowlte," a combination of a mattress and a bedcover.

Crusaders returning from the Middle East were responsible for bringing quilting to Europe around the 11th century—the quilts apparently softened the impact of the knights' armor chafing their skin. And with their batting, quilts were also used as blankets to keep people warm, as they are today.

At first, quilts were made simply by sewing together pieces of cloth with sturdy stitches, but the introduction of quilting frames made the process easier. Soon quilters were using finer and more decorative types of stitches.

The Colonial era ushered in the quilt's heyday. European settlers brought the quilting techniques they'd learned on the Continent to the U.S., and the hobby thrived here for the next 200 years. Quilting bees, in which women would get together and make quilts, became popular in the 1800s.

getting started

Quilting entails three basic steps: piecing the components together, layering them on top of each other, then binding them together. To make your own square quilt, you'll need to figure out what pattern and design you want to use. Consult a website or books for ideas (see resources). Start with a simple design. For beginners, the easiest shape to work with is a square. After you've chosen your fabrics, wash and press them. Then cut the pieces into the shapes you've chosen. Now arrange your square pieces, called blocks, in the design you've chosen, pattern side down, and use a ruler to line them up. With your fabric pencil, mark the fabric about ¼ to ½ inch (64 to 127 mm) from the edges—this is where you will make your seams.

Now you begin assembling the quilt top. This will basically involves pinning two pieces of fabric with the lines facing each other, right sides together, and sewing them together along the line. You will continue to sew pieces together along one edge at a time, according to the pattern you've chosen, until you use up the remainder of your blocks.

When the quilt top is finished, you can take it to a quilt guild who will put the backing on the quilt.

project: "lazy" quilt

Here's a quick quilt that's perfect for beginners. All you need is two store-bought flat bed sheets, polyester batting cut about 1 inch (2.5 cm) smaller, and some yarn in a contrasting color. Position the sheets right side in and sew them together, leaving about 12 inches (30 cm) open on one side. Turn right side out, insert the batting, and whipstitch the opening closed. Using some chalk, mark the quilt from top to bottom and left to right every 6 inches (15 cm). Thread the yarn through a heavy yarn needle and insert the yarn ties through the chalk marks, stitching all the way through the quilt each time, then tie off the yarn and trim it.

profile: queen of the mini quilt

"Quilts are as much and as little as you put into them," says JENNY RYAN, proprietress of the online craft store SewDarnCute.com. Ryan focuses on the "little" part by making quilts for babies, and their diminutive size makes you wish (1) you were that small, (2) you had a baby, or (3) you could somehow triple the quilt's size to make it fit your bed (and, in fact, her patterns show you how you can). She uses vintage-inspired fabrics—like illustrations of Betty Boop, cowgirls swinging their lassos, or cupcakes with hand-embroidered sprinkles, all surrounded by polka-dotted fabrics, for example—that appeal to people of all ages.

Ryan knows herself well enough to plan her quilts according to her attention span, which is brief. "The small quilts are quicker, easier, and satisfy my need to move on to the next idea," she says. For beginners, especially, it should be a relief to hear that you don't have to spend weeks and months of your life on one quilt—unless you really want to. Ryan steers away from complicated patterns, which she says can "tax the brain cells a bit—so many measurements, so little time!" Although she tends to keep things simple, she still relishes the process of planning and sewing quilts. She carefully chooses each fabric design and changes thread colors often for the detail stitching to give each piece its own signature finish. "The end result is totally worth it, though," she says. It's the potential for endless possibilities that Ryan loves most about quilting. "It can be anything you want it to be," she says. "Even the most basic pattern will turn out differently from person to person, depending entirely on your personality and the fabrics and techniques you use. A traditional six-patch quilt can look chic and modern when done in a subtle color palette, but make the same design using a boatload of scraps from old clothes, and it has a wacky farmhouse/hobo feel."

radio control vehicles

FOR THE LEFT-BRAINED SET—amateur engineers and those who love to tinker with mechanics—radio control vehicles are the dream hobby. Taking apart and putting back together the guts of model airplanes, cars, trucks, and motorboats are just part of the fun. Racing them is the other half of this playful equation.

what you'll need

- *Local RCV club you can join*
- *Radio control vehicle*
- *Open space*

overview

Radio control (RC) vehicles are available in two categories: toy-grade and hobby-grade. Toy-grade models are found in most toy stores and come preassembled. They're targeted at kids, typically run on battery power, and have simplified circuits that can't be transported to other remote control vehicles. Hobby-grade vehicles are another story. They're more sophisticated in the way they're made and how they function, usually require some assembly, are customizable, and include many features. These types can also accept RC equipment from a variety of manufacturers and vehicles. In addition to cars and trucks, RC vehicles take the shape of boats, airplanes, helicopters, ships, submarines, tanks, bulldozers, motorcycles, and robots. Hobbyists like to race their RC vehicle's, which can be either electric-or gas-powered. Some of these machines can really zoom: Certain types of aircraft can go as fast as 250 miles per hour.

history

Though difficult to confirm, it's thought that radio remote control was first conceived of by British aeronautics enthusiast Patrick Young Alexander, who came up with the idea of wireless aircraft control in 1888. He had also worked on developing wireless telegraphy methods, and wrote a paper about directing airplanes wirelessly. But because of the weight of the machines used at the time, the idea did not come to fruition until the 1900s. During World War II, radio control was used by Germans to direct missiles and bombs. In the 1950s, miniature vehicle models became mobile with the use of internal combustion engines but were still controlled by wires. It wasn't until the 1980s, when small computer chips were developed, that RC vehicles for the consumer market became light enough to move on their own, wirelessly.

getting started

- *THE EASIEST TYPE of vehicle to start with is a ready-to-run model, which saves you the trouble of assembling a complicated kit—unless you're interested in that sort of thing. In that case, the unassembled kits allow hobbyists to construct a vehicle from scratch (ideal for those who like to build models: see Model Aircrafts, Model Railroading, and Model Ships.) Kits typically come with the necessary hardware (all those tiny screws and nuts), and require builders to construct different parts of the vehicle, such as the transmission and differentials. Some kits don't include electronics like motors and engines, or even body parts, allowing hobbyists the opportunity to truly customize their vehicles.*

- *THE BEST WAY to get acquainted with the world of RC racing is to join a club. (Ask your local hobby shop about clubs near you or search the internet for ideas.) You'll meet other enthusiasts, who can show you the ropes, telling you which races to enter and giving you tips and strategies to win. Go to a few races to get a feel for the intensity of these events and to watch how the winners perform, then sign up when you're ready. After you've chosen your vehicle and all the specificities it requires (cars, for example, come in gas or electric, rear-wheel or front-wheel drive, and a variety of suspension types), then practice as much as you can. You'll need to learn how to anticipate other racers' moves and react in order to stay in and win the race. Visit the venue where you'll be racing to get familiar with the set course, and practice there if you can.*

project: clean your rc vehicle

Every 3,000 miles, you change your car's oil (or at least you should). After every landing, real airplanes are cleaned and checked. Just as with these, remote control vehicles need to be regularly maintained too. After every race or run, give your vehicle a good once-over, checking for nicks, cracks, or any other damage that might need to be fixed. Then it's time to carefully clean the vehicle, using a damp cloth. For those tight spots, you can use Q-tips or an old toothbrush. If you know you won't be using your vehicle for a few days, empty the fuel tank. And just as you would with your own car, clean the air filter to make sure it runs as smoothly as possible.

hobby hazard: RC vehicle racing has enough excitement without the need to add any more, so when it comes time to charge your batteries, whether they're nickel or lithium poly batteries, be sure you read the manufacturer's instructions thoroughly and take all required precautions. These types of batteries have known to heat up, vent smoke, and even explode!

resources

Radio Control Airplane How To's, by Rom Atwood (Air Age Publishing, 1995).

Take Off: All about Radio Control Model Aircraft, by Alex Weiss (Nexus Special Interests, 2002).

www.beginningrc.com: For beginners, a comprehensive guide to the differences between RC vehicles and which to choose.

www.hobbytron.com: All varieties of radio-controlled vehicles available for sale.

www.radio-control-model.com: Instructive site comparing different RC models.

robot building

MARY SHELLEY'S SEMINAL BOOK *FRANKENSTEIN* **should have convinced us of the dangers of building lifelike creatures that humans think they can control. But it's an irresistible human compulsion—we need to take risks! We hope that your first attempt doesn't result in a homicidal android, but if it does, don't say we didn't warn you.**

what you'll need

FOR A KIT:

- *Robot-building kit and any supplies called for in the instructions*
- *Computer (if required by kit)*

resources

Robot Building for Beginners, by David Cook (Apress, 2002).

JunkBots, Bugbots, and Bots on Wheels: Building Simple Robots with BEAM Technology, by David Hrynkiw, et al. (McGraw-Hill Osborne Media, 2002).

www.gorobotics.net: Links to books, articles, clubs, and other robot-related topics.

www.hobbyengineering.com: Kits and parts for beginners and advanced robot builders alike.

overview

Building robots—machines meant to mimic the behavior of humans or, occasionally, other animals—is an extremely complicated and time-consuming hobby, requiring a fair amount of familiarity with electronics and computer programming. Robots can be put together with kits that include everything a beginner needs or they can be built from scratch by advanced engineers. In essence, robot builders model their creations after humans and strive to make them look and act accordingly. Robots are built on five components: the composition of the body, "muscles," sensory abilities, a central brain system that controls the other functions, and a power source. Robots can be lifelike and sophisticated "humans" that work on voice command, or more rudimentary creatures that can just teeter around on two legs. A robot operates by a computer that controls all its functions, from mobility to the astounding ability to smell, taste, and speak. Just as a person's brain commands all of his functions, the computer commands the robot's operations. Unlike humans, however, robots run on rechargeable batteries.

history

The first robot-type machine is commonly believed to be the water clock, built in 250 B.C.E. by Greek engineer Ctesibius. Fast forward a few centuries to the late 1890s, when Nikola Tesla figured out how to harness electricity, which aided in the development of a self-regulated machine. The term robotics entered the vernacular in a play by the Czech writer Karel Capek called *Rossum's Universal Robots*, or *RUR*, in which the robot kills the man who built it. The idea of life-like mechanical beings gained popularity with the science fiction novels written by Isaac Asimov in the early 1940s. In 1950, scientist Grey Walter created Elsie the Tortoise, an animal-like machine that had phototube "eyes" and vacuum tube amplifiers. Around the same time, industrial robots called Unimates were developed by George Devol and the "father of modern robotics," Joseph F. Engelberger. Today, robots are being developed that can recognize and respond to human emotions and can "learn" from their mistakes—which is more than can be said for some humans.

getting started

For someone who's never built a robot before, the best way to go is to buy a robot-building kit and follow the instructions closely *(see resources)*. Kits include every necessary piece (except, of course, batteries). There are robot kits made for every level of engineer— so make sure you choose a starter kit. As you become familiar with the tools and components (typically made from metal, plastic, and rubber), you can graduate to higher levels of robotics. It's a good idea to start with toy robot kits to get accustomed to the basic mechanics of how robots work; these may come with their own built-in brain or may be operated with a remote control. The next step up would be to buy a programmable robot kit, which presents you with the basic technology of robotics to work with. Advanced kits use infrared, alternative energy sources, muscle wire that moves robot parts, and computerization. Many kits can be customized, and some require a computer to program the robot.

"Robots are difficult to build from scratch, so start with a robot kit to get things moving along."

project: program a robotic dog

Who says money can't buy love? Shell out $2,000 and Sony's robotic dog, Aibo, will instantly become your best friend. In addition to sadness and anger, Aibo emotes joy and surprise and has the capacity to interact with his owners, nudging them to come play when left alone too long. Just like with a real dog, you can teach him tricks. Best of all, there's no poop-scooping required.

1) Teach your pup his new name by pushing his sensor button, then saying his name in two seconds. In ten seconds, he'll repeat it back to you.

2) Teach him specific movements by moving his legs in the direction you want him to go and pressing the paw sensor on his front legs.

3) Have him take your picture by pushing his sensor while saying "Take a picture." After he nods and his tail lights up blue, the countdown starts and Aibo takes a picture. You can then retrieve the picture from his hard drive.

profile: the magic of machinery

While ROGER ARRICK's preteen friends were engrossed in after-school cartoons, Arrick found pleasure in the confines of his garage, taking apart inanimate objects and putting them back together again. He built gadgets with anything he could get his hands on—Erector sets, Legos, Tinker Toys, broken radios. He's now a dad in his forties living in Tyler, Texas, but nothing has changed. "I'm always tinkering with something," he says.

Learning the mechanics of what is essentially an attempt to create a living being is what motivates Arrick. "When parts come together right, I just get a rush," he says. "It's like bowling a strike or discovering treasure." Among his trove of treasures, Arrick boasts about his latest creation: a geckolike walking robot that can move its tail and head in an eerily lifelike way.

"Balancing a four-legged walking robot is an interesting challenge," he says. "Component placement, software, and linkages are very tricky." Indeed. If his day job allowed him more leisure time, Arrick would have perfected his reptilian version of Frankenstein by now. That project may be on hold, but Arrick will always find another. "I find anything that moves without human interaction the most fun to build," he says. "It usually involves mechanics, motors, computers, software, everything I love working with."

For Arrick, seeing his little beings respond to commands is one of life's great joys. "There's something addictive about seeing a creation awaken," he says.

rubber stamping

RUBBER STAMPING GOES FAR BEYOND making stationery and cards. You can customize just about any surface with your favorite design using rubber stamps. Cover your clothing, your walls, your furniture, even your plates with the motif that most captivates you. What may have begun with a potato stamp when you were a kid can easily turn into a sophisticated form of art as a grownup.

what you'll need

- *Rubber stamp*
- *Ink*
- *Surface such as paper, for stamping*
- *Markers, paint, or chalk*

if you like this hobby, you might enjoy:

- Beading *(see page 34)*
- Collage
- Decoupage *(see page 70)*
- Faux finishing *(see page 96)*
- Framing *(see page 104)*
- Gilding *(see page 110)*
- Glue gun décor
- Latch hooking
- Scrapbooking *(see page 176)*
- Soap making *(see page 190)*
- Stenciling

overview

Rubber stamping involves using a stamp and ink to print an image—whether a letter, word, or picture—onto a surface. The stamp is made of rubber into which an image has been carved or vulcanized (treated chemically), or in the case of commercial stamps, laser-engraved. Paper is the most common receptor for rubber stamping, but many other materials can be stamped, including glass, plastic, wood, metal, and fabric.

The most widely used inks are either dye-based or pigment. Dye-based inks are less expensive than pigment and can be washed away with water. Because they're prone to bleeding, they typically come with markers and chalks in a matching color to help clean up lines and borders. Pigment inks are of higher quality and are more costly. They can be washed off with water but don't bleed in heat or in high humidity. Metallic inks impart clean edges and come in rich hues; these inks contain petroleum, so solvents are needed to clean the stamps, which result in their deteriorating more quickly.

Rubber stamps are often mounted on wood to make for easy gripping. They can also be placed on rubber or foam mounts (less expensive), or acrylic mounts, which allow stampers to see the design through the mount. Stamps also come unmounted, which allows for easier storage. These stamps must be temporarily mounted onto a reusable acrylic mount with rubber cement or double-stick tape.

history

Before the invention of the rubber stamp, brass stamps were used for printing. The process of curing rubber was first developed by Charles Goodyear in 1844, who experimented by cooking rubber and sulfur together and discovered that the elasticity held. Taking his cue from the rubber molds used to make denture bases, James Woodruff made letter molds using the same procedure. Since then, rubber stamps have been used in banks and businesses and in post offices all over the world. These days, rubber stamping is also very popular with scrapbookers, who use stamps to embellish their pages. *(See Scrapbooking.)*

getting started

You can do almost anything with rubber stamps. Want to make greeting cards? Start collecting stamps with general themes, like floral or geometric patterns for all-occasion cards or letter stamps so you can spell out "Happy Birthday" or "Congratulations." You can use candles to represent birthdays, bassinets to symbolize the arrival of a baby, Christmas trees for the holidays, and so on. If the stamp you want can't be found online or at a store, you can have one custom-made with the image of your choice. (This costs more than buying readymade stamps, but no one will have another stamp like it.) You can also carve the stamp yourself *(see project)*.

Paper surfaces of all kinds are suitable for stamping: gift wrap and bags, paper bags, stationery, and such. You can also decorate fabric (such as jeans, T-shirts, quilts, and bedding), candles, lampshades, dishes and ceramics, walls, and shower curtains. There are different types of inks to use in each case, ones that will stay fast even when washed, so ask your rubber stamping source or hobby store clerk about what type of ink works best for your medium. All you need is the stamp and inkpads. Most inks are washable with water, but some metallic inks need solvents to be completely washed out of the stamps. You can also use paint, markers, or chalks in combination with rubber stampings to embellish your design (note that some of these materials might leave an indelible mark).

When choosing rubber stamps, go for fine-lined images, which you can stamp in one color, then use paint or markers to fill in for a more personalized effect.

resources

Storytelling with Rubber Stamps, by Joanna Slan (Memory Makers Books, 2002).

Glorious Rubber Stamping: Ideas, Tips, and Techniques by Judy Ritchie, et al. (Hugh Lauter Levin Associates, 2005).

www.rubberstamper.com: Must-read online magazine for rubber stamping enthusiasts.

www.rubberstamps.net: Custom rubber stamps.

http://rubberstampstore.com: Retailer for all types of rubber stamping accessories and equipment.

project: customized rubber stamp

For a project that'll introduce you to the hobby, try making your own rubber stamp.

1] Come up with a symbol or a simple design with a clear silhouette that will fit onto an eraser—one of those large white vinyl, pink rubber, or green rubber rectangles. A heart, star, or letter of the alphabet would work nicely. Draw your image onto tracing paper with a soft pencil, making sure to fill the lines in darkly.

2] Position the tracing paper so that the image is centered on the eraser—with the pencil marks facing the surface of the eraser. With a rounded stick, rub the back of the tracing paper to transfer the marks onto the eraser. You'll see the reverse image on the eraser.

3] With a sharp tool such as an X-Acto knife, carve out the areas around the lines, leaving the design raised on a recessed background. Try scooping out and away from the lines for the best results.

4] Press your new stamp onto an inkpad and make your mark on any surface you choose.

scrapbooking

PEOPLE MARK SIGNIFICANT MOMENTS of their lives in different ways. Some videotape every occurrence, some take photos *(see Photography)*, and some people make scrapbooks. For the latter, these books provide a personalized keepsake for storing memories and represent an extension of their personalities.

what you'll need

- *Scrapbook with photo-safe or acid-free pages, preferably a three-ring binder*
- *Page protectors*
- *Scissors or paper cutter*
- *Hole punch*
- *Glue*
- *Photo corner mounts*
- *Photos, receipts, tickets, and other memorabilia*
- *Decorating supplies such as die cuts, rubber stamps and ink, stickers, ribbon, glitter, art pens, embossing tools, brads, and beads*

overview

Scrapbooking is a way of preserving important documents, photos, and mementos in book form. Modern scrapbooks come in a variety of sizes and are typically made of blank pages, onto which keepsakes are glued or otherwise fastened. They usually have a theme, like a birthday book, which documents the activities of a person's year: important travels or events, tickets to a movie or show, photos from outings, receipts of purchased items, anything that relates to what happened during the course of the year. Some "scrappers," as they're called, get together and have scrapbooking parties, where they combine resources such as stamps, stickers, stencils, paints, colored pencils, and die cuts (illustrated images or patterned cut-outs), and make scrapbooks together. Though most scrapbookers still prefer the tactile qualities of physical scrapbooks and the original memorabilia they contain, some have begun putting together digital scrapbooks—they can scan in photos, receipts, and notes, and compile them onto a website, then circulate the URL to friends and family.

history

Notebooks have been used to collect and hold information since the time of Aristotle, who kept his notes in what would now be called scrapbooks. During the Renaissance, when Greek and Roman cultures were intensely studied, literary types wrote down poems and stories in handmade books. During the Age of Enlightenment, the philosopher John Locke published an essay entitled "New Method of Making Common-place Books." Such keepsake albums were a popular way to preserve ideas, proverbs, speeches, and other significant items. A few decades later, William Granger wrote a history of England and left blank pages at the end of the book for people to write their notes in. Thomas Jefferson was known to be an avid scrapbooker, saving newspaper clippings, speeches, and illustrations in albums. By the 1800s, scrapbooking had become very popular. In the 1980s, Marielen Christensen, a Mormon mom who wrote a book about scrapbooking called Keeping Memories Alive, opened the first scrapbook retail store, called the Annex, in Utah in 1981, paving the way for a thriving scrapbooking industry.

getting started

With scrapbooking, it's best to come up with a theme before getting started. Do you want to mark an anniversary, a birthday, or another special occasion? Is it a gift, or something you're going to keep for yourself or your kids? Once that's decided, it's time to go shopping. Just about any craft store, even drugstores, will carry scrapbooking supplies. You'll be looking for the necessities, like acid-free scrapbooks and pages, scissors, and glue. You want the paper to be acid-free because the acids contained in some kinds of paper can harm the documents that are attached to it. As for embellishments, there's no end to the variety available. Rather than grabbing every bead and bauble, consider a few tips. Less is more when it comes to scrapbook design; a cluttered page will be hard on the eyes and difficult to follow. Use each embellishment thoughtfully and give it meaning. For example, use die-cuts and shiny, metal accents as a way to highlight an item, not as background design. Always keep your theme in mind when choosing your décor. A wedding scrapbook might look nice with a couple of ribbons glued on that match the colors chosen for the wedding.

If a photo is the focus of the page, use trimmings to attract the eye toward it. For photo-filled pages, use two or three different pieces of color-coordinated, acid-free paper as "frames" or mats, onto which you'll adhere the photos. Try to use one or two photos at most per page, so as not to overcrowd it. You can also crop your pictures to focus on just the part of the image you want to highlight.

Collect the pieces you want to include in your scrapbook in one spot, and start designing your pages. Try each piece in different spots on the page before you permanently glue it in place. If it's a chronologically organized scrapbook, all the more reason to set up the pages first before gluing in place.

project: make a baby birthday book

Is someone you love (or even you) expecting a baby? Create a scrapbook that will give the new arrival a glimpse into what life was like when he or she entered the scene. Start cutting out headlines from local and national newspapers and magazines close to the time the baby is due. Include photos of celebrities and tidbits of gossip that pervade the public consciousness at the time. Be sure to use headlines from the day the baby is born, and feature them prominently in the book. Cut out your favorite outfits from catalogues and fashion magazines. Use movie ads from the local paper, as well as advertisements for food and kitchen staples. Include the day's crossword puzzle, the weather, the horoscope, and anything else that seems appropriate.

To add some context to current events, you can also put together a brief family history. Talk to the grandparents and create a family tree (see Genealogy). If you have the time and inclination, write a narrative history about the baby's lineage, all the way up to the time he or she was born. This project will take some time and effort, but the child who receives it will forever be grateful for this priceless gift.

resources

A Designer's Eye for Scrapbooking, by Ali Edwards (PriMedia, Inc., 2004).

Clean and Simple Scrapbooking: Ideas for Design, Photography, Journaling & Typography, by Cathy Zielske (PriMedia Inc., 2004).

www.creativememories.com: Retailer that sells scrapbooking supplies.

http://scrapbooking.com: A magazine about scrapbooking, with articles on tips and ideas.

scuba diving

JACQUES COUSTEAU'S UNDERWATER ADVENTURES in the 1950s revealed an entire world that had never before been seen by the general public. Since then, the possibility of viewing ethereal marine creatures through scuba diving has fascinated humans. Thanks to Cousteau, meeting an octopus on his own turf is just an oxygen tank's breath away.

what you'll need

- *Scuba gear*

- *Certificate from the Professional Association of Diving Instructors*

- *Transport to the dive site*

resources

Dive: The Ultimate Guide to 60 of the World's Top Dive Locations, by Monty Halls (Ultimate Sports Guide) (Firefly Books Ltd., 2004).

Dive like a Pro: 101 Ways to Improve Your Scuba Skills and Safety, by Robert Rossier (Best Pub, 1999).

www.padi.com and *www.naui.org*: Everything you need to know about the hobby and requirements for certification is addressed on these comprehensive websites.

www.scubadiving.com: The magazine for scuba enthusiasts, with information about gear, diving destinations, links to photography, and a community board.

overview

SCUBA stands for "self-contained underwater breathing apparatus." Scuba gear allows divers to go deep underwater and observe marine life that can't be seen from or near the surface of the water. Divers, who usually wear wetsuits and fins, can use the gear to breathe at extreme depths and remain underwater for long periods of time. It adjusts the atmospheric pressure on the chest and lungs and provides breathing gas at the appropriate pressure. The diving mask, which covers the diver's nose and eyes, is connected to a two-stage regulator. The first stage decreases the cylinder pressure, while the second stage transports the breathing gas to the diver's mouth. There are some special skills to master before undertaking this potentially risky endeavor. Before being allowed to dive independently, divers are required to become certified through the Professional Association of Diving Instructors (PADI).

history

An Assyrian fresco that dates back 3,000 years depicts humans swimming with a simple breathing tool, but fishermen and divers started snorkeling with rudimentary tools like hollow reeds around 100 C.E. In the 1500s, large barrels, which divers carried with them, contained a few breaths of air, but that was a cumbersome proposition. About 100 years later, Robert Boyle started working with underwater compression and decompression. British engineer John Smeaton then invented the air pump in 1771, followed by the hose that connected the air pump to the diving barrel. Throughout the 1800s, inventors continued to add to and perfect the system, and by 1943 Jacques Cousteau and his partner Emile Gagnan devised the first "aqualung," which compressed air on demand, making scuba diving available to the public at large. After a few tragic drownings, however, it was clear that a certification and instructional process was necessary, so in 1960 the National Association of Underwater Instructors began implementing certification courses, followed by the formation of the Professional Association of Diving Instructors.

getting started

The first thing to consider is how often you'll be diving. If you just want to dive at popular tropical resorts once a year, you don't need certification; plan on going on supervised dives. If you think you might pursue the hobby more regularly, you'll need to get certified. To find a reputable certification agency, refer to lists on PADI's and NAUI's websites *(see resources)*. The sites will also describe the variety of classes offered and help you find the ones that are most appropriate for you, based on how much they cost, how big they are, and the duration of the course. When asking the agency about their charges, make sure they include (or at least address) things like equipment, boat fees, NAUI certification card, dive tables, and log books, all of which can add up. The certification process will end with a written exam, as well as a swimming test to determine your preparedness to dive into the deep sea.

To qualify for your certificate, you'll need to demonstrate that you're in good physical shape with no heart conditions and show that you're a strong swimmer (you'll be asked to swim about 200 yards using any stroke and then tread water for about 10 minutes). You'll also learn how to breathe through your mouth and how to equalize the pressure in your head by popping your ears, and be prepared to face large, intimidating waves calmly.

profile: come on in, the water's fine

KEVIN DWYER compares scuba diving to being able to walk off the edge of a building without falling. "Being in the water is the closest feeling to being able to fly," he says. "You can move in any direction, upside down and everything. You can be swimming along, and then the ocean floor might drop off 60 feet."

Despite bumping into a shark and being attacked by a large triggerfish while swimming through its nesting grounds, Dwyer, who lives in San Francisco, California, is a certified diving addict and dives every chance he gets. Off the coast of Cairns in Australia, Dwyer was followed around by a giant Mouri wrasse—a brilliantly colored fish with canine teeth that lives in tropical seas—which let him and his buddies pet him, but "got jealous and hunted away other fish that we were interested in," he remembers. The next day, swimming out of a cave, Dwyer looked up to see a giant turtle "the size of a huge TV" swim over his head. Dwyer is perfectly at home in the water and has never felt anything but excitement at the prospect of donning 30 pounds of scuba gear and diving headlong into the abyss. He doesn't fear the ocean, but he has a healthy respect for it. He simply follows his instructor's immortal words: "Look, but don't touch."

project: learn scuba sign language

Down in the open water, where words can't be heard and lips can't be read, communicating with your diving partners is crucial. Before taking the plunge, learn how to convey these important messages.

- **"Watch me"**—point to yourself.

- **"Out of air"**—keep the regulator in your mouth, swipe your flat hand across the neck, toward the right.

- **"Stop"**—palm out parallel to your body.

- **"Trouble"**—with palm flat out, make the "so-so" sign, your hand tilting right and left.

- **"Pressure not equalizing"**—tilt your head and point to your ear.

- **"Go up"**—point thumb up.

- **"I'll follow you"**—point toward the direction you want to go with both hands, positioning your right hand just ahead of your left hand.

- **"Hurt"**—both index fingers crossed in front of you.

- **"Shark"**—flat, vertical hand placed against your forehead.

- **"Danger"**—arms crossed with fists closed, like a skull and crossbones, faced in the direction of the dangerous element.

sculpture

SOMETIMES, ARTISTIC EXPRESSION can't be confined to only two dimensions. By building a sculpture, budding artists can freely create a piece that articulates their complete vision, whether it's made of marble, bronze, or even scrap wood.

what you'll need

- *Sculpting material such as clay, wood, or stone (beginners might want to try a clay such as Sculpey, which hardens in the oven, or plastilina, which does not harden)*

- *Carving tools appropriate to your chosen medium (for example, stone would require chisels, a mallet, hammers, and picks, while clay would require clay modeling tools)*

- *Work space*

- *Work clothes*

overview

A sculpture is a three-dimensional work of art that is carved, molded, cast, or otherwise constructed out of stone, wood, clay, metal, ice *(see Ice Scupting)*, or other material (or a combination of materials). Sculptures can include mobiles *(see Mobile Making)*, busts, statues, and garden ornaments, and are made using a variety of techniques. With the additive method, materials are added and combined to make a sculpture. With the subtractive method, the artwork is created by carving away pieces of the material, whether that's wood, stone, or ice. Free-standing sculptures are typically built or placed on bases or pedestals. Relief sculptures are carved in such a way that the figures seem to be emerging from a flat, vertical surface.

history

The history of sculpture is almost as old as humanity itself. Some historians consider the caveman's club to be first example of it. Throughout the ages, every important civilization created its own type of sculpture. Miniature statues in the shape of humans and animals carved out of ivory or soft stone were made during the Stone Age. In ancient Mesopotamia, wealthy people used gold, silver, and precious stones like lapis to create sculptures. A famous Egyptian sculpture, dating back to 3100 B.C.E., is the Palette of King Narmer, a relief sculpture depicting scenes of the leader's victorious battle. Of course, the Egyptians are also responsible for the famous Sphinxes built in 2500 B.C.E. They're impressively large: 60 feet (18.3 m) high and four times as long. A few of the most significant and influential sculptures throughout history are Michelangelo's David, Rodin's The Thinker, and the ancient Greek work the Venus de Milo, but there are countless others worth viewing and appreciating. In modern days, many large sculptures have been mounted in public places, such as in parks and in front of civic buildings.

getting started

Sculpting can be as tricky or as easy as you want to make it, depending on the kind of material and process you use. So your first decision is what you want to sculpt. If you want to start small and build a sandcastle, head out to a sandbox or the beach and start piling up your blocks of sand. If you want to begin with building a marble bust of your grandfather, it's best to take a class and learn the right techniques and tools to use. Talk to a sculptor and read books and websites about sculpting to get an understanding of what it takes. Once you have an idea of what direction you want to follow and what materials you want to use, you'll think of all sorts of inspiring sculpting projects to attempt. Sculpting is, above all, a tactile art form, so the best way to become familiar with it is to throw yourself into the creative process.

project: build a sculpture with scrap wood and found objects

There are sculptures waiting to be built out of just about anything. Look in your garage. You can probably put together an abstract piece using the scrap wood, paint, and other objects you've got lying around.

WHAT TO LOOK FOR:

Scrap wood
Epoxy
Hammer
Nails
Drill
Screws
Paint
Other found objects, such as old toys, a spare bicycle wheel, broken terra-cotta pots, rusty silverware, chipped glasses, and so on

Spread all your pieces out on the ground and consider how each one could fit or complement another. You can make a completely abstract shape or try to construct a building, an animal, or other object. Use different shapes to create contrast; a triangle might balance on the edge of a rectangle, for example. Then start nailing, soldering, screwing, or otherwise fusing your pieces together. Pick up odd ends like wires to add ears or appendages. Glue on buttons, pen caps, pieces of paper, or dull glass for texture and variety. When you feel finished (this is totally subjective, by the way), you can paint your wood or other pieces, either by spray painting (try a metallic color) or with a brush. Let dry, and display your *objet d'art* in a flattering environment.

resources

A Sculptor's Guide to Tools and Materials, by Bruner F. Barrie (A.B.F.S. Publishing, 1998).

Sculpture, Principles and Practice by Louis Slobodkin (Dover Publications, 1973).

www.dickblick.com: Beginner's kits and tools.

www.sculptshop.com: Mold-making kits, plaster casts, and all sorts of tools.

www.sculpture.net/community: A community blog, news, and events listings.

www.sculpturetools.com: Tools of the trade.

seed trading

FOR GREEN THUMBS, THERE'S NOTHING MORE GRATIFYING than watching flourishing plants grow from a tiny seed. There, in front of our eyes, the complete life cycle transpires—from germination, to growth, to blossom, and perhaps even fruit. By trading seeds with other likeminded gardeners, not only can you expand your collection, but you can do it for free.

what you'll need

- *A flourishing garden with a variety of plants that can be seeded*
- *Storage bags, glass jars, or sealable plastic containers*
- *Computer with internet access*

overview

Seed trading is a hobby enjoyed by avid gardeners who want to cultivate new plants by taking seeds from other gardeners in exchange for giving seeds from their own garden. It requires gathering, drying, and storing seeds from your plants and flowers, and finding others who are interested in your varieties. Many gardeners now post their seeds available for trade on online garden forums.

history

Spices and seeds have been traded and sold for thousands of years. Seeds from the Chinese derivative of rhubarb, which was first cultivated in 2700 B.C.E., had found their way to Europe by the 1600s. Botanists and scientists traveling to different countries have for centuries made a point of bringing native plant seeds to their own countries, both for cultivation and for study.

The preservation of heirloom varieties of fruits and vegetables has been a major motivation for seed trading. Thomas Jefferson is said to have tried to grow fruits and vegetables that came to the U.S. from the "old country" (Europe), where they had been harvested for centuries. At Monticello, Jefferson's home in Virginia, hundreds of varieties of fruits and vegetables continue to grow, many of them heirloom varieties. Because the thousands of varieties of vegetables and fruit have dwindled over the years, there's a movement to preserve these old and valuable heirloom plants.

seed trading etiquette: *Experienced seed traders abide by a set of unwritten rules that helps the entire community function. Here are a few guidelines to remember when you join the community.*

- Always include a self-addressed stamped envelope (unless the person you're trading with requests another form of communication). Write the name of the seeds you're sending, as well as the variety of seeds you're seeking, on the inside flap of the envelope.
- Each pack typically contains about 24 seeds. If your seeds are particularly rare or heavy, be clear about the amount you're going to send in your communication with the other trader.
- Ask for an equitable number of seeds in relative value to what you're offering.
- Though seeds last for many years, be sure to inform the person you're trading with if your seeds are older than a year.

getting started

- *EACH PLANT has a different way of storing its seeds, but there are a few fundamentals that apply to all plants. Look at the flower closely after it's bloomed and starts to wilt—try not to jostle it around too much. When the bottom of the flower starts to swell, you'll know that seeds are being formed there. Soon, the stem will start to droop and turn brown, and the pod that holds the seeds will begin to open up, indicating that it's time to collect the seeds. You can remove the pods from the plant and keep them in a safe, uncovered place, like a plastic bowl. Over the course of a couple of weeks, they'll dry naturally. Then you can safely remove the seeds from the pods. After letting the seeds dry for several more days, put them in plastic storage bags or envelopes, and be sure to label them. Keep the seeds away from heat or sunlight, ideally in a drawer.*

- *NEXT, find a seed-trading forum (see resources) and list your seeds along with your own wish list. When you get a response, package up the seeds in protective wrapping, like Bubble Wrap or a padded envelope, and send them to their new home.*

project: grow a plant from a seed

Now that you've got your new seeds in the mail, it's time to cultivate.

1] Choose a container with drainage holes, fill it with planting soil, and water the soil to make sure it's moist. You can use small pots, or long, rectangular wooden container boxes—it depends on what type of plant you want to grow and the space available. Make ¼-inch-deep (64 mm) dents in the soil where your seeds are going to go (in a row, if you'd like), drop them into place, and gently tap them in. If they're seeds that need to be covered, cover them with plastic wrap, making sure there's enough air for them to germinate (you may need to poke holes in the cover). You can also use a water sprayer to mist the air under the wrap for added moisture.

2] Follow the directions for the seeds you've procured when choosing where to let the seeds sprout—for many, this will mean placing the container in a warm place that gets full sunlight. If the plastic wrap does not bead with moisture, mist the seeds.

3] When you notice a sprouting of leaves, your seeds have successfully germinated, and they're almost ready to be placed in their own containers. Allow the soil to dry over the next few days (but don't let the sprouts get to the point of wilting), and once the plants are 1 or 2 inches (2.5 or 5 cm) tall, move them to a container with potted soil, making sure that the soil is moist at the bottom.

resources

The New Seed Starter's Handbook, by Nancy Bubel (Rodale Books, 1988).

The Gardener's A–Z Guide to Growing Flowers from Seed to Bloom: 576 Annuals, Perennials, and Bulbs in Full Color, by Eileen Powell (Storey Publishing, 2004).

Saving Seeds: The Gardener's Guide to Growing and Saving Vegetable and Flower Seeds, by Marc Rogers (Storey Publishing, 1991).

www.amseed.com: The American Seed Trading Association helps to connect seed growers and aids in the planning of seed trading conventions.

www.gardenhere.com: An active forum for beginning and experienced gardeners, with step-by-step instructions for seeding and seed trading.

www.seedswapper.com: Swap your seeds here.

sewing

SEWING CAN BE MORE A LIFESTYLE THAN A HOBBY. Once you start to sew your own clothes, you'll notice all the other useful items around your house you can make: napkins and tablecloths, an apron, curtains, sofa slipcovers—the potential is limitless. All you need is a sewing machine (or needle and thread), steady hands, a little bit of instruction in the techniques, and inspiration.

what you'll need

- Sewing needle
- Thread
- Sewing machine
- Fabric
- Pattern
- Scissors
- Pins
- Thimble
- Buttons
- Zippers

resources

Sewing 101: A Beginner's Guide to Sewing, by Editors of Creative Publishing International (Creative Publishing International, 2002).

Sew Basic: 34 Essential Skills for Sewing with Confidence, by Threads Editors (Taunton Press, 2002).

Sew U: The Built by Wendy Guide to Making Your Own Wardrobe, by Wendy Mullin with Eviana Hartman (Bulfinch Press, 2006).

www.sewing.org: The Home Sewing Association's website offers tips, patterns, and sewing project ideas.

www.threadsmagazine.com: A monthly supply of ideas and patterns.

overview

Sewing entails using fabric, needle, and thread to create a piece of clothing or other item. You can sew just about anything that's made of cloth. You can mend holes, fix hems, or sew buttons by hand, and for larger projects use a sewing machine. Sewing patterns instruct sewers on how to cut out and attach pieces of fabric together to create a complete piece. Of course, as your skills improve, you can improvise on the pattern and even, one day, create your very own patterns from scratch.

history

Humans have been sewing with one tool or another since Paleolithic times, around 30,000 B.C.E. Back then, people used bones and animal horns for needles, and animal tendons for thread. The invention of iron needles in the 1300s made matters a tad easier. About 100 years later, someone figured out that looping the thread inside the needle might also help, at which time the first eyed needle was invented.

The invention of the sewing machine sped up the process tremendously. In 1755, the British engineer Charles Weisenthal was issued a patent for a needle connected to a machine, and in 1790 another Englishman, inventor Thomas Saint, received a patent for a sewing machine. It was the French tailor Barthélemy Thimonnier who is credited with inventing the first functional sewing machine, much to the chagrin of other tailors, who believed the sewing machine would render them obsolete and apparently rioted and destroyed the machines. In the U.S., Isaac Singer brought the sewing machine to the masses in the 1850s with a foot-pedaled machine. Today's electronic sewing machines can add all types of fancy flourishes and decorative stitches with the push of a button.

getting started

If you're serious about sewing, you'll need to invest in a sewing machine. Do some research and find one that is appropriate for your skill level and needs. If you don't need to do fancy stitches, stick to the simple models. Once you've got your machine set up, familiarize yourself with the mechanics. You'll need to learn how to thread your machine, wind a bobbin with thread, slide your fabric in at the right place, bring down the presser foot, push the pedal, and finish a stitch. It's best to practice this on scraps of fabric before you tackle a pattern. A few tips: Be sure to hold on to both the top thread and the bobbin thread while sewing the first few stitches so they don't get tangled. Keep the tension with the thread even with both spools, so your stitches don't turn out too loose or too tight. Use both hands to keep the fabric in place, one in front of the presser foot, and one behind.

When you feel you're ready, start with a simple project like sewing napkins, whereby you fold over 1/4 inch (64 mm) of the border on a square piece of fabric, and sew a straight line. When you're ready to move on to more complicated projects, find a pattern you like and follow the instructions to the letter.

project: sew a button

If you don't know how to sew anything else, you should know at least how to sew a button back on when it pops off.

First, either find your button (many clothes come with a replacement) or buy another. Find matching colored thread and cut it to about 2 feet (61 cm) long. Thread your needle—that is, pass the thread through the eyehole—and tie a knot at the loose ends of the thread to hold them together. You can tie off your knot by wrapping the string around your index finger a few times, then pulling it off and tightening the knot at the end. Make sure your button fits the buttonhole, then put it where it needs to go. Now push the needle from underneath the fabric through one of the holes in the button and pull until the knot in the thread is tight against the fabric. Push the needle from above the button down through another hole in the button to the underside of the fabric and pull the thread tight. Repeat that step a few times, going through the same holes. If what you've got is a two-hole button, you're done. Your last stitch should bring the needle to underneath the fabric, where you can sew a couple of small stitches to tighten it up and knot the thread before cutting it.

profile: sew smart

BECKY EATON would never be caught wearing an off-the-rack hoodie from the Gap—at least not without some serious modifications to give it her own signature flair. Browse through the closet of her San Francisco home and you'll see her style stitched across every piece. A humdrum crewneck sweater is ripped diagonally across the front to make way for a white plastic zipper. A pair of ordinary khaki pants has been slashed into a micromini skirt with bright green stitching going across at varying angles. Flashdance-era sweatshirts have been turned upside down, with the elastic becoming the waistband for a skirt. Old pants, sweatshirts, tees, and dresses are transformed into street wear that turns the heads of even the most discerning fashionistas.

If she creates covetable pieces that would be snapped up by any talent-hounding fashion designer, it's not because she's trying to draw attention to herself. Eaton is a designer, and with those God-given skills (plus a few lessons from Mom), making cute clothes is part and parcel of her identity. "I've always been intrigued by the design process," she says. "Instead of spending a bunch of money on clothes, I keep my eyes open and sketch things I like. It's great to know that I can create a piece and be the only person in the entire world wearing it."

silk-screening

FOR BURGEONING DESIGNERS who are itching to get their original works out into the world, silkscreening is the fastest and most efficient way to go. The variables in the process leave as much room for inventiveness and experimentation as do the designs themselves, so you can't really go wrong.

what you'll need

- *Screen-printing kit, such as the Ultimate Screen-Printing Kit (see resources), which includes paint, screens, emulsion liquid, instructional book, and video*

- *150-watt incandescent lightbulb or Photoflood lightbulb*

- *Wheels (if not included in kit)*

- *Fabric or paper for screen-printing medium*

- *Black cardstock*

- *Glass or Plexiglass to keep image on screen*

- *Squeegee or plastic spreader*

- *Design or image on photo transfer paper*

overview

Silk-screening is a process used to print images onto T-shirts, posters, and other media by transferring the image through a screen made of silk, nylon, or polyester mesh. The process starts with transferring an image to the screen, which is stretched taut over a wooden frame. You can do this a few different ways, including painting on the screen by hand, or using photo emulsion paper and shining a light on transparent paper laid on the screen. Once the image is transferred to the screen, the screen is laid down on the medium and paint is pushed through the screen with a sponge or squeegee (rubber blade). The screen is lifted off the medium and the design is printed. The same screen can then be used to make multiple copies of the design, as is typically done with T-shirts and limited-edition posters.

history

Silk-screening is a form of stenciling, an artistic technique used 4,500 years ago by the Egyptians and the Greeks, and later by the Japanese. Though a simplified screen-printing process was used in the 1800s with fabrics like organdy, the invention of the silk-screening process itself is credited to Samuel Simon, an Englishman who won a patent in 1907 for using silk as a printing screen. In 1914, John Pilsworth used the process to make prints in multiple colors in San Francisco, and by the 1930s the process was becoming widely used by graphic artists. In the 1960s, Andy Warhol created his iconic silk-screened posters of images of Marilyn Monroe, Elizabeth Taylor, and Campbell soup cans, among many other pop images, which brought the process into the forefront of the art world. These days, silk-screening is done commercially and by individual artists to print images on fabrics, ceramics, glass, paper, wood, and even different types of metals.

getting started

The best way to get started with silk-screening is to buy a kit, which contains most of what you'll need *(see resources)*. For more complicated silk-screening processes, you'll probably need to take a class. You can also consult recently produced books, videos, and websites that illustrate step-by-step instructions *(see resources)*.

- *THE MOST COMMON technique used in silk-screening is the photographic emulsion method, which you can easily do using a silk-screening kit and a few household tools. First decide what image you want to use and what medium you'll be transferring the image onto. Take whatever design or image you like to a copy store and have it printed onto transparency paper. Next, coat your screen by pouring a drop of the photo emulsion solution on one end of the bottom side of the screen, then spread it evenly and thinly over the screen with the squeegee or another type of plastic spreader. You can pour whatever excess solution you've got back into the container. Set the screen horizontally on a flat surface, bottom side down, and let it dry overnight in a dark, dry spot, like a closet.*

- *WHEN YOU'RE READY to do the transfer, it's important to set up your basic equipment first. You'll need a table and a 150-watt incandescent lightbulb, or a specialized Photoflood bulb that will hang anywhere from 12 to 17 feet (3.7 to 5.4 m) away from the screen, depending on the size of your screen. It's best to hang the bulb overhead using a utility lamp cord, but you can also use a desk lamp.*

- *NEXT, rinse the photo emulsion solution from your screen using a faucet sprayer (don't use hot water), then let it dry completely. Place black cardstock on the table, then your medium (fabric or paper) on top of that, then lower your screen onto the fabric or paper, and place a piece of glass or Plexiglas on top to hold everything in place. Let the light shine over the screen for anywhere from 45 minutes to an hour and half (again, depending on the size of your screen), then lift off the glass. Now pour your dye over the screen, and using a rubber squeegee, spread the paint all the way across the screen evenly and smoothly. This forces the ink through the screen and onto your medium. Let the paint dry overnight before framing or wearing your new piece of art.*

project: stencil a t-shirt

Since silk-screen printing is a more complicated form of simple stenciling, you can take your first baby step toward silk-screening by stenciling a design on a T-shirt. First, buy a stenciled pattern from a craft or hobby store, or if you have a design you haven't seen anywhere else, make your own stencil by carving it out on stencil paper with an X-Acto knife. Place the stencil over your T-shirt and secure it with pins or fabric tape. Using fabric paint and a roller brush, fill in the stencil design on the T-shirt, lift up the stencil, and let it dry. If anyone asks where you scored it, just tell them your shirt is a one-of-a-kind!

resources

The Complete Book of Silk Screen Printing Production, by J.I. Biegeleisen (Dover Publications, 1963).

Silk-Screen Printing for Artists and Craftsmen, by James A. Schwalbach and Mathilda V. (Dover Publications, 1981).

www.americanapparel.net: Soft, well-made tees, hoodies, and other clothing ready for silk-screening.

www.reuels.com: Silk-screening kits, materials, and step-by-step instructional books and videos are offered on this comprehensive website.

www.silkscreeningsupplies.com: Everything you need for silk-screening.

soapbox derby

THE THRILL OF RACING CARS AT THE INDY 500 can be experienced only by professional racecar drivers. For the rest of us, there's the soapbox derby, a hobby that invokes nostalgia for simpler, more carefree times. For some, the thrill comes from assembling a soapbox car; for others, it's feeling the wind blowing through their hair as they race along in a small wooden contraption with nothing but gravity pulling them.

what you'll need

- *Soapbox car kit*

- *Necessary tools may include a screw gun with Phillips bit, wrenches, pliers, vise-grips, C-clamps, and a file*

- *Wheels (if not included in kit)*

- *Paint, glue, sandpaper (for finishing the car)*

- *Helmet for safety*

resources

Soap Box Derby, by All-American Soap Box Derby (Novar Electronics Corp, 1987).

I Want to Go to . . . the All-American Soap Box Derby Race, by Kathy Johnson (Creative Image Publishers, 2003).

www.aasbd.com: The official website of the All-American Soap Box Derby, for kids ages 8 through 17.

http://waycoolkits.com: Supplier of excellent soapbox car kits.

overview

Soapbox cars, also known as billykarts, are small moving vehicles made of wood, aluminum, or fiberglass that are propelled by gravity and can reach speeds of 30 miles (48 km) per hour. Typically, the races are for kids, but adults also engage in this hobby. Once a year, the official Soap Box Derby is held in Akron, Ohio, where the winners of races across the country converge to race each other, but other derby races also take place all across the country.

In order to compete in these annual races, your soapbox cars can't cost more than $300 to build, can't have a motor, and must be equipped with four wheels and brakes. Once the driver (who cannot be older than 18) is pushed from the top of the hill, gravity does the rest of the work. Most people buy kits from hobby stores and assemble the pieces like a puzzle.

For those over 18 years old, you can most certainly help in building the car, but if you want to race you'll have to organize your own unofficial contest *(see project)*.

history

In 1933, a photographer and Ohio native named Myron Scott was assigned by the *Dayton Daily News* to find out what children were doing for fun. He found a small group of them racing cars made of crates, sheet metal, scrap wood, soapboxes, and whatever other random scraps the children had managed to collect. Soon after, Scott arranged a larger race, and the following year he decided to do it on a national level. Within a few years, largely because of Scott's influence, every state had its own soapbox derby. The winners of each race were sent to Akron to compete in a championship contest. The event is now played out in every corner of the world.

getting started

Soapbox car building is one of those hobbies best begun using kits. If you're a handy person, you might decide to experiment with the aerodynamics of a car built with real soapboxes, pallets, and wine crates. You can also look for local classes that teach soapbox car building. But for those who like the structure provided by building plans and the carefully chosen tools and materials that go with the kit, it's worth the investment. Find a reputable dealer and weigh your options, considering who will be driving this car—is it you, a kid, both? Many of the cars can carry an adult up to 200 pounds or more, so if you're inclined to race, it's your prerogative. The kits come with all the wood and hardware necessary to build the car, including screws, steering wheel, and axles, but some require you to purchase your own wheels, paint, and glue. The holes are even predrilled to make the car as simple as possible to assemble—easy enough for a kid to make, with supervision.

Car kits come in a variety of sizes and have different strengths. Some don't steer well but can speed down hills. Some are designed for paved surfaces, others for dirt. Consider where and how you'll use the car to help you choose which kit to purchase.

project: organize an adult soapbox car race

If you're older than 18 and you want to race a soapbox car, you'll have to organize your own race. The best place to start is by talking to the parents of junior soapbox racers to see if they're interested in joining a grownup race. It's your race, so you can make up the rules, but you can also consult the rule books of official kids' races for reference. Also, check with members of other organized groups around the country for ideas—in Salem, Oregon, for example, there's an annual adult soapbox race.

profile: speed racer

At the age of nine, when most kids become obsessed with video games, DAN FINK followed in the footsteps of his grandfather and his mother and started building a soapbox car with his dad. Now, with seven years of experience under his seatbelt, the clever Cleveland-based teenager races six to eight times a year, and last year qualified for a race that took him to Sioux City, Iowa. The soapbox derby bug has also bit his siblings—his younger brother and sister are racers, too. "My 10-year-old brother can put a whole car together by himself," Fink says, pointing out that while parents often serve as guides, kids end up doing a lot of the work themselves.

Though assembling a car from a kit is challenging enough, it's far easier today than 50 years ago. "Things have changed quite a bit from the time my grandpa was racing," he says. "The cars were all built from scratch then—[race organizers] just supplied the wheels and some steering

parts, but you'd have to build the car from the ground up." To put together a derby car, racers have to know how and where to place the weights that propel the car forward, how to tighten or loosen the suspension, and, most importantly, how to handle the car on steep roads. Though the contests typically last just 30 seconds, racers whiz downhill at up to 35 miles (22 km) per hour.

Apart from working on his racing skills, Fink also runs a business. The young entrepreneur found a niche in the soapbox car building market—custom-made weights—and sourced a nearby metalworker to make the steel plates, which come in a variety of sizes, and began selling them online (www.derbyweights.com). The thrill of racing a car, meeting new friends, and running a business are all enjoyable diversions, but for Fink the best part is hanging out with his father. "Just building the car with my dad is so fun," he says. "It's a total family event."

soap making

IF YOU PREFER GIVING HOMEMADE GIFTS or are really particular about your own bath products, soap making could be the right hobby for you. Easy-to-assemble kits allow you to hand-pick your favorite scent, shape, and even pattern. You'll never have to set foot in the Body Shop again.

what you'll need

- Melt-and-pour soap base
- Soap mold
- Fragrance and dye (optional)
- Knife
- Cutting board
- Scale
- Large glass measuring cup
- Double-boiler (if you use the stove)
- Measuring spoons
- Whisk
- Plastic wrap

if you like this hobby, you might enjoy:

- Aromatherapy
- Candle making (see page 52)
- Coffee roasting (see page 60)
- Making preserves (see page 136)
- Olive oil infusions (see page 154)

overview

Soap is basically made by combining fats with lye (sodium hydroxide) to create a chemical reaction called saponification. There are a few different home-making techniques to make soap. With the cold-processing method, lye is mixed with cold water and cooked fats, scents, and coloring, then blended and poured into molds. The soap takes a few weeks to cure in order to evaporate the excess moisture before it can be used. The melt-and-pour process involves, as the name suggests, melting and pouring mixtures of premade blocks of soap (glycerin is widely used with this method) and infusing the new mixture with your preferred scent. With the hot process, fats and scented oils are boiled in a solution containing lye, then salt is added and the remaining liquid is drained. Then there's rebatching, which involves chopping existing soap into small pieces, adding milk or water, and heating the mixture until it becomes thick. It's then poured into molds and cooled.

history

Evidence exists from as far back as ancient Babylonian times, around 2800 B.C.E., that some version of soap was known. Containers from that era show images that indicate fats being boiled with ashes, which contain lye. Egyptian records from around 1500 B.C.E. show that vegetable and animal oils were mixed with salt to create a soaplike material. Romans used soap in the infamous Roman baths, built around 300 B.C.E. By the 7th century in Europe, soap makers had learned to combine vegetable and animal oils with plant ashes and added scents to make something approaching a pleasant soap. Animal fats were used in most soaps until 1916, when World War I caused a shortage of fats so scientists began using synthetic ingredients, what we know as detergents, to make soaps.

getting started

For beginners, it's best to start with a kit, most of which use the melt-and-pour method with glycerin *(see resources)*. First, you'll chop the soap base into cubes, then melt the soap in a glass bowl in the microwave (though some people use Crock-Pots). You can melt as little or as much soap as you want, and the melting time will depend on how much soap you're using. Then you'll add fragrance and color, which are included in the kit, then stir the mix together thoroughly. You'll pour the mixture into soap molds (you can choose from a wide variety, from dragonflies to heart shapes to modern geometric shapes), place them in the freezer for about an hour, then take them out. The soaps should pop out of the molds easily, ready for use.

project: make a bath bomb!

While you're in the mood to make soap, add a little fizz to the cleaning process by making a bath bomb. All you need is a spray bottle filled with witch hazel, dome molds, which you can buy from soap-making suppliers *(see resources)*, baking soda, and citric acid. Combine two parts baking soda and one part citric acid, also available at soap-supply retailers and health food stores (as little or as much as you want, in those proportions) and mix them together well. If you want to add a dry colorant or fragrance, you can do that, too. Begin spraying witch hazel onto the mixture while stirring it. When it starts to stick together, it's time to press it into the molds. After a few minutes, the bombs should pop out on their own. Allow them to dry for about four hours, then you're ready to bomb your bath.

resources

Soapmaker's Companion: A Comprehensive Guide with Recipes, Techniques & Know-How, by Susan Miller Cavitch (Storey Publishing, 1997).

Essentially Soap, by Robert McDaniel (Krause Publications, 2000).

www.soapcrafters.com: Soap-making supplies.

www.sweetcakes.com: Well-designed soap molds and soap-making kits.

www.teachsoap.com: Formulas, recipes, and a colorful photo gallery.

hobby hazard:

Making soap requires handling extremely toxic substances at very high temperatures. The danger of getting burned is serious, so proceed with extreme caution.

- Always wear safety goggles, rubber gloves, a long-sleeved shirt, shoes, socks, and long pants.

- Set out and organize all your ingredients, tools, and containers before you start mixing solutions.

- When preparing caustic solutions, make sure the room you're working in is well ventilated. Even better, go outside to stir toxic contents if there's no wind.

- Keep a bottle of vinegar nearby, which will help neutralize the lye if you get it on your skin.

- Make sure there are no kids around when you're making soap. Lye can be fatal if swallowed.

- The best kinds of containers to use are made of stainless steel, enamel, plastic, or glass.

species protection

WE ALL KNOW THE IMPORTANCE OF SAVING ENDANGERED PLANTS AND ANIMALS from becoming extinct. The good news is that, though it's a big job, it can be approached in manageable ways. Each one of us can work on a daily basis in contributing to this cause, which will affect us for generations to come.

what you'll need

- Time
- Inclination
- Computer and email account

resources

The Endangered Species Act at Thirty: Vol. 1, Renewing the Conservation Promise, by Dale Goble, et al (Island Press, 2005).

The Penguin Atlas of Endangered Species: A Worldwide Guide to Plants and Animals, by Richard MacKay (Penguin, 2002).

www.audubon.org: The website of this revered organization lists how to take local steps to help the conservation cause.

www.saveourspeciesalliance.org: A grass-roots campaign that works on many levels to protect environments and species.

www.worldwildlife.org/endangered/: The organization helps to protect endangered species.

overview

The value of saving plants and animals that are in danger of becoming extinct are multifold. Humans rely on a precariously balanced ecosystem to survive. Estuaries, prairies, and forests help absorb carbon dioxide from the air, clean the water, and supply provisions. As an animal species becomes endangered or extinct, the ecosystem it inhabits undergoes a change via chain reaction. According to the U.S. Fish and Wildlife Service, if just one plant species is lost, up to 30 different plants and animals can also be threatened. The possible loss of the now-famous spotted owl foreshadowed the disappearance of old-growth forests in the Pacific Northwest, where more than 100 other species that rely on that habitat are at risk as a result of rampant logging. Due to commercial fishing practices, coral reefs all over the world are dying off and simultaneously putting the well-being of many types of sea life at risk. Thousands of books and studies have been written about the subject, but these are just a few examples.

history

Animal and wildlife preservation has been a human aspiration for centuries. St. Francis of Assisi, born in 1181 C.E., was arguably the first champion of animals. Stories about St. Francis describe him preaching to birds and taming a wild wolf, and emphasizing the need to respect all of God's creatures. In the U.S., concern for the safety and preservation of endangered species and the environment was formalized with the passage of the Endangered Species Preservation Act of 1966. Initially, the legislation was limited in its capacity to protect habitats, so another, more powerful version was created in 1969, which gave the government authority to extend land acquisition, and expanded the definition of the phrase "fish and wildlife." Another amendment was made in 1973 that broadened the act's protective powers to all wildlife and plants. Now, the act includes subspecies, races, and populations. But even before these acts were ratified, the World Wildlife Fund was formed in 1961 to protect endangered wildlife. About ten years later, the internationally known organization Greenpeace was founded in Vancouver, British Columbia. It engages in nonviolent tactics to call attention to high seas whaling, endangered species protection, and the destruction of ancient forests.

getting started

You can join organizations and community groups that work on conservation causes and help them organize petitions, rallies, and meetings to educate people. Spread the word via email and phone calls to your friends and family, and enlist their help in getting the word out. When visiting national parks, ask rangers about the endangered species on their designated land and what can be done to help protect them.

On a local and personal level, there are many specific actions you can take that will positively impact the environment and wildlife on a broader level. In your own backyard, instead of spraying weeds with pesticides, just pull them out. Try your best to conserve water by planting drought-resistant plants and taking care not to use water you don't need. Plant native species flourish in their natural environment and encourage native animals to return. Attract wildlife to your home by building or buying birdfeeders. This is just a start. See resources for many, many more ideas.

profile: one parcel at a time

When someone calls ANN BONNELL a treehugger in derision, she always answers back with a "thank you." In fact, Bonnell, a passionate conservationist who lives in Littleton, Colorado, has been known to literally hug trees she's fond of. The Ponderosa pine, for example, which is found throughout the west and smells of vanilla or butterscotch, is one of her favorites.

Her first foray into the world of wildlife activism began with the simple idea of saving beavers from being trapped in a favorite local site, Chatfield Lake. "That was my first crusade, and it was successful," she says. "I learned that you can go to the press and you can get results."

Since then, Bonnell has been a familiar face in public meetings related to wildlife in her area. As the vice president of the board of directors at the Audubon Society of Greater Denver, she's worked hard to create a buffer for the Chatfield area, participating in lawsuits to stop developers from building a brick quarry and to designate open space.

Bonnell is devoted to saving big portions of land by connecting small pieces to bigger parcels, in order to make a broad impact. "Animals have to have their native habitat, and enough of it to survive," she says. "If we keep taking a piece at a time and isolating the habitat, and they can't exchange DNA, they get isolated. That's what causes extinction. It's not just saving one species, it's saving diversity."

project: plant a tree

Planting a tree goes a long way toward attracting wildlife and improving the quality of the air. First, choose one that you know grows well in your neighborhood, ideally an indigenous species. The best times to plant a tree are spring and fall to avoid extreme temperatures. The most important part of planting a tree is to dig the right type of hole—if it's too narrow, it won't allow roots to grow, and if it's too deep, the roots won't get enough oxygen. Make the hole about three times the diameter of the tree's rootball or of its container. Break up the hard soil around the edges of the hole so it'll be easier for the roots to expand. Remove the tree from the container and examine the roots. With your fingers, gently loosen tight clumps. Place the tree inside the hole and fill the remainder of the hole with compost-rich soil, which will help the tree stay healthy and grow quickly. Don't forget to water the tree once a week for the first two years while the tree's root system becomes established, after which time you can water less frequently.

> **"We have to somehow slow down the materialism and the consumption. You can start small: donate your used things to Goodwill."**

stained glass

IF THE VIEWS OUT YOUR WINDOWS AREN'T AS FETCHING as, say, a gorgeous stained glass design, maybe it's time to consider this hobby. The process is not as cumbersome as you might think. Piece together a lovely coastal vignette or a Frank Lloyd Wright—inspired geometric design and hang it in your window, and you'll find your eyes repeatedly drawn to the view.

what you'll need

- *Colored glass*
- *Pattern*
- *Glass cutter and glass cutter oil*
- *Pliers (specialized pliers for breaking scored glass are available and are very helpful)*
- *Soldering iron, solder wire, flux, and a flux brush*
- *Copper foil tape, with an adhesive back (wide enough to cover the edges of the glass pieces and hang over a small amount—¼ inch, or 64 mm, is a typical width)*
- *Copper wire*
- *Straightedge or ruler*

resources

Stained Glass: Step by Step, by Patricia Ann Daley (Hand Books Press, 2003).

Basic Stained Glass Making: All the Skills and Tools You Need to Get Started, by Eric Ebeling (Stackpole Books, 2003).

www.glassmart.com: Stained glass tools.

www.stainedglass.org: The Stained Glass Association of America's website, with links to a periodical, discussion forums, and a list of members.

overview

Making stained glass is like putting together a puzzle, only first you have to make all the puzzle pieces out of glass, then attach the pieces together. Stained glass projects can include windows, lampshades, candleholders, or sun-catchers, but beginners should probably start with flat projects before going into three-dimensional sculptures.

We've all seen stained glass—in churches, Arts and Crafts—era houses, and those famous Tiffany lamps (and infamous "Tiffany-style" ones). To make it, colored glass pieces are put together to form a picture or an abstract design. Many different kinds of glass can be used, ranging from uniform, transparent pieces to artisan glasses with textures and patterned effects, and even opalescent or smoky opaque glass.

There are two methods of creating stained glass: One involves using copper foil tape and solder to bond the pieces of glass, and the other makes use of a preformed border called lead came. Beginners often start with the copper tape and solder method because it's easier and more forgiving, as solder can fill in gaps between the cut glass shapes.

history

The oldest piece of glass dates to ancient Egypt, between 2750 and 2600 B.C.E. By 100 C.E., Romans were making windows with stained glass for the villas and palaces of the wealthy. Stained glass appeared in the Byzantine, Moorish, and Arabian empires in the 10th century. With the growth in power and influence of the Christian religion, decorative stained glass windows became highly popular in churches.

In modern history, Louis Comfort Tiffany is recognized as a celebrated stained glass artist of the late 1800s and early 1900s whose lamps and leaded glass windows are prized collectors' items and displayed in museums. Frank Lloyd Wright, a seminal 20th-century architect, is another important stained glass artisan whose work epitomizes modern geometric stained glass design.

getting started

Completing even simple stained glass projects can require the assistance of a guide or tutor the first time around, so consult a book or website *(see resources)* or sign up for a class at a local art school or community college. For context, here are the basic steps for making a small stained glass panel.

First, choose a design that has only straight lines—cutting glass into curved pieces is tricky and involves either grinding (with a motorized glass grinder) or grozing (nibbling the glass into shape with special pliers).

Make two copies of the design, one in the actual size of your planned project that is drawn on a piece of thick paper, and a second copy (which can be smaller) for reference. Cut the life-size design into pieces to use as templates as you cut the glass.

Place a portion of the paper template on the color of glass you want for that piece. Wearing safety glasses, use a straightedge and a glass cutter to score the glass along a single line, running the cutter along the length of the glass, from edge to edge. Make sure to use the glass cutter oil (some cutters have a reservoir to automatically lubricate the cutter). Once the glass is scored, align the score line with the edge of a table and use pliers to break the glass along the score. Repeat this process for each side of the glass shape.

Once all the glass pieces have been cut to size, arrange them in the planned pattern to make sure they fit together. Make any adjustments needed so that they do.

Wrap copper foil around all the edges of each shape. The foil should uniformly overlap onto the front and back of the glass. Using a credit card or small piece of cardboard, smooth the foil against the glass. After applying the foil, put the glass pieces back together and begin soldering them in place.

Using a soldering iron and solder, "tack" the pieces together with small dots of solder—this will hold the pieces in place while you work. Be sure to apply flux with the flux brush to each spot you are going to solder.

To finish the stained glass panel, solder each seam between pieces, melting a uniform line of solder in between and on top of the copper foil. Once the entire panel is soldered, flip it over and repeat the process on the other side of the panel.

Attach loops of copper wire to the top using solder. You can use these to hang the stained glass.

project: faux stained glass window

If you want instant gratification (and promise you'll do the real deal later), here's how to make a quick-and-dirty stained glass window, using an old wood window.

1) First, make yourself a life-size design on heavyweight paper that exactly fits each pane of the window.

2) Gently use sandpaper or a wire brush to remove loose paint from the window frame. Clear away any paint or dust and clean the glass with glass cleaner. Tape the design to the back of the glass (and to each pane, if the window has more than one).

3) Tape the patterns in the position where you want them, attaching them to the back of the windowpanes, so you can see the designs from the front.

4) Lay the window on a flat surface and apply simulated leading (sometimes called "liquid lead") along all the lines in your design. Make sure there is a line of leading between each section of the design that will be a different color.

5) After the liquid leading has dried, use glass paint to color each shape outlined by the leading.

stargazing

LOOK UP IN THE SKY! Is that a bird, a plane, or a falling star? The universe puts on a spectacular performance every night, just at the time we're used to closing our doors and windows and turning on the television. Forget *American Idol*—the cosmos offers a much more entertaining spectacle for your enjoyment.

what you'll need

- *Telescope*
- *7-power binoculars*
- *Red filtered flashlight*
- *Constellation guide or sky chart*
- *Chair*
- *A clear view, and as dark a night as possible*

resources

Stargazing: Astronomy without a Telescope, by Patrick Moore (Cambridge University Press, 2000).

Simple Stargazing, by Anton Vamplew (Collins, 2006).

http://curious.astro.cornell.edu/stargazing.php: Cornell University offers tips and helpful information.

http://skymaps.com: Vendor of beginner's guidebooks, astro calendars, and telescopes.

www.wunderground.com: Type in your zip code and see what the constellations will look like from your vantage point.

overview

Stargazing is super simple: Just walk outside at night and observe the sky. Stargazers can use binoculars or telescopes to focus in on specific planets, stars, the moon, and other celestial bodies. Because of the Earth's rotation, we can see different things from the same position on different nights. There are 88 constellations, and on a clear and moonless night, you can see more than a thousand stars, depending on your location. You can see five of the solar system's nine planets, star clusters, and galaxies, as well as comets.

Planets, which appear to move through the constellations, can be tracked with the use of maps, available online or in books or magazines. Stargazers can also be treated to meteor showers, which look like fireworks, can last for hours, and are caused by the Earth's movement through the orbit of a comet's "debris." Comets can be seen without telescopes, but are rare.

Stargazing is getting more difficult for those without telescopes because of an increase in light pollution. In cities, lights left on all night long, even when not necessary, make it impossible to see much more than the very brightest celestial bodies.

history

Astronomy is perhaps the oldest form of science, going back to the Babylonians, who studied celestial bodies back in 2000 B.C.E. The ancient Greeks contributed to the development of astrological science with their theories about the Earth's relation to the universe. Understanding astrology was the first step in learning about astronomy. During the 2nd century C.E., Ptolemy developed the model of Earth as the center of the universe, which was accepted as the truth for more than 1,300 years, until Nicolaus Copernicus entered the picture in the 1500s and convinced the world that the sun was actually the center the universe and the Earth and other planets revolved around it. Galileo's improvements to the newly invented telescope in the early 1600s led to many more discoveries about the celestial movements and positions. In the 1950s, satellites launched into outer space gave astronomers an even better understanding of the worlds beyond Earth's orbit.

getting started

It's important to find a good spot for stargazing. For those living in dense, urban areas, this might be difficult, but it'll be worth it to get away to the top of a hilly residential neighborhood. The sky changes every night, so for beginners it's best to get started by finding the brightest stars and constellations. To help you identify what you see, you can print out an image of the night sky from your own vantage point, which is available on a number of websites. Look for groupings like the Big Dipper, Little Dipper, and Orion, and, from there, the North Star. Once you find one major constellation, you can look for the others in relation to its position. Consult your map on where to quickly find the easiest ones first. If you feel you're ready to take it to the next level and would like to purchase a telescope, there are three basic kinds to choose from for this purpose: a refracting telescope, which has a convex lens on one side and an eyepiece on the other; a reflecting telescope, which uses a concave mirror; and a catadi-optric telescope, a type of reflecting telescope that uses a correcting lens. For beginners, choose a simple but good-quality model. If you want to expand your knowledge—and enjoy the opportunity of viewing the night sky through the more powerful telescope of a more advanced stargazer—join a stargazing organization for regular outings.

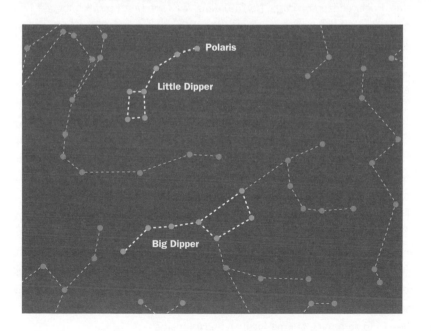

project: build a telescope

You don't have to spend hundreds of dollars to get a closer look at meteors and falling stars. You can build a telescope with a few simple tools. You'll need a large convex lens and a small concave lens, and two different sizes of cardboard tubes that fit into each other and that can accommodate the lenses (you can buy these at hobby stores). To measure where to place the lenses in relation to each other, look through the concave lens, hold the convex lens behind it, and try to focus on a distant object. Measure that distance, then double it to calculate the length of the tubes. Place the convex lens on the wide end of the tube and fasten it in place using epoxy. Place the concave lens on the other end of the tube, which will serve as your scope. You can use pieces of Styrofoam to snugly fit the smaller piece. When the pieces are perfectly aligned with the center of each lens placed directly in the middle of the tube, you should be able to see the stars.

storm chasing

LIGHTNING BOLTS FLASH, THUNDER JOLTS THE GROUND, a tornado spirals through town—it's nature's most dramatic show. You can watch it transpire on the Weather Channel, or you can jump in your car and see these astounding sights with your own eyes. You will be humbled by Mother Nature's inarguable supremacy.

what you'll need

- Mode of transportation, preferably a four-wheel-drive vehicle to access muddy roads

- Camera (still or video)

- Weather radio or access to internet

- Police scanner

- Small TV

- First-aid kit

- Road maps and atlases or GPS tracking system

- Two-way radio for communicating with other chasers

resources

Big Weather: Chasing Tornadoes in the Heart of America, by Mark Svenvold (Henry Holt, 2005).

Storm Chasing Handbook, by Tim Vasquez (Weather Graphics Technologies, 2002).

www.cloud9tours.com: Offers storm-chasing excursions around Tornado Alley.

www.nssl.noaa.gov: The National Severe Storms Laboratory's site explains weather patterns and phenomena in detail.

www.stormtrack.org: The website for the newsletter started by David Hoadley (see history). Everything a beginner storm chaser needs to know.

overview

Storm chasing involves tracking weather systems and following storms as they approach. The fact that the hobby requires the storm chaser be in the center of a violent weather system makes it a somewhat dangerous recreational activity. Storm chasers consider exposure to extreme weather and scary road conditions all just part of the fun. They often drive thousands of miles to witness quickly changing weather, racing to arrive in time. Though they're not meteorologists, storm chasers have spent a lot of time learning about storm movements and track weather conditions for days in advance. The busiest time and place to view storms are the months of May and June across the Great Plains.

history

The pioneers of storm chasing were scientists who studied volatile weather systems. Roger Jensen of Fargo, North Dakota, was the first known hobbyist hurricane chaser. He began pursuing Minnesota storms in the early 1950s. A few years later, another North Dakota native, David Hoadley, took up the pursuit, using information from local weather bureaus. Oklahoma meteorologist Neil Ward collaborated with the state police, who helped him study and track storms.

In an effort to better predict storms and warn people of their approach, the federal government began to focus on the issue in 1952. The Weather Bureau's Severe Storm Forecasting Unit in Washington, D.C., enlisted volunteers to help them find and track storms. In 1964, the National Severe Storms Laboratory was created in conjunction with the University of Oklahoma to take on a formalized study of such weather patterns. In 1977, David Hoadley started Stormtrack, a bimonthly newsletter for the community of likeminded hobbyists. Despite having a fair number of followers, storm chasing remained a relatively obscure pastime until the release of the movie Twister in 1996, after which the hobby exploded into the public arena. The Weather Channel and websites that track weather systems also contribute to the fascination. The invention of the Doppler radar, which is radar that uses the Doppler effect to measure velocity, has also helped storm chasers to determine storms' location and intensity.

getting started

The first thing you'll need to do is learn how to forecast storms. Those who can reliably predict storms can arrive in time to watch the best part: the brewing. Sometimes computer models can be inaccurate and cause chasers to actually miss the storms, so it's important to broaden your own knowledge of meteorology. During your studies, start connecting with experienced storm chasers to learn about different tactics and techniques.

In most cases, chasers have about a day's notice if they carefully monitor forecasts. Severe weather patterns are formed with the right combination of lift, wind shear, moisture, and instability. When all the ingredients are there, chasers can target exact areas by looking at weather maps and satellite pictures and, if they're in the right spot, simply by looking up at the sky. The dangers related to this hobby are numerous. Apart from having to drive in extreme conditions, there's the chance of being hit by lightning, struck by huge hailstones, swept away in a flash flood, trampled by frightened livestock, or overturned in your car by gusty winds. Chasers accept the possibility of some of those hazards by putting themselves near the storm. But if you're cautious, drive slowly on wet roads, and keep an eye out for obstacles, a lot of dangers can be averted.

project: keep a weather diary

Successful storm chasers must understand how weather works. What better way to build a foundation of meteorology than by keeping tabs on conditions in your own backyard? Here's some advice on keeping a weather diary:

- Look up! Take note of the sorts of clouds or fog you see.
- What's the temperature? A maximum/minimum thermometer will track the highs and lows of the day. How humid is the air? Measure the amount of rain with a rain gauge.
- Post an anemometer to measure wind speed and direction.
- Check the barometer, which measures air pressure—an important indicator of weather systems.

profile: in search of the squall

On May 29, 2001, in the Texas panhandle, CHRIS KRIDLER witnessed a remarkable sight: a giant, revolving storm that looked like a rotating wedding cake "lit brilliant orange by the sun." "I've never seen anything like it," says the veteran storm chaser, who's been trailing tempests for 10 seasons. "The whole storm was a spinning top." Her car has been battered by hail the size of softballs that left the body dented and the windows and taillights shattered. "The barrage was preceded by a gorgeous white tornado, which lessened the pain a little," she says.

On another chase in 2004, Kridler and her buddies watched a tornado as it lifted the roof off a house, utterly destroying it. Later that day, as they were pursuing a large tornado, they looked around and saw that they had satellite tornadoes to the north and south of them. Which way to go? "For a few moments, I was wondering if we were going to have to get into a ditch," she says. Thankfully, the tornadoes cleared and they zipped out of danger.

> "Beginning chasers should learn as much as they can about storms and how they behave. A wrong move can put you in danger, and not just from tornadoes—hail, lightning, flooding, and other hazards can ruin your day."

Though she says these incidents are exhilarating, storm chasing is "not about the thrill." "The most rewarding element of chasing is experiencing the storms in their infinite variety. Every one is different, and they can be breathtaking," she says.

tarot card reading

READING TAROT CARDS REQUIRES A BIT OF FAITH IN THE PARANORMAL, or at the very least in your ability to intuit meaning from symbols. You certainly don't have to be Nostradamus—all you need is some understanding of the meaning behind the cards and a willing participant. The cards reveal the information—it's just a matter of being open to receiving it.

what you'll need

- Tarot cards
- Open mind
- Receiver (this can be yourself)

overview

There are two participants in tarot card reading: the reader and the receiver. The receiver chooses cards from the tarot deck, which are interpreted by the reader. There are typically 78 cards in a deck, which is divided into two parts: the Major Arcana, which has 21 trump cards plus the Fool card, and the Minor Arcana, which has 56 cards divided into four suits. The suits are cups, coins (or pentacles), batons (also called wands, rods, or staves), and swords.

Each suit has an ace and four court cards (king, queen, knight, and page, the equivalent of traditional deck's jack). The receiver picks a succession of cards, each of which symbolizes something in that person's life. For example, picking the Fool signifies new beginnings, either spiritual or physical, a new life cycle. It's associated with happiness and optimism and lucky accidents. But if it's upside down when picked from the deck, it symbolizes instability and foolishness. The meaning is interpreted according to both the card's face and its position (upright or reversed) when it was picked.

history

Most people agree that tarot cards originated in northern Italy in the 1400s. They began as an addition to a traditional set of playing cards—a queen for each court and 22 unsuited cards with symbolic pictures of such aspects of life as the Wheel of Fortune, Death, the Moon, and the Pope. As in the game of bridge, the cards were used as trumps that outranked all the other suits. The game was popular with the wealthy classes, and it spread to neighboring countries. As it changed hands, new symbols were added and rules were changed, varying the ranks of the cards. A few hundred years later, magicians in France and England started to divine supernatural meaning in tarot cards, which brings us to the present-day practice.

getting started

- *THE FIRST THING you need is a deck of tarot cards and a dependable reference book. You can find one online and at stores that sell games or mystical items. There is a wide variety of artwork available in tarot cards, so choose one that appeals to you on a spiritual level, one you think you might form a trusting relationship with. Conduct a small blessing ritual of your deck, and clean it with a scarf or other fabric. You can use the same cloth to cover your cards when you're finished with the reading. Some advise "seasoning" the deck by placing it near where you sleep.*

- *WHEN YOU'RE READY to read, ask yourself a question and concentrate on it as you shuffle the deck. Then cut the deck and put together the tarot spread. There are many arrangements to choose from; an easy one to start with is to place four cards in a diamond shape.*

- *NOW IT'S TIME to interpret the cards. Many readers subscribe to the following reading: the top of the diamond represents the romantic aspect of your life, the one in the middle right symbolizes money issues, the bottom card represents health, and the one on the left indicates career and work. Assuming that you're reading for yourself, the ones that are right side up facing you are in the positive position, while those upside down are reversed. You can either choose to avoid or encourage reversed cards by how you face them before you shuffle. Refer to a guide (see resources) to interpret what each card indicates.*

resources

Tarot for the Beginner: A Simple & Easy Step-by-Step Guide to Reading the Tarot Cards in One Hour or Less!, by Dayle Schear, Dayle (Blue Dolphin Publishing, 1994).

The Enchanted Tarot: Book and Cards, by Amy Zerner and Monte Farber (St. Martin's Press, 1990).

www.bewitchingways.com/tarot/class/intro.htm: A step-by-step guide to reading tarot cards.

www.paranormality.com: Find out the meaning behind each card on this comprehensive site.

project: conduct a reading

When you feel confident enough to pass along the benefits of your skill and intuition to others, you can offer to conduct a reading for a friend. Find a quiet room away from outside noise and spread a cloth out on a table, then cleanse the space with either sage, incense, or candles.

Place your cards on the table and ask your receiver to shuffle the deck so she feels she's got her own personal energy working on those cards. (Some readers prefer that they be the only ones to touch the cards so that their aura is not diluted.) Next consider your preferred methodology. You can ask your recipient to either cut the deck, after which you will deal the spread, choosing cards from the top, middle, or bottom of the deck—or whatever way you decide will yield the most telling results. Ask your recipient to focus on the question as you're interpreting the cards, and to take notes in order to remember important points from your reading. Remember, the Major Arcana cards are the most significant ones, so pay close attention to those particular cards.

At the end of the reading, sum everything up in a clear and concise way for the recipient, and allow her to ask any questions she might have. If you have intuited an answer, offer what your reading of the cards has revealed to you.

taxidermy

THIS HOBBY IS NOT FOR THE FAINT OF STOMACH, but for those who have high tolerance for gore and a scientific bent taxidermy can provide a fascinating look into animal anatomy. For hunters, taxidermy is a natural extension of the activity and a way to provide a dignified perch for the animal in its afterlife.

what you'll need

- *Taxidermy tool set that includes scalpel, surgeon's scissors, hook and chain, forceps, pinning needle, and brain and eye hook*
- *Taxidermy kit*
- *Tanning kit*
- *Designated workroom*

resources

Home Book of Taxidermy and Tanning, by Gerald Grants (Stackpole Books, 1985).

Taxidermy Guide, by Russell Tinsley (Stoeger Publishing Company, 1990).

www.learn-taxidermy.com: Step-by-step instructions, as well as video instructional guides for sale.

www.taxidermy.net: Forums, suppliers, and books.

www.vandykestaxidermy.com: Taxidermy kits and other supplies.

overview

Taxidermy is the art of mounting or preserving a dead animal for display. It is practiced mostly with vertebrates, though insects and other invertebrates are sometimes mounted as well.

The process entails freezing the animal's carcass, carefully removing the skin, then immersing the internal muscles and bones in plaster of paris to create a cast. The cast is then used to create a fiberglass replica of the animal, which is then recovered with the animal's tanned and treated skin or fur. A simpler method is to place the skin on a standard model or form. Taxidermy teeth and eyes, which are typically made of glass, are then attached to the mount.

Freeze drying is another, newer technique used by taxidermists. This process removes the moisture from the frozen carcass, keeping the muscles from collapsing and shrinking. Without the moisture (the element that keeps bacteria alive), the mount can't rot. Freeze-drying businesses also inject preservatives into the body to repel bugs and moths. The animals don't need to be skinned with this process. The result is a fairly accurate replica of the live animal, and the mounts last just as long as with the traditional method.

history

Hunters and gatherers were the first kind of taxidermists—they discovered that the skin of the animals could be used for making clothes, housing, and containers. By the 19th century, hunters would bring their trophies straight to the tanner, who would stuff the animal, preparing it to be displayed. This practice resulted in some dreadful-looking mounts. In the early 1900s, American professional taxidermist Carl Akeley and other likeminded scientists perfected the taxidermy process by paying careful attention to re-creating all the animals' parts through anatomically correct methods. The mounts were also placed in lifelike environments to evoke a look of authenticity. British explorer Captain James Cook, who traveled the world in the 18th century, brought home taxidermied species, and British naturalist Charles Darwin used taxidermy to preserve species he found on his epic voyages on the Beagle in the 1830s. Today, taxidermists always attempt to create the most realistic version of the animals—both inside and out—through the use of modern materials.

getting started

For neophyte taxidermists, it's best to get started by observing a taxidermy class or instructional video. In class, tools for you to use are typically provided, and an instructor walks you through the complex process step by step. Attending a class will also allow you to discover just how squeamish you are about cutting open an animal before you decide to invest in your own taxidermy setup. If you feel you are ready, first decide what animal you want to start with and research the kinds of tools you'll need. If you've got a specific animal in mind, look for a retailer that sells taxidermy kits by animal category *(see resources)*. You'll find kits for deer antlers, squirrels, game birds, geese, bobcats, red foxes, raccoons, coyotes, and even turkeys. The kits come with explicit instructions, as well as pickling and tanning solutions (types of acids), earliners, eyes, hangers, clay, hide paste, and a mount. All you add is the skin from your hunting trip.

profile: wild about animals

In the Texas wilderness, handling dead animals is not as taboo as it is in other parts of the country. Hunting is a popular hobby, and taxidermy is the next logical step after coming home with the prize. So when TIM MUTINA began dabbling in taxidermy more than 22 years ago, it was a natural extension of hunting. "I've always been a hunter and a fisherman, and that sort of grew into wanting to re-create the animals and bring them back to life," says the resident of West Columbia, Texas.

For someone who loves wildlife as much as Mutina, taxidermy is a way to ensure the hunted animals their dignity. He is repulsed when he sees an animal that "doesn't even look like what it is" mounted on a wall, and takes pride in achieving the detail work that really makes the animals look alive. "Some people might not view it as an art form, but I think it really is," he says. "Just like pencil drawings of wildlife, you really have to have an eye for it." What he calls the finishing work is the most challenging—and artistic—part of taxidermy. "You have to sculpt back the muscles that were there to make the animal look alive, airbrush paint onto certain animals, and that's where the art comes in. The nose, the eyes, the color of the animal all have to resemble the animal when it was alive," he says.

Mutina has probably mounted 400 or 500 animals over the years, most of them in his garage. Though it can be gory, Mutina is not fazed. "It's a labor of love for me," he says.

project: clean your mount

Now that you've done the hard work of mounting, the time will soon come to groom your model for presentation. (Keep it in a cool, dry place, away from direct sunlight.) When it's time to clean, don't break out the vacuum. Instead, dust as well as you can with a feather duster in the direction of the fur or plumage. The more frequently you do this, the more you'll discourage vermin from visiting. If the feathers get ruffled, you can steam them to help flatten and smooth them down by aiming the steam from a boiling kettle of water directly at the mount and stroking the features with a piece of fabric.

If pesky insects come calling, you can use an insecticide in the room (ask a taxidermy specialist or supplier what type is most appropriate for your specific mount) or you can put the mount in a plastic bag along with moth crystals and leave it in there for a week. And if all else fails, have a professional fumigator take over the task.

> "find a good mentor who practices the proper techniques and learn it the right way from the beginning."

topiary

THERE'S SOMETHING ABOUT METICULOUSLY GROOMED TOPIARY that evokes a civilized, aristocratic lifestyle. Perhaps it's because they are found in the formal gardens of British estates, on the grounds of elegant French chateaux, and in Martha Stewart's backyard. Whether it's a rabbit made of boxwood or an enormous ball made out of holly, you can shape a living plant into almost any form that strikes your fancy.

what you'll need

- Potted plant
- Topiary frames
- Sharp shears, pruners, and scissors
- Wire and wire cutters
- String for guiding straight edges
- Wooden stakes for support
- Ties
- Sphagnum moss (optional)

overview

Topiary is the art of pruning trees, shrubs, or plants into decorative shapes. Plants commonly used include boxwood, bay laurel, holly, myrtle, ivy, yew, and privet. Topiary plants held in smaller containers include herbs like rosemary, French lavender, scented geranium, lemon eucalyptus, and thyme. They can be bought already shaped or you can start with a natural plant and train it yourself. The plants need consistent watering, monthly slow-release fertilizing, and careful trimming to keep their shape and to thrive.

history

The ancient Greeks are said to have been the first to develop the art of topiary. They pruned evergreen trees and shrubs into cones, columns, and spires that complemented their ornate buildings. The Romans picked up the topiary practice, and by the 1st century C.E. the gardens of the wealthy were filled with living plant sculptures. Pliny the Younger, a writer who lived from 62 to 110 C.E., describes shrubs cut into figures, boxes, and letters. Topiary sprang back up again during the Renaissance. Italian gardens in the 1600s were designed with boxed bushes and shrubbery, while the French preferred more elaborate patterns evocative of embroidery. English gardeners wove together thyme, germander, rosemary, and other herbs into tidy little designs. Topiary peaked in the 17th and 18th centuries, when the gardens of aristocrats were bedecked with bushes shaped into ships, hounds, and hunters. Though different design trends have waxed and waned over the centuries, the art form has persevered.

resources

Quick and Easy Topiary and Green Sculpture: Create Traditional Effects with Fast-Growing Climbers and Wire Frames, by Jenny Hendy (Storey Publishing, 1996).

Topiary and the Art of Training Plants, by David Joyce (Firefly Books, 2000).

http://timelesstopiary.com: Tips and facts about topiary.

www.treehelp.com: All sorts of topiary pruning and shearing tools.

getting started

- *START WITH a small potted plant with a promising full shape for sculpting. You may have to wait a bit to get started. If it's a slow-growing plant with small leaves (English boxwood, for example), it should be about a foot tall before you begin; if it's a fast-growing one (a creeping fig, for example), you should let it grow to at least a foot and a half. Put a stake alongside the plant and tie it to the stake with a piece of string. When you see the plant starting to grow new shoots along the lower sides of the trunk, cut them off immediately to ensure that the plant grows vertically, not horizontally. Make sure the plant is getting sufficient sunlight and growing evenly. Water and feed your plant with fertilizer regularly.*

- *NOW CHOOSE the design for your topiary—a sphere, a box, or a pyramid are all easy ways to go for beginners. Start pinching out the tip of the trunk (that means removing the new growth with your fingers), and allow only three new branches to grow at a time so you can carefully monitor and control their growth. Over time, the trunk will grow long and thicken. Pinch the tips of new growths to direct them in the way you want them to grow. If you're training vines, keep the shoots tucked inside the form.*

project: make a standing topiary

You don't have to start with live plants or flowers to make an eye-pleasing topiary. Dried flower topiaries are a long-lasting and lower-maintenance option. To make standing topiary with dried lavender, collect a large bunch of lavender and hold it upright. Using twine, bind the herbs together tightly around the middle of the stems and test the bundle to see if it can stand on its own. Now, just put the bundle in a basket that is roughly as deep as half the length of the stems, and garnish the basket with tiny roses or baby's breath around the bottom of the basket.

gardens to visit:
Visit any one of these renowned topiary gardens and you'll see why this form of garden art has endured through the centuries.

CHATEAU VERSAILLES
The gardens of this magnificent chateau outside Paris warrant an entire day to explore, so consider skipping the indoor tour. The elaborately designed hedges are laid out in geometric patterns that can be appreciated as much from an aerial point of view as from the ground.
Versailles, France (33-1) 30 83 77 89
www.chateauversailles.fr

GREEN ANIMALS TOPIARY GARDEN
Just outside Newport, Rhode Island, you'll find a whole menagerie of topiary animals, as well as other elaborate topiary sculptures.
Portsmouth, RI (401) 847-1000
www.newportmansions.org

LADEW TOPIARY GARDENS
These gardens span 22 acres and feature walking trails, Italian-style garden "rooms," beautiful flower gardens, and what has been called the best topiary garden in America.
Monkton, MD (410) 557-9466
www.ladewgardens.com

LEVENS HALL AND GARDENS
For visitors to the English Lake District, this 17th-century garden boasts magnificent topiaries in an idyllic setting that has remained almost unchanged for 300 years.
Lake District, U.K. 44 (0)15395 60582
www.levenshall.co.uk

LOTUS LAND
Within this 37-acre estate and botanic garden is a "zoo" of 26 topiary animals, including a camel, giraffe, gorilla, and seal. You'll also find a boxwood maze, and enormous topiary chess pieces.
Santa Barbara, CA (805) 969-3767
www.lotusland.org

train- and planespotting

SOME PEOPLE LIKE TO COLLECT MATERIAL THINGS *(see Collecting)* **and some, like train- and plane-spotters, like to collect experiences. For these hobbyists, a comprehensive knowledge of their most beloved transportation mode is ample reward. Like avid birdwatchers, the notebook that holds the list of all the models they've seen is more valuable than anything they could buy.**

what you'll need

- *Mode of transport to railroad tracks, railway station, or airport for best viewing*
- *Camera*
- *Notebook*
- *Pencil*

resources

Spotting Planes, by Bill Gunston (Gloucester Press, 1979).

North American Railyards, by Michael Rhodes (MBI, 2003).

www.airliners.net: Photos and articles about everything related to airplanes.

www.jetphotos.net: Videos, photos, and forums for jet lovers.

www.railcams.com: Watching trains from the comfort of your home.

overview

Trainspotting is enjoyed by railroad fans who take great pleasure in watching the passing of trains and locomotives. They're drawn in by the romance of riding the rails and wish to relive the glory days when railroads were the most efficient form of transport. They want to see as many different varieties of train as possible and become knowledgeable in the way they operate. They take note of serial numbers and list the models they spot in a notebook. They learn about all the different parts of the train and detail information about how they move, what equipment they're carrying, and what their destinations are. Though the spotting part of the hobby may draw the rail fan in, typically it's photographing trains that keeps them interested. Documentation is key.

Hobbyists engage in planespotting for the sheer joy of watching aircraft fly—this might be any type of craft, be it jet planes, helicopters, gliders, or even hot-air balloons. The aim here is to spot as many different types of planes as possible, and if it means traveling from airport to airport to see them, that's all part of the pleasure. They also like to document the evidence by taking photos, filming, sketching, or otherwise capturing the aircraft they've seen. The information can be shared with others on websites and online forums. Another way to see airplanes in action is at organized air shows, where professional pilots fly historic aircraft or new jets perform tricks.

history

Planespotting started as an effort by civilians who volunteered to look for enemy aircraft during World War II. That was the case in England, during the Battle of Britain, as well as in cities and states across the U.S., such as in Connecticut, where thousands of people took shifts on airplane-spotting towers to warn their fellow citizens if enemy aircraft approached. Each tower was typically manned around the clock by volunteers who were told to report to the local military if they observed enemy planes heading in their direction.

Trainspotting had a completely recreational origin. People have been spotting trains since the invention of the locomotive in the 1700s, purely for pleasure.

getting started

Trainspotting and planespotting are very similar hobbies. For each mode of transport, spotters need to find the best location for viewing purposes. At the railway station, that will most likely be on the platform, where you can closely inspect the trains during their stops. Take your notebook and camera with you and jot down the details of what you see: any serial numbers, the colors, the model and type, whether it's a passenger or cargo train, where it's headed, and anything else you find interesting or important.

For planespotting, head to your nearest airport and perch yourself close to one or more of the runways (in between runways would be ideal). As you watch these graceful machines take flight and land, take note of their physical features: the type; the model number; the number and position of the engines; the kinds of wings, their relation to the fuselage, and their movement; the location of the tailplane; the speed in the air or on the runway; the name of the carrier; and even the plane's colors. Check to see if you can spot the cockpit and the pilots. You can also try listening for air-traffic control commands on a radio. When you see the perfect shot of the plane ascending into the sunset, snap your photo.

project: look for an airbus airliner

Intrigued by planespotting? Try your hand at recognizing the Airbus Industrie, a twin-engine jet with a wide body.

Go to your nearest airport and find a good location for watching airplanes. Airbus airliners will be fairly easy to spot because of their wide structure—they're around 18 feet (5.5 m) across. They also have extremely large fuselages in contrast to their wings. Each model has its own distinguishing features. The A-320 is short and smaller than the A-310, which can accommodate up to 170 passengers. The largest models are the A-330 and A-340, and the latter has four engines.

profile: plane fun

For some people, the white-knuckle thrill of flying in an airplane is quite enough excitement, thank you. But for the likes of PHIL DERNER, JR., of New York City, it's just a small part of the vast joy of all things aeronautic. It's not just flying that delights him. Derner and his ilk will get excited about watching an American Airlines 767-300 land at New York's La Guardia Airport (those are unique at that particular landing field). Binoculars in hand, zoom lenses focused, they're perennially on the lookout for new paint schemes on jets, new routes for airliners, and different landing patterns. "Any chance for a special photo opportunity gets our blood jumping," he says.

Derner's love of airplanes emerged at a young age, when from his third-story window in Queens he watched the activities at runway 13/31 at La Guardia through the trees. At age nine, the lucky kid got to walk a mechanic's clipboard over to the cockpit and relay an important message to the pilots: "No ice." "I remained calm, as though this was normal duty for me," he says. "The pilots showed me how the plane flew, the actions of the yoke, and I assured them that I knew what the yoke did. Derner's fascination grew into a consuming hobby, motivating him to found NYCAviation.com, an airplane enthusiast's website. Derner and his colleagues congregate in public spaces near major airports (some airport management officials don't allow photography on airport grounds or in the terminals, especially after the 9/11 attacks). "Aviation enthusiasm was greatly affected in the wake of the terrible attacks," he says. But on the five-year anniversary of the tragedy, Derner showed up at La Guardia Airport's Planeview Park shortly after sunrise; a few hours later he was joined by 19 others. "People from here in New York stood beside friends from England, Germany, and the Ukraine to share in their passion," he says.

treasure hunting

YOU NEVER KNOW where a good treasure hunt will take you. You may end up in your backyard or, if you're game, clear across the country. You might find a valuable prize or simply take satisfaction in knowing you achieved a goal. The true joy, of course, is in the hunt itself.

what you'll need

- Puzzle or hunt
- GPS system (for geocaching)
- Mode of transport
- Metal detector
- Camera

resources

Treasure and Scavenger Hunts: How to Plan, Create, and Give Them!, by Gordon Burgett (Communication Unlimited, 2005).

The Essential Guide to Geocaching: Tracking Treasure with Your GPS, by Mike Dyer (Fulcrum Publishing, 2004).

www.geocaching.com: Type in your zip code and learn about caches in your area.

www.theproblemsite.com/treasure_hunt: Email your contact information, and you'll be connected to the next big hunt.

www.treasureclub.net: An armchair treasure hunt club based in both the U.S. and U.K., with a fascinating newsletter.

overview

Treasure hunting is a game that requires one or more players to look for hidden "treasures" based on solving clues. One clue leads players to a spot where another clue is found, which then leads to another clue, and so on. Eventually the last clue leads to the treasure. The game is now played in several different types of formats. Armchair treasure hunting requires solving a puzzle that's written in a book or via another widely available medium, like the internet. The solution reveals where the prize is hidden.

Another form of treasure hunting is called maritime salvage, whereby hunters search for treasures in sunken shipwrecks; this requires scuba equipment (see Scuba diving). There are also road rallies, which are similar to scavenger hunts, requiring participants to follow puzzle clues (word games, actual puzzles, and the like), and scavenger hunts organized by social groups and businesses as a team-bonding exercise.

Geocaching is a more modern version of this game, whereby players use global positioning systems (GPSs) to find "treasures"—caches—stored in waterproof containers and hidden. Geocaching works in a variety of ways: Sometimes geocachers are provided with just the coordinates; other times they're required to arrive at a designated site at a specific date and hour. Once they find the cache, to prove that they were really there they must either write down their identification number on a log at the site or take a photo of themselves at the site.

history

Treasure hunting goes all the way back to the pirates, who terrorized the seas for centuries and became legendary. In the 16th century, Spanish ships carrying treasures from Mexico to the Caribbean were attacked by British pirates hunting for treasure. Blackbeard, an English pirate, who lived in the 1600s and early 1700s, is said to have left a large stash of treasure buried somewhere along the Virginia or North Carolina coast, though it's never been found.

getting started

Embarking on a treasure hunt requires simply finding one that interests you. Browse websites that offer treasure hunts or geocaching expeditions *(see resources).* Be prepared to get down on your hands and knees, dig through dirt, and spend a good deal of time on your outing. The treasure may not be found in one try, or even in one day. Many of these hunts last for months before someone finally locates the loot.

Treasure hunters must abide by both written and unwritten rules of decorum. They cannot trespass or dig on private property, unless the owner expressly agrees. And, of course, those organizing the hunt must not put hunters in any danger.

If you're planning a treasure hunt, here are a few things to take into consideration. The most important aspect of organizing this kind of event is coming up with the rules. Every game should have a clearly articulated set of regulations, such as what areas of search are off limits, what technical help the participants can use (computers, compass), and the time limit. If the clues are for specific people to read, mark their name on the paper so it's perfectly clear. What happens if more than one person finds the treasure at the same time? And once it's found, what should players do with it? Have a plan for every stage of the game.

profile: the ultimate map quest

In 2000, JON STANLEY waited until the snow had melted around his family's cabin at Priest Lake, Idaho, and as soon as he saw a clear path, he headed up to a nearby peak with a stunning view of the lake. There, he hid the very first cache placed in Idaho. "I named it 'Camel's Prairie Stash,'" he says proudly.

Stanley, a map aficionado, had bought one of the earliest consumer models of a GPS receiver in 1995, which he used to map out mountain bike trails around his home in Sammamish, Washington. After five years of patiently waiting for the government's more sophisticated GPS system to be made available to the public, he was rewarded with a stronger GPS signal. Not long after that, he learned about people's fascination with geocaching, and as soon as he discovered the existence of a treasure hunt in his neck of the woods, Stanley dove right in. He found his first cache near Snoqualmie Pass in September 2000. "Caches then started showing up regularly nearby, and I've been hooked ever since," he says.

> "When you get to the area of the cache, don't worry too much about monitoring the GPS receiver at first. Instead, focus your initial search on those places where you would put the treasure if you were the hider. You might be surprised at how frequently that leads you right to the container."

For a self-professed "map freak," technofile (Stanley works in the computer industry), and outdoorsman, geocaching seemed like it was invented just for him. "This combines my strongest interests into one neat package," he says. As with most geocachers, the journey is the best part of the hobby. For example, Stanley was delighted when he found a hand-knit hat from Uzbekistan in a cache in the Canadian Rockies a few years ago.

"Had I found that hat in a suburban park cache, it might not have made such an impact," he says. "But I was on a trip with my wife to visit family in Calgary, and we headed out to search for this cache." They hiked up a narrow canyon surrounded by craggy peaks, observing ancient petroglyphs along the way, and ended up in a grotto with a lovely little waterfall. "It was a very memorable experience, and I still have that hat," he says.

urban animal husbandry

WHY IS IT MORE COMMONPLACE TO HAVE A DOG as a pet than a chicken? Or a parakeet instead of a pigeon? Keeping and caring for these untraditional pets can be just as rewarding, if not more so: No dog or cat ever repaid you with eggs.

what you'll need

- Backyard
- Coop, cage, or pen (depending on the animal)
- Food suitable to the animal
- Water
- Protection from other animals

if you like this hobby, you might enjoy:

- Ant farming (see page 16)
- Beekeeping (see page 36)
- Birding (see page 44)
- Dog breeding (see page 78)
- Pet rescue
- Species protection (see page 192)
- Vegetable and herb gardening (see page 212)

overview

Raising farm animals in your backyard is very similar to raising pets. Both types of animals require time, energy, and commitment. And every animal obviously has its own particular needs and requirements (check your local ordinance about keeping farm animals in residential neighborhoods.) Pigeons have to be kept in enclosed aviaries covered by a solid roof and, in colder environments, need doors and windows to protect them from storms. Chickens are said to be very friendly, easy pets to keep. Some even respond to their names and sit on laps to be petted. In addition to clucking, they sing and purr like cats. They come in a variety of colors and plumages. Fancy Bantams have feathered feet, silky coats, hairless necks, beards, and curls in their feathers. It's crucial to keep chickens safe from predatory animals, like cats and hawks. As part of their "rent," chickens will give you eggs and fertilizer for your garden. You can purchase live chickens through mail-order or at some farmers' markets.

history

First and foremost, animals have been domesticated throughout history for the purpose of providing food for their keepers and for farming labor. The Chinese have been keeping chickens strictly as pet companions for hundreds of years. The Brits and Americans took a liking to these striking-looking birds, and began importing them around the late 1800s. The hobby of poultry raising for presentation became popular for Americans, who then bred their own varieties of chickens. Pigeons were reportedly trained by ancient Egyptians and Romans to carry messages, and they continue to be kept as pets and trained to race.

resources

The Complete Handbook of Poultry Keeping, by Stuart Banks (Van Nostrand Reinhold, 1979).

Small-Scale Pig Raising, by Dirk Van Loon (Storey Publishing, 1978).

www.gamebird.com: A bird conservation magazine that offers instructions on how to raise pigeons and doves.

www.mcmurrayhatchery.com: Supplier of everything you need to buy and raise poultry.

getting started

Check with your city's planning department about the legality of raising the animals you're interested in.

Each pet has its own requirements. Pigeons, for example, need a coop big enough to move around in with ease. An ideal size for 8 to 10 pigeons is a 6-by-7-foot (1.8 by 2.1 m) structure. Each pigeon needs a nesting box full of straw or long pine needles. Containers of food—you can buy bags of "pigeon chow" or give them a variety of grains, as well as vegetable leftovers and bread from your kitchen—and water are also necessary. Pigeons are social creatures, so ideally you'll have three or four mated pairs. Croppers, white and silver kings, and Indian fan tails make great pets.

Chickens need varmint-proof quarters and a place safe from predators. When you're ready to take the chicks home, place them in a small warming box or aquarium and be sure to give them commercial chick starter feed for the first two months. Make certain water is replenished and easily accessible. Chicks also need lots of warmth, so use a 250-watt infrared heat bulb to keep the temperature at about 90°F (32°C). You'll eventually move the chicks to a bigger coop, and their new feathers will keep them warm. Their new digs, which should have perches or a roosting area, should be kept as clean as possible to deter disease. You'll need nesting boxes for when the chickens lay their eggs, too.

profile: fond of feathered friends

On a quiet, stately block in a residential Oakland, California, neighborhood, one mile from downtown skyscrapers and the subway, there are eight happy chickens clucking around in MAUREEN FORYS's sunny backyard. They are named Clementine, Isabella, Exene, Lucy, Ethel, Ava, Audrey, and Anais. Each has its own personality. "Exene knows her name," Forys says. "She's vocal and loves to eat, especially tomatoes and cucumbers."

As with any pet, chickens can be wonderful, happy-go-lucky companions who bond with their caretakers, but they can also fall ill or be attacked by animals higher up in the food chain. "In urban areas, chickens face threats from raccoons, possums, hawks, snakes, cats, and dogs," Forys says. She learned about chickens' tenuous existence when she was 12 years old and came home one day from school to find that wild dogs had attacked her chickens and killed all but two. After that incident, Forys couldn't face the idea of going through that trauma again, until four years ago, when she rustled up the courage to raise chickens again.

"They're really fun animals that have a lot more smarts than people know," she says. "And when you raise them from baby chicks, they really consider you part of the flock. They cluck at you and come running for snacks and petting and lap time."

The eggs are also a welcome by-product of raising chickens. "They're amazing," she says. "Happy chickens make delicious eggs that are nothing like the eggs you get at an average grocery store, she says." They have shells that are thick and strong, yolks that are bright yellow and perky."

> "It's a rewarding hobby, but you have to make sure that you are set up to handle more birds than you initially get (you always want more birds) and that your setup is predator proof."

As a result of living just a few feet from the next house—as opposed to a few acres from the next farm—Forys's chickens have inadvertently united the neighborhood. "It's brought our block closer together," she says. "The adults learn; the kids get to see what a chicken is and where eggs come from. This is so important, since we are so distant from our food in modern society. It is important to know and respect your food."

vegetable & herb gardening

HOBBY PERSONALITY: adventurous · animal-loving · artistic · crafty · dexterous · **epicurean** · extroverted · history-loving · independent · meditative · meticulous · musical · **nature-loving** · **nurturing** · outdoorsy · **patient** · social · sporty · technical

NOTHING IN THE FRIDGE FOR DINNER TONIGHT? If you had a vegetable garden in the backyard, you could simply walk outside and pick a few tomatoes, some squash, and some carrots for a stir-fry. And if your spice cupboard were bare, you could simply pinch off a few sprigs of rosemary and thyme to season your delicious meal.

what you'll need

- *Vegetable starter plants or seeds*
- *Herbs starter plants or seeds*
- *Soil and compost* (see Composting)
- *Backyard space*
- *Gardening tools such as shovel, trowel, and weeder*

resources

Burpee: The Complete Vegetable & Herb Gardener: A Guide to Growing Your Garden Organically, by Karan Davis Cutler, et al (Wiley, 1997).

Easy Vegetable Garden Plans, by Pamela Peirce, et al. (Ortho Books, 1997).

www.backyardgardener.com: Hundreds of ideas for what kinds of vegetables and herbs to plant.

www.gardenweb.com: How to grow different types of vegetables and herbs, and forums where gardeners trade advice.

www.johnnyseeds.com: All manner of seeds and gardening tools.

www.sunset.com/sunset/garden: Step-by-step instructions on how plant herb and vegetable gardens and beds.

overview

Each type of vegetable and herb has different needs—water, light, temperature, and space—to grow. For example, artichokes grow well in coastal regions with cool summers, and can't withstand freezing temperatures. Tomatoes, on the other hand, grow best in hot weather and need lots of nitrogen, phosphorus, and potassium. Tomatoes can spread along the ground or climb up a trellis. Adding mulch to the soil surrounding the plants will help keep them from drying out quickly.

Vegetables and herbs can be grown from seed, then transplanted into healthy soil in either a raised bed, 3 or 4 feet (.91 or 1.2 m) wide and about 1 1/2 feet (.46 m) tall, or put directly into the ground. Most varieties need plenty of sunlight, an important part of deciding where to plant them. The best time of year to get your garden going is in the summer, when plants will benefit from eight hours of sun per day. Transplanting starter plants involves digging holes about 8 inches (20 cm) into the soil, adding about 4 inches (10 cm) of compost, placing the plants in their respective holes, and filling in the holes with more soil. Seed planting requires spacing the seeds out at intervals that vary depending on the plants. They need regular watering, but too much or too little will kill them. Hooking up a drip system on a timer is ideal, but a hose can also be used. Weeds need to be pulled immediately to prevent them from choking the herbs and vegetables. Once the vegetables have grown to their appropriate ripeness, they're ready to be harvested.

history

Horticulture has been practiced in one form or another for more than 11,000 years. The Chinese grew rice and cabbage in about 5000 B.C.E., the civilizations in Mesopotamia grew vegetables, wheat, and barley starting around 8000 B.C.E., and by 2800 B.C.E. Egyptians had devised irrigation systems, which simplified the process of growing vegetables and plants. The Egyptians grew vegetables like peas, onions, beans, garlic, leeks, cucumbers, radishes, cabbage, asparagus, and lentils, all of which we still enjoy today.

getting started

First, research the types of plants you're interested in growing and find out what time of year is best to start your plantings. Look at your backyard and determine how much space you can allot to your vegetable or herb garden *(see project)*. If you don't have a sizeable outdoor lot, you can also grow vegetables in a window box that receives lots of direct sun.

If you decide to go with a raised bed, which allows for easy access to your veggies (no need to bend over to the ground to harvest), you can either buy one readymade or build one yourself. If you're planting straight into the ground, dig out the appropriate-size hole and loosen the soil around it, making sure to clear it of all rocks and debris. Go to the nursery and buy your vegetable starter plants, keeping in mind what you like to use most in your cooking. The more apt you are to use the veggies or herbs, the more invested you'll be in their growth. Seeds are less expensive to begin with than grown plants in pots or packs, and should be purchased in the early spring, when you have the most choice. However, growing plants from seeds adds time and effort to the process, so it's best to use starter plants for your first garden. If you're planting in the summer, choose warm-season crops like cucumbers, melons, tomatoes, corn, or squash. If you're getting started in the winter and live on the West Coast, go with cool-season veggies like cabbage, carrots, lettuce, beets, and broccoli.

Now add your compost soil to the raised bed, or to the dug-out hole. If you're planting from seed, read the directions on the packet and space them out accordingly. Add bark or wood-chip mulch to discourage weeds from taking over your vegetable or herb garden. You can also plant small onions, garlic, and marigolds to repel pests. When your vegetables or herbs are ready to harvest, you'll know by the way they look (whether they are soft and ripened or have grown to a certain size, for example), or if they pull off the plant with ease.

project: build a raised garden bed

Raised beds are an ideal choice for medium-sized back-yards that don't have acres of land to devote to vegetables and herbs. The bed also creates a tidy, picturesque display for the fruits of your labor.

First, decide the length, width, and height of the bed you want to build and mark the perimeter with string wrapped around four stakes, so you have a visual of the size of the bed. A good size for your bed is 12 inches high by 6 feet long by 3 feet wide. Cut a piece of wire netting the exact length and width of the planned bed and place it on the ground—this is to keep gophers and other animals from sneaking from underneath into your plants.

To build the walls, you can use concrete blocks, bricks, stones, or wood. If you're using wood, opt for fir or redwood, which are resistant to rot. Avoid using pressure-treated woods, which have been treated with toxic chemicals. You will need to cut two pieces of 2-by-6-inch wood for each side of the rectangular box (eight total), which will be stacked on top of each other; four will be cut 6 feet long, and four will be 3 feet long. For each of the corner posts, use 4-by-4-inch wood, each cut to 12 inches high. Attach the stacked 2-by-6-inch sides to the corner posts with rust-proof carriage bolts or wood screws. Add soil to the raised bed, let it settle, and you're ready to plant!

watercolor

ALTHOUGH IT'S SIMPLE ENOUGH FOR KIDS TO DO, painting with watercolors can also produce remarkable works of art. From Vincent van Gogh to Paul Cezanne, Winslow Homer to Georgia O'Keeffe—some of the world's most revered artists have created brilliant works of art using watercolor paints. Take your inspiration from these luminaries, and start mixing your colors.

what you'll need

- Selection of paintbrushes—round, oval, and flat and in various sizes
- Watercolor paints in tubes or in solid form
- Watercolor paper
- Watercolor trays
- Easel (optional)
- Rags, sponges, and paper towels
- Water container

overview

Watercolor paints are made of pigment that's been ground in gum arabic, which is water-soluble. To paint with them, you add a bit of water—as much as needed to make the color saturated or pale, according to your vision—then apply it with a brush onto a medium (watercolor paper is best). The result is a transparent color, which can be made more opaque by mixing in whiting.

Watercolor painting can be done with different brushing techniques. Typically, the brush is dipped into water then into the paint, then onto the paper. With the dry-brush technique, the brush picks up the paint but uses very little water. It's dragged across the coarse part of the paper and looks very much like the work of a crayon. A flat wash means covering the entire paper horizontally with a color. This can be done in color gradations or in the same color, and can serve as the foundation for the painting, or can be the final work. Glazing adds another layer to the flat wash to even out the color. Wet-in-wet means painting with a wet brush on wet paper, which results in amorphous shapes. Lifting off invovles dissolving a color after it's already dried by wetting the area and blotting away the color with a rag or paper towel.

history

Unofficially, watercolor painting dates back to prehistoric times, when humans mixed crushed pigments with water to adorn the walls of caves. Ancient Egyptians used water-based paints on sheets of papyrus, and artists in Japan and China used them to paint on silk and, after 100 C.E., on paper. In the West, watercolors were used to decorate the illuminated manuscripts of the Middle Ages, and Renaissance artists used them to make studies and sketches for larger works. But it wasn't until the 18th century that watercolor painting really came into its own, especially in Britain; in fact, the mid-18th to mid-19th century in Britain is called the "golden age of watercolor."

At first the paints were mostly used to add faint washes and tints to drawings, but artists eventually began to explore bolder uses of color. Watercolor clubs and societies sprang up, and specialized brushes and paper were developed that fueled the trend. Late-19th- and early-20th-century American artists like James Abbott McNeill Whistler, Winslow Homer, Mary Cassatt, and Edward Hopper pushed the medium to its limits, creating sophisticated paintings that rivaled their works in oil. Although mid-20th-century artists tended to favor brasher media, Abstract Expressionist painters like Mark Rothko and Helen Frankenthaler used oil painting techniques that mimicked the subtle color-washes of watercolor paints, but on a grand scale.

getting started

- *WATERCOLOR painting requires you to spread out a little, so you'll need either an easel or a worktable. When buying paper, you can choose from a variety of weights, from 90 to 300 pounds (refers to the weight of a ream, which is 500 sheets of paper). Some are smooth, others are rough or textured. Whatever you choose, invest in acid-free paper to prevent fading.*

- *NOW IT'S TIME to mix your colors. From your tubes, squeeze out the shades you've chosen into individual slots in your tray. You can experiment with mixing colors to get the precise shade you're looking for. Study a color wheel to understand how color mixing works. The purest colors result from mixing two primary colors together; the more colors mixed in, the more diluted and muddier the color will get, so try keeping it to no more than three colors. Begin with the two lighter colors, then add the darkest one to the mix. Keep in mind that as the paint dries, the hue will become lighter. Colors also look different mixed in your tray than they do on the paper. Now that you've got your paper and watercolor paints organized, start painting!*

resources

The Big Book of Painting Nature in Watercolor, by Ferdinand Petrie (Watson-Guptill Publications, 1990).

Watercolor for the Serious Beginner, by Mary Whyte (Watson-Guptill Publications, 1997).

www.fountainstudio.com: Step-by-step instructions for successful watercolors and tips for beginners.

www.pearlpaint.com: Watercolor paints and supplies are available on this comprehensive site.

www.watercolorpainting.com: Step-by-step tutorials and tips on how to paint with watercolors.

project: stretching watercolor paper

If the weight of your watercolor paper is less than 140 pounds, you'll need to stretch it so the paper doesn't warp when you apply watercolor paint.

1] Cut four strips of gummed brown tape long enough to cover the four sides of the paper and set them aside.

2] Submerge the paper in a sink full of cold water for a few minutes, then take it out, let all the water drip off the paper, then place it on a drawing board, or a flat piece of wood, then place that on a flat surface. With a sponge, smooth the paper down.

3] Use the sponge to moisten the tape pieces one at a time. Attach the paper to the board with the tape pieces, working so that the paper is stretched as tight as possible.

4] Let the paper dry, then remove it carefully from the board, or leave it there if you want to use the board as an easel.

whittling

JUST AS COUNTING WORRY BEADS OR CRACKING KNUCKLES is a form of expending nervous energy, so is whittling wood. But with this hobby, you actually produce a material product: a lovely little sculpture. Once you get the hang of it, you'll be whittling away your hours.

what you'll need

- *Whittling kit or a piece of wood and a design idea*
- *Whittling knife*

resources

Art of Whittling and Woodcarving, by Elsie Hanauer (Oak Tree Publications, 2000).

Whittling Twigs and Branches, by Chris Lubkemann (Fox Chapel Publishing Company, 2002).

www.chippingaway.com: Whittling kits and tools.

www.traditionalwoodworker.com: Whittling and other woodworking tools.

overview

Whittling is the art of carving figures and objects with a knife from scraps of wood. It's the younger cousin of carving, a more elaborate process that makes use of chisels, mallets, and gouges. Whittling can be done using a pocket knife, though more specialized whittling tools are available. Some blades are better for deep cuts, while others are attached to round handles that make it easy to rotate the knife in the hand while cutting the wood. There are also fine blades made to work with smaller, lighter pieces of wood.

history

Ancient whittling tools like stone hand axes found in Olorgesailie, Kenya, 100 miles south of the equator, show that whittling was practiced more than 400,000 years ago. In an Iraqi desert, archaeologists have found blood spilled by a man they believe was whittling wood that dates back 180,000 years. Whittling has been practiced all over the world to create everything from spoons and bowls to larger pieces of furniture like chairs and wooden chests. In China, ivory was whittled into puzzles and folding fans as far back as the 9th century c.e.

The art of whittling was brought to the U.S. by European settlers, who bartered their carved pieces for necessities like food and clothing. In the 19th century, sailors whittled whale teeth and bones into small and large decorative objects—called scrimshaw—to pass the time during their long journeys, and around the same time whittling became a form of relaxation for people who were used to working with wood to make farm tools, hunting tools, and fishing poles. They used pocket knives to make toys, little sculptures, and puzzles. One challenging project, the wooden chain, involved whittling wood into links. Such chains were typically about a foot long, though more motivated woodworkers could work with 8-foot (2.4 m) planes of wood. Woodworkers and hobbyists whittled abstract shapes like rectangles, ovals, and circles, then added embellishments to them.

getting started

As with most hobbies, practice makes perfect when it comes to whittling. Especially with any type of woodworking, the more you handle the tools, the more refined your pieces will turn out. The place to start is figuring out what you want to carve. If you just whittle haphazardly, you might never make a decision and just end up with a toothpick. Of course, the end result is suggested by the original shape of the wood. To get an idea of how this works, you might want to start with a whittling kit *(see resources)*. It'll come with pieces of basswood precut into profiles of shapes of animals or other figures that are either drilled or marked with carving guidelines to show you where to start. Kits even provide you with a plastic scale model so you can compare your work to the model as you progress.

You'll use a few different techniques here. The "cut" is simply that—cutting chunks of wood in the first few steps. "Shaving" uses the knife as a plane for making wide, horizontal cuts. The "channel cut" entails making one deep cut into your wood, then another one parallel to it, but at an angle toward the first cut, so you can gouge out an entire piece. And the "scrape cut" is when you scratch the dull end of the knife across the wood to smooth the surface.

Some tips to remember:

- *Start with small cuts rather than gouging out huge chunks, as you might remove more than you intended to.*
- *Be sure your blade is sharp. Surprisingly, this is safer, because a dull knife is more likely to slip as you apply extra pressure to force it into the wood.*
- *Always cut away from yourself. This way, if the knife flies out of control, it won't strike any of your precious body parts.*
- *Rest your hands often so you don't get cramps, and try massaging them when you need a break. Go slowly and relax your grip so you don't tire out easily.*

project: add color to a whittled sculpture

When you finish your best whittled piece, you can add layers of colored varnish to give it a polished, professional look.

1) First, clean the piece with water and soap, using toothpicks, Q-tips, or toothbrushes to thoroughly clean the crevices. Allow it to dry thoroughly.

2) Apply rabbit skin glue (found at craft and art supply stores) to seal the surface.

3) When that's dry, you can start painting the piece with a straight stain, or add a light watercolor mix to the stain. (Make sure the stain is water-based.) You can also apply the stain first and apply another coat of watercolor paint over it when it's dry. If you like, color in the features of your figure: a woman's mouth, clothes, and shoes, an animal's fur—anything that would benefit from a spot of color.

4) When all the paint has dried, coat the surface with beeswax to protect the color, then buff it with a soft cotton cloth.

so many hobbies, so little time

THE HOBBIES WE DETAIL IN THIS BOOK ARE JUST A STARTING POINT. The potential list is almost infinite. With that in mind, we offer you a list of other diversions you might enjoy trying.

altruistic: In the long run, it's you who feels better about yourself.

- Building preservation
- Coaching a sports team
- Community gardening
- Leading tours of museums or neighborhoods
- Letter-writing campaigns
- Literacy or ESL tutoring
- Pet therapy
- Public place clean-up
- Soup kitchen volunteer work
- Volunteer grandparenting
- Voter registration

artistic: Unleash your creative powers.

- Amateur theater
- Animation
- Cabinetmaking
- Cake decorating
- Collage
- Dancing (ballet, ballroom, belly, country, exotic, folk, Highland, line, square, step, tap)
- Figure skating
- Glass blowing
- Lace making
- Latch-rug hooking
- Macramé
- Marquetry
- Metalwork
- Mime
- Mosaic
- Musical composition
- Painting (acrylic, encaustic, gouache, ink, oil paint, pastels, spray paint, tempera)
- Pastry making
- Printmaking (relief printing, intaglio, lithography, screen-printing, giclée, Ukiyo-e)
- Singing and playing musical instruments
- Trapeze artistry
- Weaving

cerebral: Keep those brain cells active.

- Book club
- Bridge (and other card games)
- Crossword puzzles
- Games (Chess, D&D, Go, Pente, Tournament Scrabble)
- Interactive fiction (IF)
- Learning a musical instrument
- Learning another language
- Spelling bees
- Sudoku

spiritual: Achieve the ultimate equilibrium.

- Acupressure
- Aromatherapy
- Chanting
- Massage (Swedish, Shiatsu, reflexology, deep tissue)
- Meditation
- Mudras
- Reiki
- Tai Chi
- Yoga (Hatha, Ashtanga, Kundalini)

travel related: Venture off the grid.

- Adventure travel (extreme destinations)
- Airport mapping
- Ballooning
- Barefoot hiking
- Eco-friendly travel
- Finding and standing on latitudes/ longitudes
- Geyser-gazing
- Hobo-ing
- Long-term RV-ing
- Maze-walking
- Mountaineering
- Long-distance sailing
- Spiritual retreats
- Urban exploration
- Winter camping

index

acknowledgments

I'd like to thank the vast number of people who helped this book take shape. Katherine Sharpe, who helped with research; Lloyd Farnham, who vetted the manuscript from an engineer's point of view; Natalie Friedman, Harrison Pollak, Todd Jackson, Stefanianna Moore, and Elizabeth Ashford, for switching on my lightbulb; Diane Hiatt for Thursdays; the staff of *ReadyMade* magazine, who is responsible for all things good; all those who agreed to be profiled and who explained patiently the minutiae of their crafts; Ana Deboo, Betsy Beier, and Liana Krissoff for their eagle-eyed edits; Lynne Yeamans and Tanya Ross-Hughes for their stylish design; Nancy Leonard for her on-the-spot illustrations; Sharyn Rosart for coming up with the idea in the first place; and finally Sarah Scheffel, this book's editor, who made a first-time author's experience utterly gratifying.

about the author

TINA BARSEGHIAN is a contributing editor at *ReadyMade* magazine, a do-it-yourself art- and design-focused publication based in Berkeley, California. Her hobbies include playing classical piano, taking photographs using the quaint medium of film, trawling for treasures at flea markets, gardening, and playing dress-up with her three-year-old daughter. She lives in the San Francisco Bay Area.

NAME THAT HOBBY ANSWER KEY

1) Cross-stitch
   Gilding
2) Origami
3) Beading
4) African violet cultivation
   Bonsai
   Topiary
5) Tarot card reading
6) Framing
   Faux finishing
7) Needlework
   Sewing
8) Quilting
9) Fly tying
10) Basketry
    Herb gardening
    Drying flowers
    Ikebana
11) Vegetable gardening
    Seed trading
12) Beer brewing
13) Beekeeping
14) Composting
    Dumpster diving
15) Candy making
    Coffee roasting
    Deep-frying
    Olive oil infusions
    Making preserves
16) Sewing
    Quilting
17) Entering contests
    Genealogy
    Journaling & blogging
18) Dollhouse building
    Furniture restoration
    Model making
19) Crochet
    Knitting
20) Photography
    Polaroid transfer
    Train- and planespotting
21) Vegetable &
     herb gardening
22) Birding
    Taxidermy
    Urban animal husbandry
23) Scuba diving
    Sculpture
    Stained glass